THE
RITE

THE RITE

THE MAKING OF A MODERN EXORCIST

MATT BAGLIO

DOUBLEDAY

NEW YORK LONDON TORONTO SYDNEY AUCKLAND

DOUBLEDAY

Copyright © 2009 by Matt Baglio

All Rights Reserved

Published in the United States by Doubleday, a division of
Random House, Inc., New York.
www.doubleday.com

DOUBLEDAY and the DD colophon are registered trademarks of
Random House, Inc.

Book design by Lisa Sloane

Map illustration by Jeffrey L. Ward

Library of Congress Cataloging-in-Publication Data
Baglio, Matt.
The rite : the making of a modern exorcist / by Matt Baglio. —
1st ed.
p.   cm.
Includes bibliographical references and index.
1. Baglio, Matt. 2. Exorcism—Biography. 3. Exorcism. I. Title.
BX2340.B34 2009
264'.020994092—dc22
[B]
2008030759

ISBN 978-0-385-52270-0

PRINTED IN THE UNITED STATES OF AMERICA

1 3 5 7 9 10 8 6 4 2

First Edition

FOR SARA AND NOAH

CONTENTS

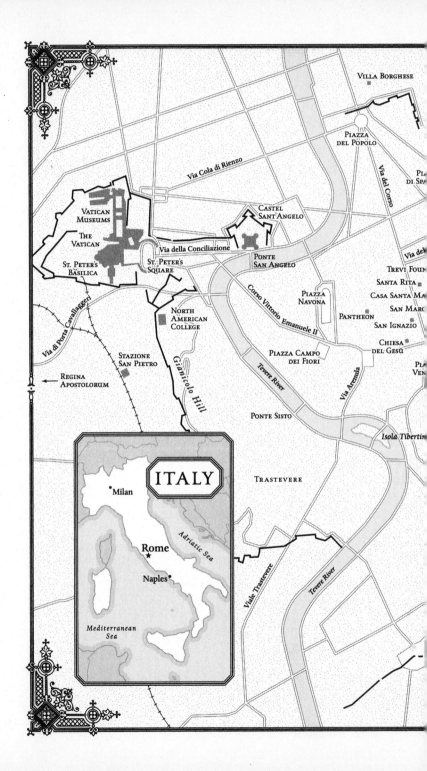

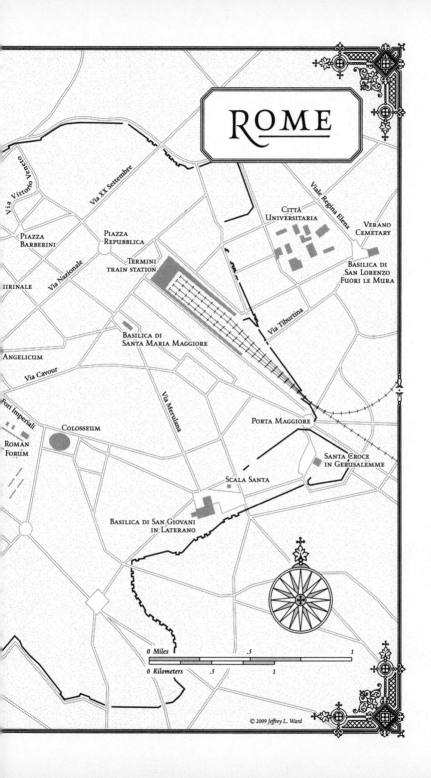

ROME

Via Vittorio Veneto

Via XX Settembre

Viale Regina Elena

CITTÀ
UNIVERSITARIA

VERANO
CEMETARY

PIAZZA
BARBERINI

PIAZZA
REPUBBLICA

Via Nazionale

TERMINI
TRAIN STATION

BASILICA DI
SAN LORENZO
FUORI LE MURA

IIRINALE

BASILICA DI
SANTA MARIA MAGGIORE

Via Tiburtina

ANGELICUM

Via Cavour

Via Merulana

Fori Imperiali

COLOSSEUM

PORTA MAGGIORE

ROMAN
FORUM

SANTA CROCE
IN GERUSALEMME

SCALA SANTA

BASILICA DI SAN GIOVANI
IN LATERANO

0 Miles   .5   1

0 Kilometers   .5   1

© 2009 Jeffrey L. Ward

THE
RITE

pRoLogue

And war broke out in heaven; Michael and his angels fought against the dragon. The dragon and his angels fought back, but they were defeated, and there was no longer any place for them in heaven. The great dragon was thrown down, that ancient serpent, who is called the Devil and Satan, the deceiver of the whole world—he was thrown down to the earth, and his angels were thrown out with him.

—Revelation 12:7–9

Among her sacramentals, the Catholic Church, in obedience to the Lord's Prayer, already in ancient times mercifully provided that through pious prayers her people may ask God to liberate the faithful from all dangers and especially from the snares of the Devil. In a truly unique way, exorcists were established in the Church who, in imitation of Christ, could cure those obsessed by the Evil One, even by commanding demons in the name of God, so that they might depart, lest for whatever reason they do further harm to human creatures.

—Decree from the Congregation
for Divine Worship of the Faith,
November 22, 1998

The thirty-five-year-old woman lay on a padded folding massage table, her arms and legs held by two men. She wore a black Puma sweat suit and her dark brown hair was pulled back tightly into a ponytail. While not heavy, she was a little on the stocky side; and as she grunted and struggled, the men fought to hold on. Nearby, another man and woman hovered, ready to intervene. The exorcist stood a few feet away, a small crucifix in one hand and a silver canister filled with holy water in the other. Surveying the scene, he had a decision to make. The exorcism had been going on for the better part of an hour, and the strain was beginning to show on everyone. Should he continue?

Suddenly the woman's head turned, her eyes fixating on a spot near the far wall. "No!" the demon said in a deep guttural voice coming from deep within her, "the one in black is here, the jinx!"

The exorcist felt a momentary ray of hope, knowing from past exorcisms that this was the demon's code to describe Saint Gemma Galgani.

"And the little white one from Albania!" the demon roared.

"Mother Teresa of Calcutta?" the exorcist asked.

The demon let fly a string of blasphemies in a rage, then his voice took on a mocking childlike tone. "Oh, look at them! Look at them! They are hugging and greeting each other!" Then, back to a deep guttural rasp, "Disgusting! Disgusting!"

To the woman lying on the table, the two figures appeared as if in a dream. Saint Gemma was dressed in her traditional black, and looked very much as she had in her twenties. Oddly, Mother Teresa also looked very young—perhaps only twenty-five.

The exorcist glanced over his shoulder to where the woman was staring and saw nothing but the blank wall. "Let us thank Saint Gemma Galgani and Mother Teresa for being here with us today," he said.

"No, him too. Send him away, send him away!" the demon wailed.

Unsure of who had just arrived, the exorcist added, "I say thank you that he is here."

Then suddenly the woman sat bolt upright, her arms extended in front of her as if she'd been yanked up by some unseen force. "Leave me alone!" the demon screamed, even as the woman flailed to break free from the invisible grasp. The two men went to pull her back down, but the exorcist motioned for them to stop. "Let's see who just came. In the name of Jesus and the Immaculate Virgin, who is this person?"

"Nooooooo!" the guttural, ferocious voice growled. "Totus tuuu-uuus!"

The exorcist smiled inwardly, recognizing the Latin motto. "Thank you, Holy Father John Paul II, for coming to help our sister," he said.

"No, no!" the demon shrieked. "Damn you! Get away from me!"

Again, in her dreamlike state, the woman watched Pope John Paul II, who seemed no older than thirty and was dressed all in white, bless her forehead three times.

Wanting to take advantage of the apparent reinforcements, the exorcist pressed on. "Repeat after me: Eternal Father, you are my Creator and I adore you," he said to the demon.

"Up yours!" the voice responded.

"Eternal Father, you are my Creator and I adore you," the exorcist insisted.

"A bomb is going to explode if I say it!" the demon shouted.

"I order you, in the name of the Immaculate Virgin Mary and in the name of Jesus Christ, to repeat those words," the priest commanded again.

All at once, the woman felt awash in an incredible feeling of love as the veiled figure of Mary appeared before her, wrapped in a gold-and-white veil that covered half her face. Watching in amazement as the figure approached, the woman was even more surprised to see that Mary was gazing at her tearfully.

As the exorcist watched, the demon once again went into a fit.

"No, no, no, don't cry!" he screamed, and the woman's body practically convulsed.

Then for an instant the woman snapped out of the trance, saying, "A tear from Mary is all it took," before falling back into the state.

The exorcist was elated to know that Mary was present and helping. He instantly launched into a Hail Mary. Everyone in the room joined in, even the woman on the table. Yet somehow the exorcist knew it wasn't over. *The demon must be hiding to allow her to recite the prayer,* he thought. "Say after me: Eternal Father, you are my Creator and I adore you," he said to the demon.

The woman thrashed and screamed. "No!" the demon barked. "I'm not going to say it! I must not say it, I can't; it is against everything."

The exorcist could feel that the demon was weakening. He asked everyone in the room to kneel. "Eternal Father, you are my Creator and I adore you," he intoned, while everyone repeated him.

The woman, sensing the torment of the demon, saw all the saints in the room respond as well.

"No, no, even those other ones kneeled down—the white one, the black one, and the little white one," the demon said. Then the exorcist noticed that the demon's voice changed slightly to a tone of forced reverence when he added, "Her, her [Mary]—she kneeled down as well."

This must be it, the exorcist thought. The demon is going to break. "In the name of Jesus Christ, I order you to repeat the phrase."

The woman struggled, but slowly a croaking noise came from her throat. "Eee . . . ter . . . nal . . . Fa . . . ther . . . , I must . . . ad . . . ooor . . . yooou."

Ecstatic, but realizing it was still not over yet, the exorcist made the demon repeat the phrase two more times. When the demon had finished, the exorcist said a phrase used at the conclusion of the Eucharistic Prayer: "Through him, with him, in him, in the unity of the Holy Spirit, all glory and honor is yours, Almighty Father, forever and ever."

"This humiliation was given for the glory of God, not because you commanded it but because God commanded it. You are damned," the demon said, addressing the exorcist.

The exorcist did not falter. *"Che Dio sia benedetto,"* he continued, God be praised.

"I go away but you are going to be damned for life," the demon sneered. "You and your companions, you are going to be persecuted for life!"

———————

WHEN PEOPLE HEAR THE WORD *exorcism*, many think of images made popular by Hollywood films—girls writhing in torment, their bodies contorting in impossible ways as they launch a continuous stream of pea-soup-green projectile vomit. In truth, such theatrics, as well as those in the woman's exorcism that took place in January 2007, in Rome, Italy, are quite rare. Instead, exorcisms can be rather mundane, almost like going to the dentist—complete with a stint in the waiting room and a card to remind the recipient of his or her next appointment. The reality is that few people realize what goes on during an exorcism, and that is true for Catholic priests as well—many of whom would just as soon forget that exorcism exists at all.

The word *exorcism* itself is an ecclesiastical term that comes from the Greek *exorkizo*, meaning "to bind with an oath," or to demand insistently. During an exorcism, a demon is commanded in the name of God to stop his activity within a particular person or place. As understood by the Catholic Church, an exorcism is an official rite carried out by a priest who has been authorized to do so by his bishop. In ancient times, exorcism was an important way for early Christians to win converts and prove the veracity of the faith. The power itself comes from Jesus, who performed numerous exorcisms as detailed in the New Testament, later instructing his disciples to do the same.

In light of the tremendous advances in modern medicine—including a more sophisticated understanding of neurological and psychological illnesses, the advent of psychoanalysis, and similar advantages—the rite of exorcism has become an embarrassment to many within the Church, who see it as a superstitious relic from the days when illnesses like epilepsy and schizophrenia were considered "devils" to be cast out.

Much of this misunderstanding comes from the nature of exorcism itself, as well as from the Devil's attributes that have more foundation in folklore than theology. A beast with horns and half a goat's body ravaging innocent virgins in the dead of night? Soul-leaching, shape-shifting she-demons on the prowl for their next victim? Without courses on demonology to educate seminarians, it's no wonder priests have turned away in droves from this exorcism stuff.

At the core of the issue lies the problem of evil. Is it a physical reality, a fallen angel called Satan (as the *Catechism of the Catholic Church*, a small but dense book of about 900 pages says), or is it a lack of good in something, an inability to live up to the designs of the benevolent Creator?

Many priests, not wanting to turn their backs on the rich history associated with their faith, while at the same time wanting to embrace the modern view of reality in which the Devil is seen as a metaphor, would like to have it both ways. Others believe in the traditional teachings, but prefer not to talk about it. On the extreme end, some priests just flat out deny the Devil's existence.

Ironically, while many priests and bishops seem bent on skepticism, the general public has become enamored with the occult, gravitating to new religions such as Wicca. According to an American Religious Identity Survey, Wicca grew in America from 8,000 members in 1990 to over 134,000 in 2001. (By 2006, that number was said to have risen to more than 800,000.) Sales of occult and New Age books have also skyrocketed, as has the number of people who believe in angels and demons (according to a 2004 Gallup poll, about 70 percent of Americans said they believe in the Devil). All this coincides with an explosion in the numbers of people who say they are afflicted by evil spirits. According to the Association of Italian Catholic Psychiatrists and Psychologists, in Italy alone, more than 500,000 people see an exorcist annually.

For many years, a small but vocal group of overworked exorcists in Italy, led by Father Gabriele Amorth, has tried to get the Church to take the increasing numbers of people who claim to be possessed more seriously. First, they said, more exorcists need to be appointed. However, the Church would have to ensure that any new exorcists be properly trained. Advocates such as Father Amorth assert that in the past, too many exorcists were appointed in name only. In addition, some of these "untrained" exorcists gave the rite of exorcism a bad name by abusing their authority. One of the most egregious cases took place in 2005, when a Romanian nun who'd been gagged and bound to a crucifix in a room at her convent was found dead; the priest who had been performing the exorcism was charged with murder.

Hoping to rectify the situation, in the fall of 2004 the Congregation for the Doctrine of the Faith sent a letter to the various Catholic dioceses around the world, starting with those in America, asking each bishop to appoint an official exorcist.

At the same time, a Vatican-affiliated University in Rome began putting together a groundbreaking course entitled "Exorcism and the Prayer of Liberation" with the intention of educating a new cadre of exorcists about the official teachings of the Church on the Devil and exorcism.

A remarkable American priest answered this call and traveled to Rome in the summer of 2005 to be trained as an exorcist. Over the span of nine months he delved deeply into a world he never knew existed, completing the course and participating in over eighty exorcisms along with a senior Italian exorcist. As a result, his view of the world—and his place in it—changed dramatically, and he later returned to the United States, determined to use his new awareness of evil and its manifest presence to help people in their everyday lives.

rOmE

We should try to be so closely united to our Lord that we reproduce his life in our own, that our thoughts and words and actions should proclaim his teaching, so that he reigns in us, lives in us.

—*Charles de Foucauld*

When Father Gary Thomas stepped out onto Via delle Fornaci at 7:45 on the morning of October 13, 2005, the road was already clogged with traffic. A long line of cars and buses inched toward the intersection of Via di Porta Cavalleggeri, funneled into the mouth of the tunnel by a canyon of four- and five-story buildings that ran along the base of the Gianicolo, one of Rome's many hills. A traffic cop, dressed like an airline captain festooned with epaulets, was doing his best to maintain order, waving cars through and screeching at the more aggressive motorists with his whistle. When the light turned green, drivers wasted no time laying into their horns.

On either side of the road, morning commuters hurried along in the direction of the Vatican, the acrid smell of cigarette smoke trailing behind them like contrails. Occasionally commuters would duck into a bar for their morning cappuccinos, and the roar of an espresso machine spilled out onto the sidewalk.

Standing on the corner, caught up in the chaos, Father Gary took a second to admire the scene as if it were some exotic postcard come to life. This was nothing like any rush hour he had experienced back home in San Francisco. The city, the cars, the people—all seemed to harmonize like some massive orchestra.

Even though he was wearing his black clerics, he blended in seamlessly with the crowds. Rome is, after all, full of priests. According to some estimates, more than 15,000 of them walk the city's narrow streets, and that doesn't even include the several thousand seminarians who also wear the Roman collar and black garb. In addition, with all the chapels, monasteries, convents, and hundreds of churches, not to mention the Vatican itself, it was no wonder that Father Gary dubbed the city the "aorta of Christianity."

As if he needed an additional reminder, the massive *palazzo* that housed the Congregation for the Doctrine of the Faith, the all-important gatekeeper of Church doctrine, stood directly across the street. And beyond that, the distant sunlit cupola of Saint Peter's Basilica floated above the tops of the buildings like an apparition. The sight of it—which Father Gary could also see out of his bedroom window—never failed to move him. In Rome he felt he was part of something bigger than himself, bigger than just the petty little day-to-day concerns that sometimes overwhelm a parish priest. "When you are a pastor, you have to wear nine hats," he said later, with a hint of regret. "It's not that it's all administration, but it does tend to take you away from the things that are more important, such as focusing on people's prayer life."

At age fifty-two he had recently left his post at Saint Nicholas parish in Los Altos, California, where he had served for fifteen years, twelve of them as pastor. While he'd enjoyed the work at Saint Nicholas immensely and had made innumerable friends, the grueling daily grind of being pastor had taken its toll. He had not only helped to completely refurbish several buildings at the parish school; he'd also raised millions of dollars to turn the old rectory into a state-of-the-art community center that pleased parishioners so much they had named it after him.

Ordained in 1983, Father Gary had been a priest for twenty-two years, and over that time he had seen—and been through—a lot. In 1997 he had nearly died in a terrible accident. While hiking with a friend in the foothills of Yosemite, he'd fallen off a sixty-foot cliff onto river rock, miraculously surviving, though during his painful two-year recovery he sometimes wished he hadn't.

With his medium height and build, thinning but neatly trimmed brown hair, and gold circular wire-framed glasses, Father Gary had the unassuming appearance of a person content to put others at ease. While not physically imposing, he exuded the quiet confidence of a man who loves his job and knows he is very good at it.

Since the rules of his diocese require that priests be relocated after fifteen years of service, Father Gary took advantage of the opportunity to take a well-deserved sabbatical. Rome, with its numerous seminaries and prestigious universities, presents visiting priests a unique opportunity. For many, studying at Pontifical universities such as the

Gregorian, where fourteen previous popes and twenty saints have studied, is an intensely sought-after privilege. Most of these students are full-time, either getting their license (equivalent to a master's degree) or doctorate. A few priests, however, are sent by their diocese for some reason, or, like Father Gary, they are taking a sabbatical year to do further study. One program that catered to this latter group was the Institute for Continuing Theological Education at the North American College (NAC), the largest American seminary on foreign soil. Started in the 1970s as a way to implement some of the calls by the Second Vatican Council for priestly renewal, the institute began offering a three-month "sabbatical" program at the NAC for priests who wanted to keep pace with current trends within the Church. At the same time, participants got a chance to enjoy Rome and to meet fellow priests from around the world.

Back in April, Father Gary had signed up to attend the continuing education program from September to November, after which he was going to take a couple of classes on spirituality at the Angelicum, the Pontifical University run by the Dominicans across town.

When he'd first arrived in the city in August 2005, he'd found Rome intimidating. Not only was there the language barrier (he didn't speak Italian), but the city, with its myriad tiny streets, proved extremely difficult to navigate. Now, after living in the city two months, he could laugh at himself for his early trepidation. He knew the bus system as well as any local and could go just about anywhere he wanted.

In addition to his time at the NAC and in other classes, Father Gary had another important assignment: His bishop requested that he take a specific course to become an exorcist. In fact, that morning he was on his way to the first session. Concerned about being late, he turned up Via de Gasperi and quickened his pace.

———

IN THE WINTER OF 2005, as Father Gary's time at Saint Nicholas was winding down, exorcism had been the last thing on his mind. At his Jesus Caritas monthly priest support group, he was surprised when his good friend Father Kevin Joyce mentioned that the Vatican had sent a letter to every diocese in the United States asking that an exorcist be appointed, and that the bishop had pegged him for the post.

Tall, lean, and studious-looking, Father Kevin personified the image of a thoughtful, composed priest. Yet perhaps most striking was his youth and vigor; despite being fifty-seven, he easily appeared fifteen years younger. Father Gary had known Father Kevin for nearly twenty years, and with his background (he had a doctorate in religious education with a specialty in spirituality), he seemed like the perfect choice to become an exorcist. But Father Kevin explained that he intended to decline the appointment. He had recently started the diocese's spirituality center and wouldn't have time to do both.

The fact that the diocese was planning to appoint an exorcist caught Father Gary off guard. The subject of evil spirits and demonic possession didn't often come up in his parish. In the previous year, he'd only spoken about the Devil during mass twice, once prompting a parishioner to ask him not to do it again for fear of frightening his kids. It wasn't a popular topic with priests in general.

While not exactly ambivalent about the Devil, Father Gary hadn't spent that much time thinking about him either. He knew there was a big difference between talking about the concept of evil behavior and the "person" of evil. Sometimes good people did evil things, he was well aware; but whether or not they were caused directly by the Devil he couldn't say. In thinking back to the little he had learned about exorcism in the seminary, he remembered that the scriptural basis for demonic possession was fairly well established. Beyond that, his mind drew a blank. In all his time as a priest, he hadn't heard of a single case of demonic possession or of an exorcism being performed. Now, however, he found himself wondering about this ancient and arcane rite. If called upon, would he be willing to do something like that?

The notion of standing in a room and squaring off against the

Devil didn't frighten him because he might see bizarre or offensive things. Before becoming a priest he had worked in the funeral business from the time he was fourteen. In fact, he was a licensed embalmer. Over the years he had seen some pretty horrible things, including disfigured bodies, some burned beyond recognition. He knew he had the stomach for just about anything. Helping people was one of the main reasons he had decided to become a priest. And wasn't that what Jesus was doing when he cast out evil spirits and healed the sick?

After submitting his name in place of Father Kevin's, Father Gary eventually got an answer about his appointment when he ran into his bishop at a convocation of priests. The bishop was delighted by the news that Father Gary was willing to assume the role. The bishop told him that in the past twenty-four years, only two investigations of possible demonic possession had been conducted in the whole diocese of San Jose. Smiling, the bishop added in his Irish brogue, "And I hope I won't have to be calling on you too much either."

As the conversation wound down, Father Gary confessed his concern about getting some kind of formal training. Then the bishop filled him in about the exorcism course in Rome. "It should work out perfectly with your sabbatical," he said.

UNLIKE IN THE AMERICAN CATHOLIC CHURCH, where exorcism is only talked about in hushed tones, exorcism is more accepted in Italy. In 1986, Pope John Paul II gave a series of talks in which he reminded the faithful not to forget about the dangers posed by the Devil, and that one of these was the real possibility of "bodily possession." And as recently as September 14, 2005, Pope Benedict XVI hosted a large group of exorcists at the Vatican and encouraged them to continue their work "in the service of the Church."

Today, Italy has gone through an exorcism boom. Not only are the numbers of officially appointed exorcists on the rise (reported to be somewhere between 350 and 400), but they also created their own guild-like association—the International Association of Exorcists—in 1992. In addition, thanks in large part to a recent spate of violent crimes linked to satanic cults, the police, in conjunction with the Church, created a special squad in 2006, called the *Squadra anti sette* (Anti-Sect Squad) dubbed SAS for short, tasked with investigating the phenomena.

Interest in exorcism had been steadily growing in Italy since 1998, when the exorcism *Ritual*, originally set down in the 1614 *Roman Ritual*, was finally updated, as per the requirements of the Second Vatican Council of 1962–1965, which called for each of the Church's rituals to be updated. (Incidentally, the ritual for exorcism was one of the last of these.) Journalists swarmed, looking for a story, and Father Gabriele Amorth was picture-perfect. The official exorcist of Rome and best-selling author, Father Amorth was already a well-known television personality in Italy and abroad. In books and interviews he condemned a wide range of things as being satanic—including the Harry Potter books—while drawing attention to what he claimed was the growing power that the Devil wielded in a secular world, which increasingly turned to the occult for answers.

Even worse, in Father Amorth's eyes, was the plight of the exorcist. In an interview published in the Catholic magazine *30 Days* in 2001, he said, "Our brother priests who are charged with this delicate task are treated as though they are crazy, as fanatics. Generally speaking they are scarcely even tolerated by the bishops who have appointed them." Time and time again he chastised bishops and priests alike for their ignorance. "For three centuries, the Latin Church has almost entirely abandoned the ministry of exorcism," he said. And while the problem might be bad in certain parts of Italy, he believed it to be downright appalling elsewhere. "There are countries in which there is not a single exorcist, for example Germany, Switzerland, Spain and Portugal." Other countries, such as France, he claimed, had appointed exorcists who didn't even believe in exorcism.

On May 18, 2001, the Italian bishops' conference, meeting in plenary assembly in the Vatican, issued an official statement: "We are witnessing a rebirth of divinations, fortunetelling, witchcraft and black magic, often combined with a superstitious use of religion. In certain environments, superstition and magic can coexist with scientific and technological progress, inasmuch as science and technology cannot give answers to the ultimate problems of life."

According to the Associazione Comunità Papa Giovanni XXIII (Pope John XXIII Community Association), about 25 percent of Italians, or about 14 million, are involved in some way or another in the occult. In the south of Italy, for instance, certain groups still practice Tarantism, the belief that a person can be possessed by the bite of a spider, while "card-readers" congest the late-night cable channels hawking their prophetic wares and "lucky" amulets. This is not limited to Italy. In 1996, for instance, France's version of the IRS disclosed that during the previous year, 50,000 tax-paying citizens had declared their occupation as healer, medium, or other such practitioner in the occult-related trades. At the time, there were only 36,000 Catholic priests in the entire country.

However, the Church was most concerned about estimates (some would say exaggerated) that as many as 8,000 satanic sects with more than 600,000 members exist within Italy.

THE COURSE "Exorcism and Prayers of Liberation" was the brainchild of Dr. Giuseppe Ferrari, the national secretary of the Gruppo di Ricerca e Informazione Socio-Religiosa (Group for Research and Socio-Religous Information, or GRIS), a Catholic organization located in Bologna, Italy, that deals with cults and other new religions.

According to Dr. Ferrari, the idea came about in 2003 when he met with a priest from the diocese of Imola who told him that a growing number of his fellow clerics were being inundated by parishioners suffering from problems related to the occult: Either they wanted to quit and couldn't, or they in some way felt afflicted by demonic forces. In many cases, the priests felt so inadequate that they simply sent the people away.

In looking into the Church's approach to appointing and training exorcists, Dr. Ferrari saw how haphazard it was, with each exorcist left to his own devices. The solution was obvious: There needed to be some kind of university-level course that would train exorcists.

Dr. Ferrari led a group of various friends and colleagues, including a few theology professors, doctors, and an exorcist, who came up with a working syllabus. Students would be introduced to a wide variety of historical, theological, sociological, and medical topics, in order to go beyond the superficial and sensationalist aspect of exorcism. The aim was simple: Give priests the knowledge they need to discern when and where Satan is active. And give the few who would go on to become exorcists (such as Father Gary) the knowledge necessary to defeat him.

But where to teach it? It was then that Dr. Ferrari got in touch with the rector at the Ateneo Pontificio Regina Apostolorum, Father Paolo Scarafoni, and the rest of the pieces fell into place.

INAUGURATED IN 2000, the sleek and modern Regina Apostolorum campus, with its large glass windows and straight lines, is a huge contrast to the old-world ambiance of downtown Rome. The manicured pathways and sprawling grounds of the hillside campus could easily be confused for the headquarters of a software company in Father Gary's native Silicon Valley—if it weren't for the groups of priests walking to and fro in their black cassocks. Run by the conservative Legionaries of Christ, an organization that some have likened to Opus Dei, the university's curriculum is decidedly right of center, following the strict teachings of the Church hierarchy on a variety of issues, including stem cell research.

The course was being taught in a large state-of-the-art classroom. And if the modern exterior seemed an odd setting in which to study exorcism, the bright, futuristic interior felt even more bizarre. Indeed, lab-coated technicians would look more appropriate bustling about among the white-on-white walls and ceilings, large windows and skylights, than would Franciscans wearing brown robes, rope belts, and sandals.

Having opted to take a five-minute train ride from Stazione San Pietro rather than the arduous hour-long slog through morning traffic on the bus, Father Gary made his way through the grounds, admiring the neatness and precision of the place. Inside, his favorable impression only grew as he climbed the marble stairs inside the brightly lit interior. By the time he arrived for the first lecture, a large crowd had already gathered outside the doors to the classroom, chatting amicably and looking over a stack of literature advertising the school, which had been placed on a nearby table. It looked to him like a good turnout, though he was surprised at the presence of the news media. Several TV cameras had been set up in the back of the classroom and along the far wall.

The first session of the course, launched in the winter/spring of 2005, had created quite a stir. Captivated by the idea of a university-sponsored course on something as arcane as exorcism, the media had shown up in force, and the headlines didn't disappoint: "Exorcists go back to school." "Priests get refresher course on exorcisms." The publicity actually served the organizers well, getting the message out that the Church was no longer ashamed of exorcism.

As a result of this success, the school decided to run the course again in the fall/winter of 2005 and 2006, with only minor changes. All the professors from the original course would be back, but this time lessons would be available via video conference to satellite locations in Bologna, Modena, and a few other cities. For the last class, several prominent exorcists were going to be invited to share their experiences and answer questions. And this time, rather than being limited to priests, the course had been opened to professionals such as psychologists and doctors who might, for example, want to hear how to distinguish between mental illness and possession.

When Father Gary had heard about the course from his bishop, he got in touch with a few Legionaries in his diocese to ask if there was someone he could talk to about it. They in turn gave him the name of a priest who was on the faculty at the university. A few weeks before he left California, Father Gary called this priest and was able to learn a bit about what to expect.

Though the course was scheduled to run for four months, from October to February, the budding exorcists would be meeting only one day a week—on Thursday morning from 8:30 to 12:30—for a total of ten classes. Five sessions would run from mid-October to late November, and the second half of the course from January to February 9. Perhaps the most important thing he found out was that the course was going to be offered only in Italian. Disappointed at first, he'd been reassured that since priests would be coming from all over the world, the school would provide him with a translator.

Now, however, when he approached a course organizer and inquired about the translator, he was told in an almost offhand way that there wasn't going to be one. Not today or, for that matter, not next week either. How was he supposed to learn anything if he didn't understand the language?

Dejected, he wandered over to the rows of desks as they were quickly filling up. The room was divided into two sections, consisting of long tables, almost like the pews of a church. At the head of a classroom stood a raised dais—the long and low kind you see at conferences and symposiums—with a blank screen behind it. Next to the dais was a cross, and on the back wall, a neorealist painting of Christ crowned with thorns. The row of tinted windows running the entire length of one wall looked down onto a large circular patch of grass, in the center of which stood a solitary olive tree.

A few minutes later, the chatter in the room died down and a line of priests and officials filed in silently behind the dais. Led by the organizer, everyone stood and recited the Lord's Prayer and then a Hail Mary in Italian. It was time for the course to begin.

The first speaker was a bishop whom Father Gary didn't recognize, though many in the room clearly did. His name was Andrea Gemma, and, at age seventy-four, he was a well-regarded exorcist and one of very few bishops who actually performed exorcisms. He had also written a well-received book, *Io, Vescovo Esorcista* (I am a Bishop-Exorcist).

As Monsignor Gemma spoke, Father Gary tried to make sense of

it, but couldn't. Here and there he'd catch a word that sounded familiar; but before he could figure out what it meant, the bishop had
already moved on to something else. After a while he gave up, becoming absorbed instead by the spectacle of media personnel who
roamed the aisles, shoving huge TV cameras into people's faces. At
the break he was tracked down by some English-language reporters
and spent the remainder of the morning fielding questions about exorcism, telling them candidly that he knew nothing about it.

Afterward, as he sat on the train heading back into Rome, he was
disappointed. He hadn't learned anything, and the circuslike nature
of the first day made him wonder if this whole course would be a
waste of time. It was an inauspicious start to his training. He certainly hoped the second session would turn out better.

CHAPTER TWO

tHe cAlliNg

In our Catholic understanding, priestly ordination is a radical, total reordering of a man in the eyes of God and his Church, bringing about an identity of ontological "reconfigurement" with Christ. This priestly identity is at the very core, the essence, of a man, affecting his being and, subsequently, his actions.

—*Monsignor Timothy Dolan,*
Priests for the Third Millennium

Back in September, once he'd gotten over the initial shock of Rome, Father Gary had settled in quite easily to life at the NAC. Originally founded in 1859, the NAC moved to its present site atop the Gianicolo in 1953. The massive six-story building—complete with its own church, auditorium, media room, library, classrooms, and dining hall—seems like a mini-oasis in the heart of Rome, set back from the noisy streets by a large security wall and gatehouse. The complex is big enough to house three hundred seminarians, with adjacent gardens and a million-dollar view of Saint Peter's Basilica. It is no wonder that Father Gary spent a few days exploring the inside.

It was also true that the priests in the sabbatical program kept a pretty busy schedule, waking up for morning mass at 6:30, followed by breakfast and then classes until lunch, with more classes in the afternoon, then evening prayer and dinner. Afterward Father Gary might have just enough time to run down to the library to check the sports scores on the Internet. A rabid sports fan, he followed the San Francisco 49ers as well as the Giants.

He got along well with a majority of the priests in the program, most of whom were around his age and hailed from different parts of the United States. As usual, a few were of the more "antisocial" type, which always puzzled Father Gary, whose concept of "priestly identity" could best be described as "being present to people," but he didn't let the aloofness of others dampen his own spirits.

One treat that staying at the NAC provided was the chance to rub shoulders with the seminarians who lived there. Like the priests in the sabbatical program, the seminarians represented a broad cross-section of cities and towns across America. Father Gary called them "kids" since most were in their mid-twenties. These were the bright young minds of the Church, priests who might one day become respected canonical lawyers or even bishops (some have nicknamed the NAC "the school of bishops"). Father Gary got into the habit of going out to lunch twice a month with a group of these seminarians, sharing with them some of the hard lessons he'd learned over the years.

———————

EVEN AT A YOUNG AGE, Father Gary knew he wanted to be a priest. His mother, AnnaMay Thomas, remembers her son at the age of eleven, pretending to say mass in the kitchen of their South San Francisco home—holding aloft the round piece of Wonder Bread, his expression fixed in reverence as he said, "This is my body, I give it up to you . . ." Gary's younger brother, David, who was six at the time, remembers how seriously his older brother went about it. Everything had to be perfect—the kitchen table covered with a white towel representing the altar, the Bible placed in just the right position, candles arranged appropriately. Gary pressed his little brother into being the altar boy. David's most important task was to make the hosts, which he'd been told had to be flat and perfectly round. Unsure how he was going to accomplish that, Gary let him in on one of his trade secrets: "Use a cookie cutter," he'd said.

Gary Thomas was born on November 2, 1953, in San Francisco, California, to San Francisco natives. AnnaMay, whose maiden name was Mahoney, was raised in a blue-collar Irish Catholic family in the Mission District. Raymond Thomas, the son of Croatian immigrants with Eastern European Catholic ties, grew up in what is now called Catrero Hills.

When Gary was four, the family moved to South San Francisco, also known as South City. At the time, South City was still a growing community, a decidedly blue-collar town populated mostly by people of Italian descent who'd settled there in the wake of World War II. The year they moved, Gary's younger brother David was born, followed by his sister JoAnn. In South City, Ray worked as an electrician, doing mostly private contract work, and once the kids were old enough to go to school, AnnaMay worked as a school secretary. By all accounts, Father Gary had a pretty normal all-American childhood. He played Little League, mowed lawns, and attended All Souls Catholic Grammar School, where he served as an altar boy until eighth grade.

Typically Gary's family would be the last ones to leave church, something Gary's dad often ribbed his mother about. For Gary, something about priests made him feel comfortable; he felt a "positive familiarity" when he was around them. He also had literal familiarity; an uncle on his dad's side was a priest and a cousin on his mom's side was a Jesuit.

In the fifth and sixth grade, when all those in his class put a picture on the bulletin board of what they wanted to be when they grew up, Gary had chosen a picture of a priest. When he told his parents about this, his dad just brushed it off, thinking his son would eventually grow out of it. While this would never happen, when Gary turned fourteen, a chance encounter knocked him off track for a while.

His mother took him to a funeral at the Nauman Lincoln Roos mortuary. After the service, Mr. Lincoln approached Gary and asked if he wanted to work part-time in the funeral home. Without much hesitation, Gary said yes. His work at Nauman Lincoln consisted of a variety of tasks: washing and waxing the cars, cutting lawns, answering the phones, arranging flowers for the ceremony, even taking people into the chapel. He found the work immediately rewarding. He appreciated the religious component of funerals (he had attended many over the years as an altar boy). Not unlike the role of a priest, the funeral director's job was to comfort people—especially in the days following the death of a loved one, when survivors need the most help.

Around the time that he was warming up to a career in the funeral business, Gary began to notice that the priesthood might not be everything he'd originally thought. In the late 1960s and 1970s, the Catholic Church went through tremendous upheaval in the wake of the Second Vatican Council, which advocated that the Church open its windows to the modern world. As a result, many priests began losing the sense of connection they'd once felt to the traditions that had attracted them to the priesthood. This had a disastrous effect. Priests began leaving the Church in large numbers. The entire order of nuns that taught at Gary's high school, Junipero Serra, disbanded. In the midst of this general confusion, Gary became disillusioned about his chosen vocation.

IN 1972 HE ENROLLED in the University of San Francisco, a Jesuit-run school in the heart of San Francisco. He and a friend, Robert Eagen, would be among the first generation of kids from South City to go to college. Thinking he might one day run his own mortuary, Gary majored in business management.

The tuition was $1,600 a year, which Gary paid himself by working as a busboy for $250 a month during the school year as well as at the mortuary during the summer. Because of tight finances, he lived at home, commuting to school in a rust-colored 1971 Chevy Camaro that he bought from a neighbor for $2,000.

As Gary matured, his responsibilities at the mortuary changed. When he turned eighteen, he went on his first "removal," mortuary parlance for picking up a dead body. Surprisingly, despite all the funerals he'd attended and his time at the mortuary, he had yet to actually see a naked corpse. This particular body belonged to a patient who'd died at San Francisco General Hospital. To this day Gary remembers that the sight of the corpse, lying bare on the metallic slab down in the morgue, made him nauseous. Eventually, he got used to that, but the experience of performing removals never became routine—especially not when he had to drive to homes and remove a body while under the watchful eyes of a roomful of grieving family members.

Meanwhile, in the spring semester of his final year at USF, mutual friends set Gary up on a blind date with Lori Driscoll (now Lori Armstrong), a freshman nursing student at San Francisco State. The two immediately hit it off and began dating, usually attending sporting events with groups of friends. "He had this ability to put other people first and make them feel special," Lori recalls.

Sometimes, however, Gary's mortuary job threw a kink into their plans. Lori remembers a few occasions when she'd gotten all dressed up, only to have Gary cancel at the last minute because he had to do a removal. Despite being disappointed, she'd soothe her bruised ego by telling herself that if he was to become a funeral director, she'd better get used to this now rather than later.

In 1975, Gary graduated from USF and immediately entered a year-long program at the San Francisco College of Mortuary Science in order to get his embalming license. He continued to live at home while attending the mortuary school, easily making friends and even picking up a nickname. One course he took was on funeral services as practiced by different religious denominations. Because of his long exposure to Catholic tradition, Gary was asked if he'd be willing to teach it to the other students. Before long, everyone began calling him "Father Thomas."

He excelled at the school, finishing the program in only nine months, after which he went to work as an apprentice for a mortuary in South City. Then in 1977, at the age of twenty-four, Gary got his embalmer's license and moved to a funeral home in Los Altos. The mortuary had a little cottage on-site, where for the first time in his life, Gary lived on his own.

During mortuary school, he had discovered a sort of "marvel to the human body as a system," especially the circulatory system, which embalmers use for draining the blood and inserting the embalming fluid. And rather than being sickened by what he witnessed, if anything the constant exposure to death helped to "elevate" his spiritual life. Oftentimes, while inserting the eye caps—small plastic devices with edged "teeth" that keep the eyes closed—he would find himself staring into the lifeless eyes of the deceased. The first time he did this, he could tell there was something odd about them; a presence was missing. To Gary, this was clear proof that there is eternal life, that the soul leaves the body at death.

During his time in Los Altos, a feeling Gary thought was long gone began to gnaw at him; he started thinking seriously about the priesthood again. Despite having a rewarding career, he felt deep down somewhere that he was destined to do something different. He began asking himself a hard question: Was the life he had mapped out for himself as a mortician the one God intended?

There was also his relationship with Lori to consider. In the end he knew he couldn't be fair to her if he continued to harbor doubts. A few weeks later, one September afternoon, he and Lori drove to Vasona Lake Park in Los Gatos for a picnic. Lori had no idea what was coming, though perhaps she should have seen the writing on the wall. For five months, Gary had been dropping hints about his interest in joining the priesthood. Lori's mind, however, had been focused elsewhere. In fact, she had expected to get a ring for her twenty-first birthday in August. At the park, the two wandered out to a shady spot on the grass, overlooking the lake. There they sat for a few minutes, watching the water, each looking at a different world and contemplating a very different future. Gary could see himself alone, a priest dedicating himself to a life of celibacy and service to God. Lori saw herself as a mother and wife of a funeral director. At some point, Gary turned to face her and their worlds collided. Though dumbfounded, Lori realized she could not stand in Gary's way.

THE YEAR AFTER he broke up with Lori turned into a time of struggle for Gary. He continued working in the funeral business while determining whether or not God was calling him to the priesthood.

In the summer of 1978, he began meeting regularly with a spiritual director, Father James O'Shaunessy, to find out "How is God in all of this?" However, the decision to apply to the seminary didn't come until after he had heard a talk at Saint Joseph's Seminary College in Los Altos on how to recognize a vocation. There, a Marian priest touched on ways a person might recognize the right vocation: "Part of it is desire, part of it is excitement for a service with people, and part of it is an inability to respond to some kind of prompting in any other way than going with what your heart tells you." The words had a huge impact on Gary. He made his decision to enter the seminary that day.

When Gary dropped by his parents' house to tell them the news, Gary's dad was shocked, telling his son that he was "nuts" to be entering the priesthood when everybody else seemed to be leaving. Gary assured him that if he didn't like it he would leave. Ray left it at that, realizing he wouldn't be able to change his son's mind. Gary's mom, on the other hand, was "thrilled." She knew he was fulfilling his calling.

Gary entered Saint Patrick's Seminary in August 1979, amid a sea of change—discipline had become lax in recent years and a new rector, Father Howard P. Bleichner S.S., had been brought in to reinstill a sense of order, which he did with an iron fist. As a result, Father Gary remembers little about the seminary as being fun.

One of the few things he did enjoy was the opportunity to work in a parish, which allowed him to interact with people. It also gave him a taste of his future life as a priest. Unlike some seminarians who preferred losing themselves in intellectual pursuits, Gary loved the fieldwork. He was a natural communicator, thriving on human interaction.

During his third year he began working fifteen hours a week at O'Connor Hospital in San Jose. He specifically requested to be moved to the "death ward." He had been around death most of his life, but his experience at O'Connor was something else entirely. Ever conscious of his priestly duty to alleviate suffering, he wanted to know what to say when people were at their most vulnerable and needed comfort. Unlike the priests who shied away from suffering, Gary experienced these as circumstances when a priest was truly called upon to be present. In the end, his hours in the ward taught him that death can sometimes be a lonely experience and that often it is best to say nothing at all.

GARY WAS ORDAINED in March 1983, during one of the worst storms to hit San Jose in twenty years. Caught out on the highway, Gary's parents braved the torrential rains and hurricane-force winds, thinking that there'd be nobody at the cathedral when they finally arrived. However, they were amazed to see the place packed, even though the storm had knocked out the power (which miraculously came back on ten minutes before the ceremony was to start).

Lori had kept track of Gary's progress over the years and, though she still felt hurt by their breakup, cared too much about Gary to miss his ordination. Newly married, she brought her husband with her.

The thought of seeing so many of his family and friends in one place made Gary incredibly nervous. The two-hour ordination ceremony for himself and just one other priest flew by. Then, as the procession was filing out of the church, Gary spotted Lori by the door and stopped to give her a hug. Blushing at all the attention, she introduced her husband, Bob, who shook Gary's hand. With that Gary rejoined the procession.

In the context of the Catholic Church, the priesthood is more akin to an identity than a job. It is not something that a priest can turn his back on or take a vacation from. As Pope John Paul II wrote, "[A] priest, by virtue of the consecration [. . .] is called to love selflessly, to put the needs of his 'flock' before those of his own."

Father Gary had seemingly internalized very early in life this desire to engage with people. Now that he was a priest, his dedication to this role carried new meaning. Because of his ordination, he felt that he had a responsibility to embrace humanity in all its beauty and ugliness. He already knew he was comfortable with death; now he looked forward to helping his parishioners confront the trials of life.

CHAPTER THREE

GoIng BaCk
to ScHooL

The Devil is present everywhere that evil
things happen within the normal laws of nature. In anyone who says: I don't accept love,
the love of my brothers and sisters, the love
of God. And in many places, in all massacres,
in every murder, in physical catastrophes, in
every concentration camp, in all evil. Sometimes he shows himself, strangely, but also in
cases of possession. But he's much more dangerous where he doesn't let himself be seen,
where he can't be done away with through
exorcism.

—*Father Pedro Barrajon,*
excerpt from interview in
Die Welt, *December 2, 2005*

When Father Gary first heard about the exorcism course, he'd wondered how such a class might be structured. Obviously the organizers had worked this out carefully and systematically.

After Dr. Ferrari contacted Father Scarafoni about the idea, they began collaborating on the syllabus and choosing the faculty. The goal was to scrape away all misinformation so priests could relearn what the Church actually taught on these matters. However, in addition to a straightforward course on the theology of demons, the organizers also wanted to ensure that potential exorcists become well rounded and decided to include lectures by a psychiatrist and a criminologist. Students would attend lectures on Satanism and youth culture, on how to discern spirits, on the powers of the Devil, as well as on the Church's teachings regarding angels and demons, taught by a Legionaire theologian. In addition exorcists would be called upon to discuss their ministry and share practical tips. Unfortunately, the International Association of Exorcists had refused Father Scarafoni's request to perform an exorcism live, in front of the students.

After the first day of the course, things had improved dramatically for Father Gary. As soon as he'd gotten off the train coming back from the Regina Apostolorum, he'd stalked the halls of the NAC, looking for a priest to translate for him. Yet after a week of chasing leads, he'd struck out. Thinking that the second day might be a waste like the first, he nonetheless took the train out on the morning of October 20, hoping to be proved wrong. As it turned out, the course organizers had scrambled and found a very competent Legionaire seminarian to translate for him, communicating via a microphone and headset. While not perfect (sometimes the seminarian had to abridge in order to keep pace), the system worked pretty well.

RIGHT OFF THE BAT, Father Gary was amazed to learn that exorcism was actually central to Jesus' gospel message. In fact in the early Church, every Christian was thought to have the power to perform exorcisms.

Back at the NAC, as he got to know some of the priests and seminarians better, he quickly realized that he wasn't the only one to have misconceptions about the real nature of exorcism. As he shared the fact that he was a fledgling exorcist, he predictably got mixed reactions. Some complimented him. Another group responded with "You shouldn't have told us. We're not supposed to know." Perplexed by this, he got in touch with his bishop and asked if his appointment was indeed some kind of "state secret." The bishop said this was the first he'd heard about it. True to his open nature, Father Gary thought that the priests in the diocese ought to know so they could come to him with questions.

Members in the third group responded to his revelation simply by giving him a blank look and saying flatly, "I don't believe in that." And while it may seem strange that Catholic priests did not believe in the Devil or exorcism, to Father Gary, who was ordained in the aftermath of the Second Vatican Council, it wasn't surprising at all.

UP UNTIL THE 1960S, the Church as a body was relatively unified in its belief that the Devil was an evil spirit, a fallen angel created by God and endowed with certain powers and free will.

In the early Church, the Devil was seen as the leader of a vast army of demons arrayed against "the community of the faithful" as represented by the apostles and the other followers of Christ. Later, Saint Augustine would come to refer to this conflict in terms of a struggle between "two cities," created when the angels were put to a test by God. As a result, Christians had to be on constant guard against this enemy who sought mankind's ruin as a way to get even with God. In this war, the chief weapon of the Devil was temptation; however, as witnessed in the New Testament, in certain circumstances he could attack an individual directly, taking control of the person's body. When that happened, the only remedy was an exorcism.

Since Satan is a created being, and therefore subject to the power of God, an exorcism is valid only when it is performed in the name of God and by the authority of the Church, to which Christ gave that power. "Then Jesus summoned his twelve disciples and gave them authority over unclean spirits, to cast them out, and to cure every disease and every sickness" (Matthew 10:1).

The New Testament is full of stories of Jesus exorcising demons, which not only proved his divinity but was also tangible evidence that he had come to defeat the kingdom of Satan and usher in a new one. "But if it is by the Spirit of God that I cast out demons, then the kingdom of God has come to you" (Matthew 12:28).

Perhaps the most dramatic exorcism in the Gospels is the case of the Gerasene demoniac (Mark 5:1–20). As Jesus steps out of a boat near a town called Gadarenes, he is immediately accosted by a man out of the tombs on the hillside. The people of the town have tried to restrain him with "shackles and chains," but he has "wrenched them apart" during his ravings. He is always shouting and bruising himself with stones. Upon seeing Jesus he cries out, "What have you to do with me, Jesus, Son of the Most High God? I adjure you by God, do not torment me." Jesus then commands the evil spirit to leave the man and asks his name, receiving the answer "Legion." The evil spirit then begs Jesus "not to send them out of the country" but instead to allow them to be sent into a herd of swine feeding nearby. Jesus grants permission and the herd of swine "numbering about two thousand" then "rushes down the steep bank and into the sea."

Although Jesus was not the only exorcist of his day, his method was special. Rather than using the complex rituals and props of his contemporaries, he simply ordered the demon to depart, sometimes even in the first person. In fact Jesus' exorcisms were considered so radical that he was accused by his enemies of harnessing the power of demons (Mark 3:20–30), a charge Jesus answered by saying simply that it was impossible for a demon to cast out a demon.

These exorcisms had a powerful effect on Jesus' followers. The evangelist Mark thought them so spectacular that the first miracle he reports Jesus performing is an exorcism (Mark 1:23–27).

In the years following Jesus' death, exorcism became an important tool for believers to win converts and spread the faith. Almost all the Apostolic Fathers (the writers who came after the apostles) wrote about it. In his *Dialogue with Trypho*, Justin Martyr, one of the earliest Christian theologians, states: "Any demon who is commanded in the name of the Son of God . . . will be overcome and defeated."

The importance of exorcism is clear in the early ceremonies of baptism, in which candidates underwent a series of formal exorcisms over a period of days while renouncing Satan (the renouncing of Satan is still used in baptism today).

Despite this early importance, a fierce debate erupted between "liberal" and "conservative" theologians in the 1960s about whether the figure of the Devil was ever meant to be taken literally. Since the Church goes about defining truth through two distinct elements— divine revelation (scripture) and tradition, which are authentically interpreted by the Church's Magisterium, or teaching authority—both sides used a mixture of historical and biblical evidence to make their case.

For liberals, it was incomprehensible that the Church would continue to believe in such things as "unseen spirits" or that the Devil was a "person" when advances in science and human reason had clearly shown most of the foundations for these beliefs to be obsolete. "We cannot use electric light and radio, or turn to modern medicine in cases of sickness," wrote Rudolf Bultmann in 1969, "and at the same time believe in a spirit world and in the miracles that the New Testament presents us." Taking aim at the Bible, they analyzed the passages that mentioned the Devil and pointed out their reliance on allegory—a literary device used by the writers of the Gospels to underline the hold that evil had over the world. And while Jesus' actions clearly indicate that at least *he* believed in the Devil, this was debunked by critics like Herbert Haag, Bas van Iersel, and Henry Ansgar Kelly, who claimed that he was simply doing the modern PR equivalent of "dumbing down" the message to get his point across to an uncultured society.

For conservatives, not only did these interpretations misrepresent scripture, but they completely disregarded long-standing traditions reported by the Apostolic Fathers. If the Church had never come out with a binding statement on the Devil's existence in the past, that was because it never had to; the reality of the Devil had never been doubted. To dispute these teachings, they said, would be to call into question the very credibility of the Church. As if to underscore the point, on November 15, 1972, Pope Paul VI spoke out on the matter to a general audience, saying that "evil is not merely a lack of something but an effective agent, a living spiritual being, [and that] it is contrary to the teaching of the Bible and the Church to refuse to recognize the existence of such a reality."

Both positions seemed to have their limitations. While the liberal view was in many respects a continuation of Enlightenment thinking, its labeling of Jesus' exorcisms as allegorical had disturbing ramifications for anyone claiming to be a Christian. If Jesus were indeed the Son of God, as every Christian believes, why would he misinform his followers by commanding them to cast out evil spirits if no such beings existed?

Meanwhile, for conservatives, while their defense of the faith on traditional grounds did agree with the Fathers of the Church, it was perceived by rank-and-file priests of the day as being medieval and out of touch with modern society.

In the end, it would be this last view that would win out, as more and more priests found themselves affected not only by a growing acceptance of a modernist worldview, but also by a kind of existential relativism that took hold as a result of the Second Vatican Council. While not necessarily rejecting the official teachings of the Church, most clergymen found the concept of the Devil a sideshow that no "serious-minded" priest would lose time considering. For all intents and purposes, it was Charles Baudelaire's well-known phrase come to life: The Devil had finally convinced the world that he no longer existed.

AT THE COURSE, Father Gary also benefited from being introduced to other novice exorcists like himself. Most were from Italy and didn't speak English. One priest, however, a Franciscan from America, proved extremely helpful.

Father Daniel, originally from the New England area, had recently been stationed at the shrines in Jerusalem. His brown robe bore the symbol—a red cross surrounded by four smaller ones—of his order. With his robe, close-cropped hair, and beard, he appeared to be from another era. And yet, upon closer inspection, the subtle hints of his New England background rose to the surface—a sliver of blue jeans below his robe, Birkenstock sandals, the frayed collar of a green button-down shirt.

During one of the breaks, Father Daniel explained to Father Gary what compelled him to take the course. That summer he'd been at a shrine in Abruzzo, east of Rome, where he'd had a terrifying experience. One day, while he listened to confessions at the shrine, a woman approached him and asked if he believed in demonic possession. Despite his lack of firsthand knowledge in the matter, he told her that he did. The woman responded, "Good, because I suffer from it and I want to confess." Unsure what she meant, he nonetheless began with his blessing and continued to hear her confession. He could see immediately that something was amiss; she began to twitch and clear her throat repeatedly. Then things got worse. All of a sudden she began to grunt and the word *zitto*, shut up, escaped involuntarily from her pursed lips. Then, when it came time for him to say his final blessings and absolve her of her sins, to his utter shock, all the muscles in her face contorted to such a degree that he could no longer recognize her. Next, her jaw completely unhinged and, dropping down, shifted over to one side of her face, giving the impression that her mouth had become nine inches wide. At this point, Father Daniel nearly panicked but kept calm long enough to bless the woman in the name of Jesus Christ, after which she got up and bolted from the church.

After he had recovered and his fears subsided, he became curious about what he had just witnessed. In order to get answers, he volunteered to help the local exorcist who worked at the shrine. It didn't take long for him to realize that he had seen only the tip of the iceberg—there was a whole world out there that he never knew existed. As a result, when he was transferred to Rome in the fall to begin his doctoral studies, he petitioned his superior for permission to apprentice with an exorcist. Father Tommaso at the Scala Santa, a church that has been long associated with exorcism, took him on shortly thereafter.

As he listened to Father Daniel, Father Gary had no reason to doubt the Franciscan's sincerity. Far from boastful, Father Daniel had been incredibly humble, even self-deprecating—almost as if even he couldn't believe what had happened. Father Daniel's story only made Father Gary realize just how little he knew about demonic possession. Before he could ever perform an exorcism himself, he would need to learn more about who or what he was going up against.

CHAPTER FOUR

KnOw YoUr EnEmY

If God the Father almighty, the Creator of the ordered and good world, cares for all his creatures, why does evil exist? To this question, as pressing as it is unavoidable and as painful as it is mysterious, no quick answer will suffice. Only Christian faith as a whole constitutes the answer to this question: the goodness of creation, the drama of sin, and the patient love of God who comes to meet man by his covenants, the redemptive Incarnation of his Son, his gift of the Spirit, his gathering of the Church, the power of the sacraments, and his call to a blessed life to which free creatures are invited to consent in advance, but from which, by terrible mystery, they can also turn away in advance. There is not a single aspect of the Christian message that is not in part an answer to the question of evil.

—Catechism of the Catholic Church *309*

The capacity to love has been annihilated from the psychology of a demon. A demon knows but does not love. The pleasure achieved in doing an evil act is the same as that which a human being feels when he gets revenge on an enemy—it is a pleasure filled with hate.

—*Father José Antonio Fortea,*
Interview with an Exorcist

The idea of the Devil has evolved over time, primarily as a way to explain the existence of evil in a world created by an all-powerful and loving God.

The word *devil* comes from the Greek *diabolos*, which means "adversary, slanderer, opposer." When the Hebrew Bible was translated in 200 B.C.E. into Greek (known as the Septuagint version), the Greeks commonly used this word in place of the Hebrew word *satan*, which meant "accuser."

In the Old Testament, which was written between 1000 and 100 B.C.E., the Devil is only mentioned a few times, and even then he is far from a coherent, personified being. Some theologians, such as Thomas Aquinas, have speculated that this is because Moses was "addressing uncultured people" and didn't want to promote any beliefs that might tempt them to worship false idols. Other theologians have suggested that the lack of a coherent demonology in the Old Testament might be because the Israelites had a strict law in place that prohibited magic. Satan's most prominent appearance is in the book of Job; but as some scholars have pointed out, here his name is really just a title. He still has access to the heavenly court and appears to be acting as God's agent, a kind of "prosecuting attorney." In this role, he convinces God to give him the power to torment Job to test Job's loyalty (Job 1:6–12).

In the New Testament, however, the Devil plays a much bigger role. At the time of Christ's coming—thanks to original sin—"the whole world lies under the power of the Evil One" (1 John 5:19). To heal this rift, God sends his only Son. The Synoptic Gospels address this concept directly and repeatedly. "The Son of God was revealed for this purpose, to destroy the works of the devil" (1 John 3:8).

The New Testament is full of the battles that these two sides wage. Satan tempts Christ directly in the desert (Matthew 4:1–11; Mark 1:13; Luke 4:1–13) and attacks him indirectly through his followers by temptation (Matthew 13:19); by inflicting bodily harm (Luke 13:11); and by possession (Mark 1:23–28). Jesus teaches his disciples the Lord's Prayer, and confronts the Devil head-on by performing exorcisms.

THE BELIEF IN SPIRITS or intermediaries between God and man exists in just about every religion. The Assyrians, for instance, had numerous books (written on clay tablets) dedicated to incantations and conjurations to ward off evil spirits.

According to the Greeks, "demons," or *daimones,* were thought to be either good or evil. Socrates, for instance, famously credited a *daimon* as being the source of his inspiration.

For Catholics, the belief in angels is an article of faith, based on divine revelation and the teachings of the Church. "The Apostles' Creed professes that God is 'Creator of heaven and earth.' The Nicene Creed makes it explicit that this profession includes 'all that is seen and unseen.'"

The creation of the angels is affirmed in numerous passages of the Bible. Saint Paul writes to the Colossians: "For in him [Christ] all things in heaven and on earth were created, things visible and invisible, whether thrones or dominions or rulers or powers—all things have been created through him and for him" (Colossians 1:16).

The angels occupy a natural order, or hierarchy of beings, whose purpose is to reflect the glory of God. As thirteenth-century theologian Thomas Aquinas explains in *Summa Theologiæ,* his great tome on angels, "There must be some incorporeal creatures, for what is principally intended by God in creatures is good, and this consists in assimilation to God Himself [. . .] hence the perfection of the universe requires that there should be intellectual creatures."

To many theologians it seems only natural to believe in higher intelligences superior to our own, especially when one considers the ordered nature and varying degrees of intelligence that exist in the world, from single-cell organisms right up to man. "It would be most extraordinary if (man) formed the last link," writes Pie-Raymond Régamey, O.P.

THE CATECHISM OF THE CATHOLIC CHURCH teaches that Satan was a good angel created by God: "The devil and the other demons were indeed created naturally good by God, but they became evil by their own doing."

As an expression of his love, God created the angels with free will so that they could love him back and "render [themselves] similar to God who 'is love'" (1 John 4:16). In simple terms, according to the Christian tradition, love is a metaphysical necessity for created beings since it is only through love that such beings can realize their full potential. And since love not freely given is not really love at all, this meant that the angels (along with man) needed to have the ability to choose. However, God knew that once he gave this freedom, it could be used either for evil or for good. "By creating the pure spirits as free beings, God in his Providence could not but foresee also *the possibility of the angels' sin*," said Pope John Paul II.

After their creation, God tested the angels before admitting them to the beatific vision (the direct experience of God in heaven). Many angels remained faithful to God while a smaller number, led by Satan, "rebelled," choosing to place themselves before God.

After their sin, the angels were immediately stripped of their everlasting grace and condemned to an "eternal punishment" (Matthew 25:46). Theologians call this punishment the "pain of loss." The fallen angels were cut off from the only source that could have given them happiness: God. In this "hell," the demons are forever tormented and remain obstinate in their hate, a hate that has deformed their very nature.

According to Christian tradition, Satan was the principal fallen angel, the brightest and most perfect of all God's creations. The Bible makes it clear that he holds a higher rank than the other fallen angels:

"the Devil and his angels" (Matthew 25:41), "the ruler of the demons" (Luke 11:15), "the dragon and his angels" (Revelation 12:7–9).

Ever since Origen attributed the fall to pride, Satan's name has been interchangeable with Lucifer. The name, taken from a verse in Isaiah, is used metaphorically to describe the king of Babylon. "How art thou fallen from heaven, Lucifer, son of Dawn! How are you cut down to the ground, you who laid nations low! You said in your heart, 'I will ascend into heaven; I will raise my throne above the stars of God'" (Isaiah 14:12–13). Some theologians have argued against this association. Indeed, some exorcists like Father Amorth say that Lucifer and Satan are two distinct demons. Despite this, however, the tradition of associating Lucifer with the Devil continues, even as the Catholic Church maintains that the name "Lucifer" symbolizes the state from which the Devil has fallen and is not a proper name.

After the angels "fell," God created the material world, including the first humans. When this happened, Satan turned his rage on mankind, and, as described by John Paul II, "transplant[ed] into man the insubordination, rivalry and opposition to God, which had become the motivation for his existence." The book of Genesis relates how Satan, taking the form of the serpent, tempted Adam and Eve to sin.

As a result of this sin and humanity's turning its back on God, Satan has been given some degree of dominion over man. In the Bible he is called "the ruler of this world" (John 12:31) and "the god of this world" (2 Corinthians 4:4).

———

IN THE EARLY DAYS OF THE CHURCH, the nature of angels caused some confusion. Writing in the second century, Justin Martyr thought that fallen angels had denser bodies than the good angels, and that they actually ate a special kind of food (Psalm 78:25; Psalm 105:40). The word *angel* is also deceiving. Deriving from the Hebrew *mal'ak* or the Greek *angelos*, it signifies "messenger," or "envoy," which indicates more of a function than a nature.

Today, the Church teaches that angels are incorporeal spiritual beings. Saint Augustine says: "'Angel' is the name of their office, not of their nature. If you seek the name of their nature, it is 'spirit'; if you seek the name of their office, it is 'angel': from what they are, 'spirit,' from what they do, 'angel.'"

There has been much speculation over the years about what might constitute the nature of a pure spirit. And while his writings on the subject are not a part of official Church doctrine, a majority of Catholic theologians follow the teachings of Thomas Aquinas, also known as the Angelic Doctor. Aquinas explains that pure spirits are not composed of matter and form, but of essence and existence, act and potentiality. Where the early Church Fathers fell short, Aquinas suggests, was in not according enough importance to intelligence. Because of their wholly spiritual nature, angels are complete beings and occupy "the first and highest place in the scale of created things," nearer to the likeness of God, who is pure spirit, rather than man, who is a mix of the spiritual (soul) and material (body).

Every angel is a distinct being endowed with intellect and free will. However, as Aquinas explains, this doesn't mean that the angels are composed only of intellect, but rather that their knowledge is derived from the intellect, compared to a human soul that attains knowledge through both the intellect and senses. As theologian A. M. Lepicier notes, "An angel possesses such penetration that he is able, at one glance, to take in the whole field of science laying open to his perception, just as we, at a glance, can take in the entire field of vision lying exposed to our eyes."

For the ministry of an exorcist, perhaps the most important distinction that Aquinas makes is that since angels (or demons) do not occupy space, therefore they cannot be physically present in a place like a person can. In this way, they are not anywhere. Instead, when a demon is alleged to move an object (slam a door, for instance, or slide a chair across a room), the demon is *acting* on that object.

Their being immaterial means that angels do not move from point A to B by any kind of locomotion, but instead suddenly shift their activity from one point or place to a different one. Some theologians have likened this movement to the human mind, which can instantly transfer thoughts over long distances or onto random objects.

Since the Church teaches that God never rejects his creatures, even when they use his gifts for evil means, the Devil still retains his former angelic stature and powers. As Saint Augustine established, though, God does not give Satan a free hand, otherwise "no man would be left alive." Theologians stipulate that the Devil and the fallen angels are limited in their actions in two main ways: by the limits of their nature as created beings, and by the will of God.

LIMITS OF THE DEVIL BASED ON HIS NATURE

The Catholic Church teaches that no matter how superior he is to humans, the Devil is still a finite creature. He cannot, for example, perform true miracles, because by definition a miracle is something that surpasses the power of all created nature. To perform a miracle requires "supernatural" power, and Satan has only "preternatural" power. He can, however, create the appearance of a miracle since his powers allow him to surpass the limits of human abilities.

The Devil is also limited in his ability to know the secrets of the inner heart, a field strictly open to God, who is all-knowing, say theologians. However, according to exorcists, the Devil can tell what we are thinking by using his superior powers of observation, just as a physician might glean some information about a man's health by checking his pulse.

The Devil cannot foresee the future, say exorcists. He can, however, fake the appearance of psychic ability by accurately "predicting" what will happen based on his knowledge of human nature and the powers he has as a spirit.

LIMITS OF THE DEVIL BASED ON GOD'S WILL

The second limitation on the Devil's power comes from God's will. In the Christian tradition, an important distinction is made between the Devil's status as a lower being created by God and his false reputation as "god of evil" (a view held by many satanic cults). As a result, the Catholic Church emphasizes that even though the Devil, because of his angelic stature, has more power than humans, he can do nothing unless God allows it. The book of Job attests to the fact that God can restrain the Devil: "The Lord said to Satan, Very well, all that he has is in your power; only do not stretch out your hand against him" (Job 1:13).

Many have asked, Why would God allow the Devil to harm us? While this question is not easy to answer, Catholic theologians such as Thomas Aquinas have tried to show that ultimately God permits the Devil to act in order to turn evil to good.

Typically, the Devil is permitted to act in ways broken down by exorcists into two categories: ordinary and extraordinary.

ORDINARY ACTIVITY OF THE DEVIL

The ordinary activity of the Devil is temptation. Temptation is essentially nothing more than an attraction to commit a sin. In order to sin, we first have to realize that whatever act we are committing is a moral evil, otherwise we would be guilty of only ignorance, not sin. Saint Paul says in the letter to the Romans: "I do not understand my own actions. For I do not do what I want, but I do the very thing I hate. Now if I do what I do not want, I agree that the law is good. But in fact it is no longer I that do it but sin that dwells within me. [. . .] I can will what is right, but I cannot do it. For I do not the good I want, but the evil I do not want is what I do" (Romans 7:15–23). It is in this capacity of tempting us to go against the good of our nature that exorcists assert the Devil is most active. However, theologians are quick to point out that it would be a mistake to assume that all temptations come from the Devil. As Thomas Aquinas says, "The devil is not the cause of every sin: for all sins are not committed at the devil's instigation, but some are due to the free-will and the corruption of the flesh." The Catholic Church teaches that overcoming temptation is a normal way for the soul to strengthen in grace and virtue.

EXTRAORDINARY ACTIVITY OF THE DEVIL

Any demonic activity that is considered more powerful than temptation is "extraordinary." Over the years, numerous terms have been used in the field of exorcism and deliverance to describe the various ways in which the Devil and demons can afflict people directly. When the new rite of exorcism was promulgated in 1998, the Conference of Italian Bishops asked the International Association of Exorcists to come up with a list of terms that could be used by everybody. The Devil's extraordinary activity was lumped into four major areas: (1) infestation, (2) oppression, (3) obsession, and (4) demonic possession.

INFESTATION

Infestation is the presence of demonic activity in a location or object, such as a "haunted house."

The various kinds of phenomena that can occur in this situation are vast and include unexplained sounds or noises like mysterious footsteps, loud bangs, laughter, screams; the temperature of a room dropping or the feelings of a cold wind with no discernable source; objects disappearing suddenly and materializing in other parts of the house; strange presences felt; the presence of offensive odors; interruption of electric current or the malfunction of electronic devices; pictures that mysteriously bang or fall off the wall; doors and windows that open and close on their own; dishes or other objects levitating and flying about the room.

One exorcist described going to bless a house and seeing mysterious, bloodlike spots appearing on various objects, including articles of clothing tucked away in drawers and even a set of brand-new bed sheets that were still sealed in plastic. In the same instance, a rosary that had been strung with ornate glass beads was found hanging on the back of a door with all the beads mysteriously removed. Later that night, the beads were found crushed into a fine powder and placed into a neat little pile outside the house.

In another instance, a woman baked a cake and placed it on the kitchen table; but when she reentered the room, the cake was mysteriously high on top of the cupboard even though no one else was in the house.

Generally, say exorcists, such disturbances occur for a number of reasons, including the presence of a cursed object in the house or the house itself being cursed; use of the location for occult activities such as séances or for a criminal activity of some kind, such as prostitution or drug dealing; performance of a satanic ritual on the premises; or gruesome murders or suicides having taken place there. Often, say exorcists, manifestations are caused by a person being attacked by an evil presence rather than attributed to an evil spirit being attached to the house.

Typically, instead of performing an exorcism, exorcists prefer to do a simple blessing and say a mass on the premises.

OPPRESSION

Also called "physical attack," oppression often takes the form of mysterious blows raining down on the individual or scratches inexplicably materializing on the body. Some people have had strange signs or even letters appear on their skin, while others claim to be pushed down stairs or out of bed by an invisible force. The Bible attests to the power of the Devil to inflict physical infirmities. In the Gospel of Luke, for example, Jesus heals a woman who has been bowed over and deformed by a "spirit of infirmity" (Luke 13:10–16). Typically, this kind of direct attack is aimed at people who are closest to God, such as the saints. Saint Catherine of Siena (1347–1380), Saint Teresa of Avila (1515–1582), Saint John Vianney (1786–1859), and Saint Gemma Galgani (1878–1903), to name a few, were all the objects of demonic oppression at some point in their lives, as was Saint Paul, whose "Thorn in the flesh" (2 Corinthians 12:7) is generally considered to have been caused by a demon.

As in the book of Job, victims of this kind of attack may also suffer in their work, health, or relationships. The purpose is to drive these people toward isolation and despair so they may turn their back on God.

OBSESSION

Obsession has also been called "demonic temptation," and it involves an intense and persistent attack on the mind of the victim. Generally these attacks include random and obsessive thoughts that, though often absurd, are so intense that the victim is unable to free him- or herself. Victims feel tormented by a fixation that completely dominates their thoughts. These thoughts can make the victim think he is going insane, which only compounds the feelings of sadness and desperation. As Italian exorcist Father Francesco Bamonte notes, "Some are thoughts and impulses that urge people to harm others; some make people think that only a pact with Satan can get them out of their troubles or bring them success; some are thoughts to profane the Eucharist; others are thoughts to drive one to suicide." Often the obsessions affect a person's dreams, and terrible nightmares are common.

POSSESSION

Also known as "involuntary possession," demonic possession is by far the most spectacular activity of the Devil and also the rarest. Some exorcists believe they have never seen a full demonic possession, while others encounter the phenomena with some frequency. Almost all exorcists are unanimous in their belief, however, that more people are becoming possessed today than in the recent past.

In a demonic possession, the Devil takes temporary control of a person's body, speaking and acting through it without the person's knowledge. This control, however, doesn't last indefinitely, but rather occurs only during "moments of crisis" in which the victim enters a trance state. Generally speaking, after the crisis passes, the victim will not remember what transpired (rare individuals will be conscious during the ordeal and will remember). As a result of this "loss of control" the individual is considered blameless for whatever happens. However, having a free will, they are responsible for their actions when they are not in the trance state, and so, say theologians, demonic possession in no way exculpates them from guilt.

In between their crisis moments, it is also possible for victims to carry on as if nothing is wrong. This does not mean, however, that they are not affected by the demon. "People who are possessed can keep undergoing influence of the demon in their mind," says another Italian exorcist. "As the Holy Spirit acquaints one with divine things such as good feelings, pleasant sensations, a state of physical well-being, a state of calm, inner peace and also an intuition of things, an evil spirit through his ugliness can do the same thing though in the opposite way, like agitation, anxiety, desperation, hate, or thoughts of suicide."

During moments of crisis, the Devil can manifest in various ways: bodily contortions that defy rational explanation; unnatural strength; knowledge of hidden things; or abilities to speak or understand foreign languages. In stronger cases, the demon will speak through the person, usually in an odd or unnatural voice that is full of rage and hatred.

It is also possible for strange occurrences to happen at the homes of possessed individuals, such as weird animals appearing or disappearing. For instance, one eighteen-year-old girl was suddenly awakened one night by a slap across her face. Looking around, she saw that she was alone. However, as she searched the room, she noticed that misshapen bugs (with antennae or wings missing, for example) began appearing on the walls. Frightened, she called out to her mother, who also saw the bugs. The two then tried to kill them with a shoe, but they kept appearing on the walls as if out of thin air.

It is important to note that, in the case of a demonic possession, say exorcists, the soul of the individual is not possessed, just the body. A great debate has raged among Christians about whether a person in a state of grace could also be possessed. According to the Catholic Church, the answer is yes (the lives of the saints bear witness to this) because the soul remains in a state of grace while the body is taken over. The only exception would be when a person "invites" a possession to take place, such as during a satanic ritual. "In this case," says an Italian exorcist, "the presence in the soul is completed, which means that the will of the person completely identifies with the demon, having given himself completely to him. In that case the person becomes constantly possessed, and is like a demon walking on the earth."

CHAPTER FIVE

OPENING THE DOOR

My dear Wormwood,
Everything is clearly going very well. I am
specially glad to hear that the two new
friends have now made him acquainted with
their whole set. All these, as I find from the
record office, are thoroughly reliable people;
steady, consistent scoffers and worldings
who without any spectacular crimes are
progressing quietly and comfortably towards
Our Father's house.

> —*C. S. Lewis,* The Screwtape Letters

Confound the race
Of mankind in one root, and Earth with
  Hell
To mingle and involve, done all to spite
  The Great Creator

> —*John Milton,* Paradise Lost

The image of a desecrated church with satanic graffiti—"666" and upside-down crosses—spray painted on the walls filled the large white screen behind the dais.

"These photos were taken in the chapel of an abandoned hospital just outside Rome," asserted the deep baritone voice of Dr. Marco Strano, a criminologist and psychologist with the state police. A brooding, bald man with an intense gaze made more pronounced by a set of thick black eyebrows, Dr. Strano appeared right at home next to the gruesome images—elaborate satanic tattoos, self-mutilations, shattered storefronts blocked off by yellow crime-scene tape—that paraded across the screen.

Because the blinds were shut and the lights were turned off, Father Gary didn't bother to take many notes, but instead sat back and tried to digest it all.

In recent years, satanic cults had been on the rise in Italy, and several high-profile satanic murders had grabbed attention in the Italian news. In 2001, three teenage girls stabbed a nun to death in a northern Italian town as a part of a satanic ritual. In the fall of 2005, members of a satanic rock group, the Bestie di Satana (Beasts of Satan) were brought to trial for the brutal murder of one band member and two female friends, one of whom was shot and buried alive. As recently as 2007, a man with amnesia wandered into a police station in a town near Milan covered with small puncture wounds and missing three liters of blood. Later, his blood was found splattered all over the walls of his apartment seventy miles away in the form of satanic writings. Police found upturned crosses and other satanic symbols there even though the man had no recollection of belonging to any cult.

Because millions of people are reportedly involved in the occult around the world and the numbers are on the rise, the exorcism course would explain the ramifications to novice exorcists.

MODERN SATANISM, say experts, borrows from a number of historical traditions, and its tenets are hard to pin down. There is no unified
belief system, as some members of the same group may become involved for more abstract practices while others do so for carnal.

The Gnostics in the mid-second century heavily promoted the
notion that Satan was a godlike being with certain powers. Later condemned by the Church as heretics, the Gnostics believed that the material world was too full of evil to have been created by a good God.
Therefore, they proposed a dualist system whereby God was distant
and unknowable while Satan was the creator of the physical world.
Later, in the Middle Ages, the Cathars took up this theory once
again, even going so far as to say that the Catholic Church was established by the Devil to mislead people. This emphasis on the material
world having been created by Satan wasn't for the purposes of worshiping him, but to more powerfully oppose him. But this view was
easily perverted by certain groups who put the Devil on an equal
footing with God.

In the eighteenth and nineteenth centuries, on the heels of the
revolutions in America and France and in the midst of the Enlightenment, Satan's desire to rebel against God was cast as a bid for freedom. The Church, seen by some as being too authoritarian, was
accused of repressing man's natural carnal desires. As a result, numerous groups sprang up, including the infamous Hellfire Club led
by the rake Sir Francis Dashwood, which, while not necessarily be-
lieving in the reality of a personified Satan, still espoused a hedonistic
lifestyle involving supposed orgies and other debaucheries done in
the Devil's name.

According to Father Bamonte, who also authored a book on the
occult, there are two currents of Satanism. In the first, known as
"personal," adepts actually believe that Satan is a physical entity, a
god who can be prayed to and who will grant certain privileges, such

as money and fame, if offered sacrifices. While in the second, known as "impersonal," acolytes hold that Satan represents more of a force or energy, a part of the cosmos that can be developed and used to serve them.

In both the "personal" and the "impersonal" currents of Satanism, the power of the individual is exalted above anything else, while the seven capital sins are celebrated. As Father Bamonte says, "The key to understanding them is to know their motto, 'Do what you want; that is the only law.'" Beyond this basic view, the groups themselves can also be very diverse.

Father Aldo Buonaiuto, a member of the Pope John XXIII Community Association, has been working with ex-cult members for some time. Small in stature, Father Buonaiuto sports a collegiate handsomeness and a perpetual five-o'clock shadow. His appearance and mild demeanor seem completely out of place in the world of devil worship and murder. And yet, author of a book on the occult, *Le mani occulte: viaggio nel mondo del satanismo* (The Hands of the Occult, a Voyage into the World of Satanism), he is considered an expert on the subject and was recently asked to collaborate with the SAS.

During the course of his work, Father Buonaiuto has come up with different designations within satanic cults. The first, which he calls "Youth Acid," consists of mostly young people into the physical trappings of Satanism, the hedonistic lifestyle mixed with drugs, self-mutilation, pedophilia, suicide, and even murder to provide human sacrifices. The second designation, known as "Power Satanism," is more sophisticated, he claims, and counts as members very wealthy and influential people who are said to sell their souls to the Devil for the promise of power and riches, which are then used to ensure a perpetual state of strife—war, famine, economic instability, and such. The third designation he calls "Apocalyptic Satanism," which, as the name suggests, has as its goal the total destruction of life as we know it (not surprisingly, he claims this is the most dangerous strain).

WHILE THERE IS NO DENYING that groups like the "Beasts of Satan" exist, and that they claim to kill in the name of the Devil, the larger question is this: Are these groups part of a bigger problem, or just deeply troubled kids?

Similar to the "satanic panics" that gripped the United States in the 1980s and early 1990s, when cases such as the McMartin Preschool trial (in which a group of teachers were accused of ritually abusing the students) turned out to be false, some critics wonder whether the Church might be overreacting to a few isolated incidents.

Italy has seen its fair share of scandals that, while garnering headlines, have failed to deliver. In 1996, for example, Marco Dimitri, the leader of a satanic cult called the Bambini di Satana (Children of Satan) was acquitted of raping a two-year-old boy and a teenage girl during an alleged satanic ritual. Likewise, in 2007, the town of Rignano Flaminio near Rome went through its very own McMartin-style scandal when fifteen students at a nursery school accused six individuals, including several teachers, of sexually abusing them in satanic rituals. A lengthy investigation, however, involving a number of child psychologists, failed to turn up any evidence.

Dr. Strano, for his part, doesn't believe the more sensational crimes attributed to satanic cults—such as human sacrifice, organ trafficking, and slavery—are going on to the extent that some people imagine. He thinks instead that many of these groups are just about rebellion, about young people doing drugs and perhaps becoming involved in petty crimes such as vandalism or theft. Most of them "do not even know what they are doing," he says.

Father Buonaiuto, however, thinks differently. For the past five years, he has been running a cult hotline in Italy, counseling individuals and family members who are trying to get out of cults. "It's not true that they are isolated groups, that a sixteen-year-old kid suddenly wakes up and decides to start a group. There is always someone who gives them the permission; there is a territory, there is always someone who initiates the group with that doctrine," he says. The hotline has opened Father Buonaiuto's eyes to a world that many people can't imagine exists. "The thing that is the most shocking is the amount of joy that these young kids, some of them sixteen years old, get out of suffering and causing suffering for others. They celebrate death. If you read what some of the people from the 'Beasts of Satan' said, you would not believe it. While they are hurting someone, they rejoice in it." According to Father Buonaiuto, the hotline gets around twenty calls a day, running the gamut from ex-cult members on the run to people just seeking attention. It can be hard to break away from these groups, in part because the destructive lifestyle is fueled by addiction. "LSD, music, sex and violence work together to form a kind of psychological dependence," he says.

However, even while he is convinced that satanic cults pose a threat, he is quick to point out that the nefariousness associated with these groups doesn't necessarily have anything to do with the demonic. "We have to be clear: The world of satanic cults is one thing and demonic possession another. Satanism is more about an exterior thing, a cultural movement in which people perpetrate crimes such as fraud and in extreme cases murder. Some people in these groups don't even believe in the Devil but use him as a shield to victimize impressionable people. Demonic possession, on the other hand, is an individual thing, which if it affects a person, does so on an internal, spiritual level."

One, of course, could lead to the other, say exorcists like Father Bamonte. If a person were to enter such a group and perform magic or certain rituals, that could open the person up to demonic attack. Or, claims Father Bamonte, the individual could sign a "pact" with a demon and thereby open a doorway to "direct contact" with him.

ACCORDING TO EXORCISTS, a variety of factors can contribute to a person becoming possessed.

The first thing to note, say theologians, is that demonic possession cannot occur unless God allows it. It may seem contradictory, but, according to the Church, while God does not wish evil upon any person, he does permit it for some good purpose (similar to temptation). In the case of someone with a very advanced spiritual life, such as a saint, God allows Satan to test that person in the hopes that the physical trials will give their soul sanctifying grace. According to Saint John Chrysostom, "Possessed persons can obtain a twofold benefit from their condition. In the first place they can become more holy and good; secondly, having paid the debt for their sins here on earth, they can present themselves pure before the Lord."

Demonic possession in and of itself is not evil; it is not considered a sin. In addition, there is apparently no physical or otherwise inherent quality in a person's nature that predisposes him or her to becoming possessed. Demonic possession is not contagious. A person cannot become possessed by sitting in a room or living with someone who is possessed. Generally speaking, say exorcists, one has to either open the door to the Devil, or be a victim of one who has opened the door. These are some ways the Church says a person can do this:

Occult ties: According to the Church, becoming involved in the occult is a form of idolatry that goes against the first commandment and is a common way to come into contact with the demonic.

In his book *Possessioni diaboliche ed esorcismo* (Demonic Possession and Exorcism), Father Bamonte lists the following occult activities that can potentially open the door to possession: participating in a séance; frequenting a medium or magician (the Church makes no distinction between "white" or "black" magic); using an amulet or talisman, especially if it is received from a magician; transcendental meditation, the use of crystals, and other such New Age practices that stress "out of body" experiences; divination or the practice of automatic writing; practicing satanic rituals, especially signing a "blood pact" with a demon. The Bible is clear (and rather graphic) on the dangers involved in practicing magic and divination: "No one shall be found among you who makes a son or daughter pass through fire, or who practices divination, or is a soothsayer, or an augur, or a sorcerer, or one who casts spells, or who consults ghosts or spirits, or who seeks oracles from the dead. For whoever does these things is abhorrent to the Lord" (Deuteronomy 18:10–12).

The *Catechism* is also direct in its condemnation of the occult. "All forms of divination are to be rejected: recourse to Satan or demons, conjuring up the dead or other practices falsely supposed to 'unveil' the future . . . All practices of magic or sorcery, by which one attempts to tame occult powers, so as to place them at one's service and have a supernatural power over others—even if this were for the sake of restoring their health—are gravely contrary to the virtue of religion."

As Father Bamonte explains, however, just participating in a card reading or using a Ouija board does not necessarily risk possession. Yet engaging in this activity repeatedly, he says, could start people down a path that could open them up to possession either through a graver sin, or through their own actions.

One American priest on staff at the NAC related his experience helping a sixteen-year-old unbaptized girl who came to him. While playing with a Ouija board, the girl had contacted a spirit named Nick, who dared her to do things that are dangerous, such as driving her car in a rainstorm without windshield wipers. But things got worse when she awoke one night with an overwhelming sensation of being surrounded by a darkness so thick it was choking the air out of her lungs. With no training in exorcism, the priest said a simple prayer of deliverance and the problem seemed to go away.

A curse: A curse causes the suffering of others through the intervention of a demon. Curses break up marriages, cause businesses to fail, induce illness, invite possession, and so on. Curses can be carried out in a variety of ways, say exorcists. Most are the result of magic formulas or rituals performed by a warlock or a witch. Sometimes a person is affected directly (by ingesting a cursed object) and sometimes indirectly (by possessing cursed objects).

One Italian exorcist knew a very wealthy person who had tried to sell her house for many years without success. People would come to look at the house, leave enthusiastic and ready to buy, but then mysteriously never return to close the deal. The exorcist said many masses, but still the house remained unsold. One day a charismatic nun came to visit and told the exorcist that something was hidden in a wall and that the house would be impossible to sell until the object was removed. The owner of the house then asked her ex-husband, who was an artist, if he had put anything inside a wall. Reluctant at first, he finally admitted that he had placed a painting behind a wall when the house was being built (in order to dedicate it to an evil spirit in the hopes of garnering favors). When the owner destroyed the wall in question, she found that it encased a painting that portrayed a satanic image. A week after the owner burned the painting, the exorcist claims, four different people offered to buy the house.

In all cases, say exorcists, the intent is the most critical part of a curse. The strongest curses (those causing the greatest harm) are those launched with true perfidy—when there is a familial or blood relationship between the victim and aggressor, such as a parent who curses a child.

Some signs that point to a curse, say exorcists, are chronic depression and sickness, infertility, breakdowns in the family and marriage, financial difficulty, and a family history of suicide or unnatural deaths. Exorcists are quick to point out that experiencing one or more of these conditions does not necessarily mean a person is cursed. Other criteria must be weighed in all cases to determine demonic activity.

The first people to be affected by a curse are often the ones who cast it, say exorcists. A jilted lover who goes to a magician to have a curse put on the girl who spurned him will perhaps fall into a dangerous pattern of returning to the magician for other reasons, such as to obtain a lucky charm to win over a new girlfriend. According to exorcists, this could not only lead to financial ruin, but in extreme cases, also to possession.

To many people, belief in curses might seem far-fetched. However, casting and removing spells are widespread in many native cultures, including some that have embraced Christianity. Haiti, for example, is a predominantly Catholic country, yet voodoo is popular.

Dedication to a demon: This category deals with people who belong to a satanic cult specifically to harness the power of evil by dedicating themselves or family members to a demon. In the case of a child being dedicated, as with a curse, the victim is blameless. It is said that parents sometimes offer newborn babies (or even fetuses) to Satan in black masses. Father Bamonte is quick to point out, however, that any such "gifts" given in return by the Devil are almost always fleeting and have the effect of "dazzling" people so that they give themselves over completely to the Devil, becoming like slaves.

A life of hardened sin: As defined by the Church, deciding to commit a sin is a free-will choice to do evil rather than good. According to the *Catechism*, "Sin is before all else an offence against God, a rupture of communion with him." One sinner who became possessed as a result of his actions was Judas Iscariot, whom the Bible describes as having the Devil enter him. According to theologians, however, sin in and of itself is usually not enough to cause possession. Certain sins (such as worshiping false idols), however, can open the door to demonic possession. Sins can also be an impediment to liberation, say exorcists. It is said that the demon can latch on to a specific sin (such as an unwillingness to forgive), accentuating it until the person is in bondage to that particular sin. Until the person renounces this sin, he will have no chance to break the bondage and become liberated. In these milder possessions, say exorcists, a sincere conversion and a good confession is usually enough to liberate the person.

SHORTLY AFTER he had attended one of these lectures, Father Gary spoke with a seminarian originally from the Midwest who'd had a frightening experience before entering the seminary. The two met one afternoon for a *panino* at a busy coffee shop near the Trevi Fountain. Amidst the busy afternoon lunch crowd they found a spot at a counter, and the seminarian told Father Gary his story.

When the seminarian was a teenager, he and his friends had been bored, so they bought a book on spells at the local bookstore and then purchased some ingredients online. First they decided to cast a spell calling forth a particular spirit. Much to their shock, as they read out the incantations (which required that they make a pact with the Devil for maximum efficacy, though they didn't do it), a flame appeared and floated in the middle of the living room before disappearing. During another incident, a huge crow appeared outside his kitchen window, even though there were no crows around the neighborhood. Scared, they performed a different spell that made the crow disappear. According to the seminarian, however, it didn't fly away; it vanished. Realizing that he was in over his head, he'd thrown away the spell book the following day.

The story got Father Gary thinking about what might be waiting for him when he went back to San Jose. He knew from the course that the occult was rampant in Italy and growing. Perhaps even more alarming to Father Gary was that in the suburbs of a major Midwestern city, where kids were relatively wealthy and had a lot of free time, the occult was far more widespread than people realized. Had he missed warning signs in his own parish?

To Father Gary, the most interesting aspect of the lecture on satanic cults was the list of reasons people became attracted to such a world. While the traditional reasons had been trotted out by Dr. Strano—namely rock music and the lack of a strong family unit—perhaps most intriguing to Father Gary was new media. With the advent of the Internet, not only were more kids coming into contact with exotic groups, but, as one course speaker said, the computer itself—as a tool of empowerment—played a role.

Carlo Climati, who has written several books on Satanism and youth culture, coined the phrase "new culture of isolation" to describe how today's young people, who often feel cut off from family, friends, and society, sometimes treat their computers as "friends," in a sense replacing the real flesh-and-blood neighbor next door with a keyboard and screen.

Such a concept, whether true or not, made Father Gary wonder about his previous parish. It was clear to him that technology brought huge advances to people's lives, but what effect did this have on a spiritual level? With almost anything one could want only a mouse click away, it wasn't hard to see how using a computer might give a person a sense of omnipotence. Without the proper grounding, would unsuspecting kids be more tempted today than in the past to use these devices to seek occult knowledge, which might in turn open them up to the demonic?

Once he'd been called out by a parishioner who asked that he bless her house after her daughter had a nightmare and saw a shadow on the wall of her windowless room. Of course, he had talked to the girl before performing the blessing, but had he dealt with the situation in the right way? Now he would know to ask if she might have dabbled with anything such as a Ouija board or tried casting spells downloaded from a Web site.

At the same time Father Gary didn't want to make people paranoid or belittle their problems by pointing to a computer or a deck of tarot cards and saying, "Aha!" The key to the problem, he realized, was not the Ouija board or tarot cards per se, but the person's desire to seek knowledge through them. More often than not this pointed to a weak faith life. As one speaker in the course had said, "Where faith decreases, superstition grows." For Father Gary, that statement rang true.

THE CASA SANTA MARIA is a sixteenth-century convent located in the heart of downtown Rome. The building had served as stables for the French Calvary when Napoleon had occupied the city; but in 1859, Pope Pius IX had given it over to the American bishops, who had it converted into the original NAC. When the NAC was moved to its present location, the Casa became a residence for American clergy studying in Rome.

Father Gary moved to the Casa in late November, after finishing the continuing education program at the NAC. Sandwiched between Piazza dell'Oratorio on one side and Piazza della Pilotta on the other, the five-story building—almost as large as half a city block—is deceptively tucked away from the noisy streets of Rome. Were it not for a gold plaque stuck to the wall of its rust-colored exterior, one wouldn't know it existed at all.

Once inside, however, the picture was decidedly different, with trickling fountains, long breezy colonnades, and open courtyards offering an almost Zen-like tranquillity. Father Gary had no trouble settling into his new home among seventy-five priests from around the English-speaking world.

As at the NAC, most of the priests were students and kept a busy schedule, attending lectures at the nearby Gregorian University all morning or spending time in their rooms, noses buried in books about canon law. *Pranzo,* or lunch, was the big meal of the day. The priests dined in the large refectory under a fresco-covered ceiling, served by waiters wearing white jackets and ties. Afterward the staff would set out trays of cookies in an adjoining tea room.

For most of the priests, the centerpiece of their daily schedule was mass in the small Romanesque church located adjacent to the dining hall. For Father Gary, concelebrating mass in the tiny church alongside his fellow priests was an incredibly enjoyable experience.

Father Gary already knew a few priests from the States and made new friends quickly. Still, because all were on tight schedules, they had little time to socialize, something Father Gary would later lament. "It was fun to be there; but unless you really reached out, you could easily get lost in that place or be dead for a few days before anyone noticed." In order to combat this forced loneliness, a few priests had formed a group (aptly named the "Lonely Hearts Club"), which got together once a week to go out to dinner. Father Gary happily joined.

SINCE HE WAS TAKING ONLY TWO CLASSES—in the late fall he'd begun his twice-a-week course at the Angelicum on the Eastern spiritual masters—he had plenty of time to read about exorcism, which
he usually did in the mornings.

There were a few religious bookshops that he would frequent
along Via della Conciliazione—the wide, majestic avenue filled with
Vatican offices, churches, and religious memorabilia shops that runs
from the Castle of Saint Angelo to Saint Peter's Square. Many of the
books were in Italian or Latin, but a few bookshops, such as the Ancora, had a decent English section tucked away in a tiny atticlike
space upstairs. He soon found out that while it was easy to find a
book on Thomistic philosophy, it wasn't so easy to find one on exorcism.

Instead, most of his research was done at the NAC library. Located on the second floor of the massive seminary, the library had the
largest collection of English language books in Rome (over 64,000),
including huge sections on reference, theology, and Church history.

Gracious and down to earth, Sister Rebecca personified the Nor-
man Rockwell image of a librarian—conservatively dressed, short
curly blondish-white hair, and a pair of glasses dangling from her
neck on a long brown strap. A Benedictine from a parish in Indiana,
she had been serving at the NAC for eleven years when Father Gary
walked through the door. Yet in all those years, she couldn't recall being asked about exorcism. "Father Gary told me he had been nominated as an exorcist and that he didn't know anything about it," she
says. "I thought exorcism wasn't real."

Nonetheless, being the accommodating soul that she was, she
gladly helped him locate a few titles.

Most of the books were somewhat outdated when it came to exorcism, some written in the 1930s. Because of his skeptical nature,
Father Gary preferred books by writers not inclined to see demons

around every corner, or blame all the world's evils on the Devil. One book, *Diabolical Possession and Exorcism*, was by Father John Nicola, an American priest and theologian who for many years was an advisor to the American Catholic bishops on exorcism, as well as a technical advisor for the 1973 film *The Exorcist*. Father Nicola's book stood out for its measured approach, describing how science and religion must work in concert, and how an exorcism should be considered only as a last resort. Father Nicola writes: "Whenever I express a fear and unwillingness to act as an exorcist, I get letters from people assuring me that they have successfully cast out many demons and that, as long as one relies on the power of Christ, there is no need to fear the demons. It is my conviction that they are thinking of something entirely different from what I am. Solemn public exorcisms are rarely performed in modern times in the Western world. When they are performed, they are as gruesome and ugly as anything in the world."

Such passages, when coupled with the information from the lectures he was attending, gave Father Gary an increasingly clearer understanding of the scope of the demonic, at least in the abstract.

CHAPTER SIX

IN MY NAME

The Devil takes advantage of all the possibilities he has to act in the world, hoping to carry as many people as possible with him to eternal damnation. This is because of the hate he harbors for God and for mankind. He would destroy the good in the world in any possible way but we are protected by the action of God, Mary, the angels, and Saints, all of whom put limits on his actions.

—*Father Francesco Bamonte*

Father Gabriele Nanni remembers the first time he ever saw an exorcism. It was 1997 and he had just been ordained a priest and was working in a parish near L'Aquila, a city east of Rome. A young married couple approached him to ask for help. Strange things were happening to the woman daily and her problems had worsened since they'd married. She suffered from numerous illnesses—stomachaches, headaches, and pains in her joints that would incapacitate her. No pain medication helped, nor did the series of doctors who diagnosed one thing and then another. Even stranger, the objects in her house had begun moving around on their own. On one occasion the lid of a pot had levitated above the stove and then clanged to the floor. Theologically, Father Nanni believed in the reality of demonic possession, but he had no experience in the matter. He decided to take the couple to the diocesan exorcist.

Waiting outside the exorcist's office with the couple, Father Nanni remembers hearing the screams of people inside. The howling and screeching that he was hearing, he realized, was coming from a demon.

When it came time for the couple's turn, Father Nanni watched in shock as the woman's arms and legs flailed and her eyes rolled upward into her head, revealing only the whites. Clearly, something was going on here; but he wasn't sure if he was seeing the work of a demon. After a month of weekly sessions, however, the "voice" finally materialized when the demon cursed the exorcist with tremendous hatred. The demon also contorted the woman's body in unnatural ways, twisting her hands into knotted claws. On another occasion she threw herself on the floor and extended her body backward, forming the letter *O*.

These experiences had a profound effect on Father Nanni. The night after witnessing the demon for the first time, he lay awake in bed, unable to sleep. He felt "impressed," "awed" by what he'd seen, and had a million questions. His eyes had been opened to a new reality, one that had given him a "palpable" sense of the theology he had studied in the seminary. "When you are outside these experiences, you have only an abstract idea of the spiritual world," says Father Nanni. "Many priests talk about theoretical things, they have faith but they are intellectuals. The spirit is something that exists for them but it is difficult to treat him as a person; usually they are just concepts." According to Father Nanni, many theological discussions would have a different outcome if such things were taken into account. "Through being an exorcist I understood that there is much more to the faith than what we think . . . there is an almost objective, almost material [level]." Unable to shake this strong impression, he approached his bishop to ask if he could be appointed as an exorcist himself.

Tall, urbane, with fair skin and short gray hair, Father Nanni, at age forty-six, gave the impression of a sophisticated and learned man—perhaps a bank president or CEO were he given a suit to wear rather than the traditional black clerics. Born in 1959 in Forlí, he would eventually get a degree in philosophy at the University of Bologna and a doctorate in Canon Law at the Pontificia Università Lateranense, writing his thesis on the Church laws that regulate exorcism. He speaks several languages—Italian, French, and Spanish—and is the author of the book *Il dito Di Dio e il potere di Satana: L'esorcismo* (The Finger of God and the Power of Satan: Exorcism), which was published by the Vatican in 2004. He is also a frequent TV commentator on the recent spate of satanic murders and has even appeared in a documentary on exorcism done by National Geographic.

Patient, contemplative, and highly educated, Father Nanni is part of a new wave—which also includes Father Francesco Bamonte—that forms the perfect counterpart to the raving fundamentalists featured in popular media whose demagoguery and fear-mongering have done so much to tarnish the image of exorcists. It was specifically for this reason that the course organizers had asked him to speak.

As always, the lecture began with the students standing and saying a Hail Mary along with the Lord's Prayer. For Father Gary and the few other priests who would go on to become exorcists, today's lecture would provide a once-in-a-lifetime opportunity. Father Nanni, used to speaking in front of large groups, was completely at ease, accustomed to the microphone.

* * *

THE *CATECHISM* MENTIONS EXORCISM ONLY ONCE, in paragraph 1673, stating, among other things, "When the Church asks publicly and authoritatively in the name of Jesus Christ that a person or object be protected against the power of the Evil One and withdrawn from his dominion, it is called *exorcism* . . . Exorcism is directed at the expulsion of demons or to the liberation from demonic possession through the spiritual authority which Jesus entrusted to his Church." According to the Church, exorcism is a sacramental, which by definition means it signifies effects associated with the intercession of the Church.

There are only two types of recognized exorcisms: "simple" and "major." As stated in the *Catechism,* "In a simple form, exorcism is performed at the celebration of Baptism. The solemn exorcism, called 'a major exorcism,' can be performed only by a priest and with the permission of the bishop" (1673).

Today, many people confuse the rite of exorcism with the practice of prayers of deliverance, which any Christian can recite. According to the Christian deliverance minister Francis MacNutt, *exorcism* "is a formal ecclesiastical prayer to free a person possessed by evil spirits," while *deliverance* "is a process, mainly through prayer, of freeing a person who is oppressed or infested by evil spirits but not possessed."

While it's technically true that any priest can perform an exorcism, not every priest should. Guideline thirteen of the *Ritual* states that the bishop can only nominate a priest who is "distinguished in piety, learning, prudence, and integrity of life." In addition, "The priest [. . .] should carry out this work of charity confidently and humbly under the guidance of the Ordinary."

With all these conditions, it may seem odd that in the early days of Christianity there weren't any officially appointed exorcists. The thought then was that any Christian could perform an exorcism because this power was derived specifically from Christ; "And these signs will accompany those who believe: by using my name they will cast out demons" (Mark 16:17). Gradually, however, thanks to the expanded role that exorcism played in the rite of baptism as well as to combat perceived abuses, the order of exorcist was established. The earliest mention of the office of exorcist is perhaps in a letter written by Pope Cornelius (251–252) stating that in the Church of Rome there were fifty-two exorcists, lectors, and doorkeepers. Around the fourth century a series of steps were taken to give the bishops more control over the nominating process. The Council of Laodicea in the middle of the fourth century established a canon prohibiting all individuals from performing an exorcism unless appointed by their bishop.

The importance of the nomination by the bishop comes from the power of the prayer being tied to the Church as well as to the obedience of the exorcist. As the current president of the International Association of Exorcists, Father Giancarlo Gramolazzo, says, "I always use this phrase: The prince of disobedience is the Devil and you beat him by being obedient, not by your own personality, or charisms." According to Father Gramolazzo, if a priest were to perform an exorcism without the approval of his bishop, the prayers would still work to some extent because of the power of Jesus Christ's name, but they wouldn't have the same effect on the demon because essentially the exorcist would be praying the *Ritual* in a state of disobedience and the demon would know it. "Some priests have tried to perform an exorcism without the bishop's permission and the demon said to them, 'You cannot do it, you are outside your diocese and you don't have permission,'" says Father Gramolazzo.

In the beginning, the actual "rite" of exorcism was pretty simple and consisted of the laying on of hands, the invocation of Jesus' name, the sign of the cross, and fasting. Later, in the third century, the practice of blowing on the person or "exsufflation" was added. In fact, rather than relying on a complicated formula, the Fathers of the Church stressed the need for simplicity. Saint Athanasius, the Bishop of Alexandria (who died about 373), notes in a letter to Marcellinus that an exorcist who uses complicated or lengthy invocations runs the risk of being ridiculed by the demons.

Statuta Ecclesiae Latinae, a collection of Church legislation that was issued about the year 500, contains one of the earliest official formulas for exorcism. Over the years, the rite developed primarily in localized form in "libelli"—small pamphlets consisting of only a few pages. Finally, prompted by a combination of widespread abuses (exorcists incorporating their own gestures, incantations, and even medicines) and a growing climate of superstition during the Middle Ages, the diverse formulas were compiled into the *Roman Ritual,* first published in 1614.

Since then, the *Ritual* has gone through a few adjustments, including a minor one in 1952 and a major one in 1998. The 1998 *Revised Ritual,* known in Latin as *De exorcismis et supplicationibus quibusdam,* begins with an introductory section followed by the guidelines, after which the exorcist is to recite the litany of the saints, a few gospel and Psalm readings, and if he so chooses, a homily. At the core of the *Ritual* lie the prayers of exorcism themselves, which are broken up into two sections, known commonly as "deprecatory" and "imperative." The difference between these two is extremely important, say exorcists. In a deprecatory prayer, the exorcist entreats God to intervene on behalf of the person; the prayer begins "Hear, Holy Father . . . ," while in the imperative prayer, the exorcist himself commands the demon to depart in the name of Jesus Christ, "I adjure you, Satan . . ." or "I cast you out." Since the imperative formula is not really a prayer but a command, and a highly suggestive one at that, the *Revised Ritual* stipulates that an exorcist may use it only when he is "morally certain" that the person he is praying over is possessed.

To follow the *Ritual* straight through from start to finish would probably take forty-five minutes to an hour. In truth, however, few exorcists pray it this way, often intermingling Psalms of their own choosing or "spontaneous" exorcism prayers ("I cast you out, spirit of fakeness"), all of which is based on their experience.

"I never follow the *Ritual* exactly the way it is organized in the book," says Canadian exorcist Father François Dermine, O.P. "You can't follow the *Ritual* like that with a reading from the Bible and then the litany. It comes as it comes, depending on the reaction of the person. I remember one time with one person, as soon as I started to pray, the person went under possession and in that case, there is not really the time to read the Bible and stuff like that. You have to pray."

Father Amorth believes that every exorcist must find his strengths and weaknesses and what works best for him. He gives this example: "One exorcist I know who performs exorcisms down at San Giovanni Rotondo is also the postulator of the cause of beatification of a Capuchin, Father Matteo, who lived four hundred years ago. He prays to Father Matteo all the time, and when he invokes him during an exorcism, the demons become very furious. Personally, I tried several times to invoke Father Matteo but nothing happens. This means that every exorcist learns what for him is more efficient." Also, since every demon is said to have a different reaction, the exorcist needs to be able to find out which parts of the prayer hurt the demon the most. However, this doesn't mean that the exorcist can just do or say what he wants.

As of late, the International Association of Exorcists has been careful about reminding exorcists to stick with the *Ritual*. "It is better for the exorcist to just pray the *Ritual* as it is," says Father Gramolazzo.

An exorcist must remember not to pray the *Ritual* in such a way that it could be confused with a magic ceremony. The reason this is so important is that "if an exorcist were to do so," explains Father Nanni, "it would be like casting out a spell with another spell, or a demon by another demon." It would negate the whole purpose of the rite, not to mention discredit the Church.

There is also the danger of suggestion to consider. Many exorcists have acknowledged the suggestive nature of exorcism and prefer to use euphemistic expressions when performing the *Ritual*. For example, instead of the word *exorcism*, they say "blessing," and they never tell people they are possessed, but rather that they are suffering from some kind of "negativity." In addition, many exorcists prefer to pray

the *Ritual* in Latin to avoid auto-suggestion. "I think it is better if people don't understand," says Father Dermine. "If I pray in a way that
the person can understand, sometimes you can risk stimulating certain reactions. If there is really a demon there, he will understand no
matter what."

In the end, the most essential thing, says Father Gramolazzo, is
that the exorcist has faith. "The power of the prayer is not in the
formula but in the faith—my faith in the faith of the Church. I can
like the prayer, it can be beautiful; but the efficacy depends on the
faith."

AT THE BEGINNING OF AN EXORCISM, the demon is loath to reveal
himself. "To be discovered is for him a defeat," says Father Bamonte. If
the demon is strong, then he can hide in the person for a lengthy period, even allowing participation in mass and other prayerful activities.
(Hiding doesn't mean that the spirit is holed up in some dark corner of
the person's body; it simply means that he does not manifest.)

Usually, if the exorcist "insists," as one Italian exorcist likes to say,
the exorcism prayers will stimulate the demon and eventually force
him out into the open. Father Nanni describes how this process works:
"It is like boxers," he says, "who can take a lot of punishment but stay
up without falling. They are stronger because they have the capabil-
ity of absorbing the blow, but they get hit anyway; and by getting hit
and hit and hit, in the end their physical endurance collapses. For
demons it is the same. If you keep going with perseverance, sooner
or later they will start to give up and manifest."

Throughout this whole process, the demon tries his best to
thwart the exorcist. The demon will attempt to convince the victim
that he or she is suffering from a psychological disorder, or if that
fails, actually inhibit the person from physically reaching the exorcist.
Cars mysteriously break down or phone calls cancel meetings—all
without the victim's knowledge, say exorcists.

When the demon is finally forced out into the open, the person will lose consciousness and enter into a trance. At this point, all movement and speech are controlled by the demon. During these times the person's eyes will often roll up or down (the demon can't bear to look at holy objects, including the priest), the hands will usually curl into claws, and the person will be taken over by a rage directed at sacred or holy objects. Typically, the person remembers nothing upon awakening. Sometimes, however, the person may be conscious during the *Ritual* and may remember some of what transpired but will typically feel as if something "alien" had taken over. Some exorcists, such as Father Amorth, describe the latter as an example of demonic obsession, while a case involving a person emerging from a trance with total amnesia would be indicative of full demonic possession.

According to Father Nanni, once he has begun praying the *Ritual*, there are five traps that the novice exorcist should be wary of: (1) no reaction from the demon for a long time, which is an attempt to trick the exorcist into thinking the cause isn't demonic; (2) the demon fakes that he has gone after manifesting, fooling the person into thinking he or she is now liberated (for this reason, some exorcists ask for a sign of liberation); (3) the demon confuses the exorcist by creating in the possessed symptoms of mental illness; (4) the demon reveals the existence of an evil spell and the way in which the exorcist can get rid of it (the exorcist must not practice superstitious acts); and (5) the demon permits the victim to receive the Eucharist as a sign of liberation.

Many people assume that during an exorcism the demon will speak through the person, but this is not always the case. According to Father Amorth, it is a misperception that demons like to speak. In fact, they will almost never do so unless ordered to by the exorcist. Some, however, do try to confuse the exorcist by talking or even threatening him during the *Ritual* to distract him from the prayers. Father Amorth has been threatened repeatedly. "Tonight I will throw you out of your bed!" or "I will eat your heart!" To which he responds, "Come on, I have my guardian angel that protects me."

However, beyond the bravado, there is a real danger of an exorcist being attacked physically, mentally, and spiritually by the demon during an exorcism, or even after.

———————————

BECAUSE OF THE UNIQUE ROLE they play, exorcists are faced with a variety of moral and spiritual dilemmas that can open them up to potential attack by demonic forces. Perhaps the most obvious of these is sexual temptation. Exorcisms are highly charged encounters, often taking place in small confined spaces that involve a lot of thrashing and moaning from the victim, who is almost always a woman. There are several theories for the preponderance of female victims: Women are more intuitive and in touch with their spiritual side; the Devil targets women specifically to use them to tempt men; or as Father Bamonte suggests, it may simply be because more women than men are willing to seek out an exorcist.

Given this gender dynamic, it is recommended that the exorcist have a "helper" in the room who is also a woman (this is listed in the guidelines of the 1614 *Roman Ritual*). Being the cunning foe that he is, say exorcists, the demon will try anything to distract the exorcist and get him to stop praying, including sexual advances. According to Father Dermine, the exorcist must also use good sense when he touches a woman he is praying over, always keeping in mind the heightened level of sexual tension.

The exorcist can also be attacked through his pride. This sense of pride can come either from the admiration that an exorcist receives from the people he helps, or from the exorcist thinking himself superior because he has a connection to the supernatural or because he believes he has some personal "power" that can liberate people. The exorcist should never claim to be a holy man or to cultivate a cultlike following. This means he should never take money for his services, which would turn him into a kind of magician or faith healer.

On the flip side, while many exorcists may be admired by the victims, they are often ridiculed by their fellow priests.

An exorcist must be equally careful about familiarity. In many cases an exorcist is the only hope these people undergoing deep pain and suffering believe they have, and there is a real danger of their becoming too dependent on the exorcist (or vice versa). The risk is that the sufferers can become addicted and develop an exaggerated affection for the exorcist. For this reason, say exorcists, it is best to keep these people at a slight distance.

The demon will also try to dishearten the exorcist through intimidation or fear, usually carried out by displays of power. In one such instance, Father Daniel (who became an exorcist in the fall of 2006) had all his instant text messages erased from his cell phone one morning. He had recently signed up for a new plan and figured it must be a problem with the company. Later that night, however, when he was giving a blessing over the same phone (exorcists claim telephone blessings can be efficacious), the voice of the person changed and the demon came out taunting: "Did you like the little joke I played on you this morning?" When Father Daniel expressed confusion, the gruff voice mocked, "If you say a prayer that I give to you, then I will give you back all your instant messages."

Another exorcist in Chicago, the day before he found out he was to be nominated by the bishop, was awakened by a terrible noise in the middle of the night, like a train wreck happening in his room. Opening his eyes, he then saw the TV at the foot of his bed levitate off the stand a few feet then crash to the floor, and the tape inside the VCR shoot out across the room. At the same time, the curtains of his room moved violently even though his windows were closed.

Sometimes the signs can be even more direct. In 2006, an exorcist from the Midwest was talking to a young man he thought might be possessed when he heard a raspy voice—as if out of nowhere—say, "Get out!"

An Italian exorcist told of an episode involving members of a Catholic charismatic prayer group who thought they had a special "gift" to cast out evil spirits. During the exorcism, the charismatics were laying on hands and talking to the demon, ordering it to comply. Without warning, the demon turned on them saying, "Who are you?" Then he launched a bookcase at them, sending them all to the emergency room with injuries.

Exorcists have seen things happening even outside, beyond the confines of the exorcism itself. Father Nanni reports that some exorcists have had their car headlights mysteriously turn off just as they were negotiating particularly dangerous curves on mountain roads. In his book, *An Exorcist Tells His Story*, Father Amorth recounted how one exorcist, after the demon threatened him with immolation, was driving home when his car caught fire. Father Nanni, while performing a blessing by phone, had the lightbulb in his room explode over his head.

In extreme instances, an exorcist may be severely injured, though this last point has perhaps been exaggerated, especially in the media. Exorcists are rarely hurt. Father Nanni recalled one example: As an exorcist was leaving the house of a demonized person in Sicily, he was shoved by an unseen force into an oncoming truck, which nearly killed him. When asked why God would allow such a thing to happen, Father Nanni seemed unfazed. "We all have to bear our own burdens," he said. In this case, the exorcist recovered, returned to the house, and liberated the person.

Throughout all of this, the only armor the exorcist has to protect him is his faith. "Faith is worth more than anything else," says Father Amorth. "The faith of the exorcist, of the person who is getting exorcised, the faith of the people who help and pray for the person, family and friends."

"I learned more in performing exorcisms through prayer and faith than from my studies," said Father Gramolazzo. "The books that you read and study become something more theoretical; you don't get inside the world of faith. When you perform an exorcism, however, you have to enter into this world; you get in touch with the supernatural."

AS THEY WALKED BACK to the train station following class, Father Gary discussed some of the finer points of the day's lecture with Father Daniel. Perhaps as a result of his experiences as an embalmer, or the fact that he had survived a near-death hiking accident in 1997, he wasn't worried about being physically attacked by a demon. If he feared anything, it was performing an exorcism on someone who didn't need it. And while the course had taught him a lot, he realized that the only way to put his fears to rest would be to actually participate in an exorcism.

CHAPTER SEVEN

SearcHing for aN ExorcIst

An exorcist works all his life between being admired and thanked by some and bitterly despised and persecuted by others . . . God desires that this ministry always be done from the cross. If a priest is not willing to bear this burden, he should not accept this ministry.

—*Father José Antonio Fortea,*
Interview with an Exorcist

On a typical Tuesday morning, a small crowd gathers outside the Scala Santa by 8:30, even though the large wooden doors won't open for another half an hour. Most are women, ranging in age from their mid-twenties to late sixties, their outfits running the gamut from shawls and brooches to hip-hugging jeans and leather jackets. Milling around, some people pass the time chatting, others avoid eye contact. In addition to the normal purses and backpacks, several carry large plastic grocery sacks filled with various items, such as religious candles and plastic water bottles.

The Scala Santa or Church of the Holy Staircase has always held a unique place among the churches of Rome, drawing countless pilgrims over the years to its venerated sanctum sanctorum (Holy of Holies), the personal chapel of the popes, which the devout reach by climbing a special staircase, thought to be the very stairs from Pontius Pilate's palace in Jerusalem that Christ climbed on the day of his death (brought back to Rome by Helena, the mother of the Emperor Constantine in the fourth century). Pilgrims climb the twenty-eight steps on their knees, pausing at each one to say a prayer. Encased now in protective wood, the original steps can still be glimpsed through small glass windows that supposedly reveal actual drops of Christ's blood.

And yet, beyond the chapel and the stairs, among Romans, the church has a long association with exorcism. For thirty-six years, the Passionist priest Father Candido Amantini performed exorcisms there until he died in 1992. Long thought of as a holy man, even among exorcists, Father Candido had an open-door policy toward exorcism, never turning anybody away. It was rumored that he saw around sixty people every day, and while not everybody needed an exorcism, he tried to at least give them a simple blessing or even just a reassuring pat on the shoulder.

When Father Tommaso took over, this open-door policy was maintained. Even as the church continues to be a major attraction for tourists and pilgrims, exorcisms and blessings are performed around the clock, screams and all.

For half an hour, most of the women wait patiently outside the church; as more show up, the ones closest to the door begin jockeying for position. A few minutes later, they hear the telltale jingle of keys from behind the door followed by the click of the lock, and even before the sour-faced custodian has time to swing the door all the way open, the women begin filing through. Hurrying past him, they sidestep the historic steps and proceed instead toward one of the two side staircases. Climbing, they move in a rush past the sanctum sanctorum, through the Saint Lawrence Chapel, until they reach the door to the sacristy. One half expects to see a red ribbon stretched across the corridor.

Instead, everyone takes a place, as if settling into a favorite chair. One woman bends onto a small wooden kneeler right outside the door while others slide into a ten-foot wooden pew that runs the length of the wall. More branch off to a nearby chapel, where they kneel in front of a life-sized representation of Christ on the cross. A few clutch rosaries, their fingers moving anxiously over the beads as their lips mouth silent prayers. Others keep their eyes down. By now around twenty people have gathered, and still more trickle in. One of these is an attractive young woman who walks past everyone to stand next to the door. A few people eye her and shift nervously, but otherwise seem not to mind that she has cut in line. One of the latecomers, a man in his sixties, asks the woman on the kneeler, "Is he seeing anyone right now?" The woman shakes her head.

Somebody nearby pipes in, "I just have to get a quick blessing and then I'll go."

The woman on the kneeler flashes the speaker a dirty look and says, "*He* decides who goes in first."

"Who gets chosen to go in?" someone else asks.

"He performs exorcisms first and then blessings afterward," the woman on the kneeler explains.

Someone pulls out a piece of paper and people begin writing

their names down, as if waiting for a table at a restaurant. Most have places to go in the afternoon and a few sigh and cluck their tongues when they see themselves at the bottom of the list.

As if on cue, the door opens and Father Tommaso pokes his head out, his tired eyes searching. A few people near the door turn to him, but his presence keeps them back; it's clear that nobody wants to get on his bad side. He nods to the attractive woman who'd cut in line, and she enters, the door shutting behind them.

In the ensuing silence, the people settle back into their slumped postures. Then, suddenly from the sacristy comes a sound like a wolverine that has gotten loose and is knocking down all the chairs. A high-pitched scream, followed by a woman's voice shouting *"Basta!,"* disrupts the silence. Then comes moaning and howling as if someone were being tortured. Some clutch their rosaries tighter. Some try to move out of earshot, but inside the cold, marble-floored sanctuary, sounds carry far.

WHEN FATHER GARY ASKED about finding an exorcist with whom to apprentice, Father Daniel's first thought was to ask Father Tommaso. However, the exorcist was too busy to take on another student. While Father Gary was disappointed, Father Daniel reassured him by saying, "You won't learn much there anyway. The place is insane."

Over the ensuing month, Father Gary continued to look for an exorcist he could work with, a task that proved more daunting than he'd imagined. Even a cardinal whom he met in the halls of the NAC one day was unable to help. With his limited Italian, Father Gary needed an exorcist who spoke a little English, and according to a reply he received from the dean of the Lateran University, there weren't any.

Finally, Father Daniel contacted one of the exorcists who helped teach the course. A few days later, he called Father Gary back with good news. Father Bamonte, who had studied under Father Amorth and who had been performing exorcisms since 2003, said he would be willing to take on Father Gary as a last resort (he was not thrilled, largely because of the language barrier). In the meantime, Father Bamonte suggested that Father Gary contact a Capuchin by the name of Father Carmine De Filippis, who he thought knew a little English.

As he got off the phone with Father Daniel, Father Gary was guardedly optimistic about this latest turn of events.

DECEMBER ROLLED IN and Rome's famous *sampietrini* cobblestones grew cold and wet. The exorcism course had shut down for the month, so Father Gary took the time to enjoy the holiday season. There was a special mass and dinner held at the Casa on Christmas Eve; and then, on the following day, Father Gary was a Eucharistic minister at Saint Peter's Basilica during the midnight mass presided over by the pope. Afterward, despite the bitterly cold wind, the square was packed with revelers. By the time he and the other priests walked back to the Casa, it was 3:30 in the morning and the streets were absolutely still.

A few days later, Father Gary and another priest from the Casa, Father Paul Hrezzo, decided to take a little side trip together, traveling to Vienna for a few days and then on to Medjugorje in Bosnia-Hercegovina for New Year's Eve. There, the two presided over mass for the English pilgrims visiting the shrine and spent five restful days meditating and praying.

ON JANUARY 9, the second half of the exorcism course commenced at the Regina Apostolorum. Much like the first half, things got off to a bad start for Father Gary. His translator was a no-show, forcing him to comb the halls looking for a replacement, which he couldn't find. As it turned out, the lecture was on Italian law, so it wasn't a huge loss.

Now that the holiday season was over and things were beginning to return to normal in Rome, he was able to finally get through to Father Carmine (pronounced Car-me-nay), the exorcist Father Bamonte recommended. In his best Italian, Father Gary tried to explain his dilemma. Father Carmine listened patiently for a few minutes and then cut in. "Yes, yes," he said in Italian, "I'd be happy to help you, but you need to check with my superior first."

Hanging up the phone, Father Gary was relieved. *Maybe this is just a formality that Father Carmine asks all his apprentices to go through*, he thought. When he finally got in touch with the superior two days later, however, he hit a dead end. Not only was the man *not* Father Carmine's superior, but he'd never heard of the exorcist. Funny, though, he did speak a little English and had relatives in San Jose, so Father Gary ended up chatting with him for quite some time. In the end, Father Gary figured that Father Carmine had probably given him the brush-off. *He doesn't know me*, he thought, *he probably just wants to get rid of me.*

The following Thursday at the exorcism course, he approached Father Daniel at the break and told him what had happened. As luck would have it, Father Bamonte was lecturing that day, so Father Daniel approached him to ask one last time if he would help Father Gary. After a few minutes, Father Daniel returned with a gloomy look on his face. "I don't know why, but he won't do it," he sighed.

This is getting ridiculous, Father Gary thought. "I am going home soon and won't know the first thing about exorcism," he lamented to Father Daniel.

"Try calling Father Carmine again," Father Daniel said.

Back at the Casa that evening, Father Gary was on the verge of calling his bishop to tell him he would have to nominate somebody else but instead decided to go to the chapel to pray. "God," he said, as he sat in a wooden pew, "if you want me to do this, you are going to have to help me."

As he climbed the long flight of stairs back to his room, he decided to call Father Carmine one last time, though he was almost certain that no one would pick up. To his surprise, the Capuchin answered. Father Gary explained to Father Carmine what had been going on. The other end of the line was silent for a long moment before he heard Father Carmine say, "Okay, okay, but I need to see you first."

"I'll come to you. Tell me when," Father Gary responded.

"Come out Sunday morning and we'll talk."

As he hung up, Father Gary couldn't believe Father Carmine had agreed to see him. Coming as it did on the heels of his prayer, he took it as a sign that God had to be involved.

SOME EXORCISTS ARE KNOWN to have a special "gift" for healing or discernment called a charism, which the Holy Spirit distributes to those who live devoted lives. One such exorcist was Father Candido Amantini. Reportedly Father Candido could diagnose demonic possession simply by looking at a person's photo. In addition, Father Gramolazzo remembers when a demonized person took a swing at Father Candido and the fist stopped only inches from his face, as if held there by an unseen force. Father Candido then blew on the raised fist and the man yanked it back quickly, as if it had been burned.

Laypeople also receive charisms, and more than a few exorcists include such individuals on their prayer teams to help with their discernment. The Second Vatican Council affirms the existence of these gifts but recommends caution: "These charismatic gifts, whether they be the most outstanding or the more simple and widely diffused, are to be received with thanksgiving and consolation . . . Still, extraordinary gifts are not to be rashly sought after . . . In any case, judgment as to their genuineness and proper use belongs to those who preside over the Church and to whose special competence it belongs, not indeed to extinguish the Spirit, but to test all things and hold fast to that which is good."

Father Carmine, who studied under Father Candido, claimed no such "powers." Instead he preferred to rely on his experience.

Father Carmine was born in 1953 in Salerno in the south of Italy, but moved to Rome with his family when he was very young. Even as a boy he had a strong desire to enter the priesthood. "It's not true that kids don't understand anything," he says. "They understand everything." When he was ten years old, he knew that he wanted to completely dedicate his life to God through prayer and penitence, leading the life of a Capuchin friar. Frequenting religious services in his parish of Saint Teresa in Corso Italia, as a boy he was always impressed by the friars, most of all by their way of praying, by their sacred liturgies. He entered the seminary in 1974 when he was just twenty-one.

His first experience with exorcism came when he was still in the seminary. One day while in the middle of a theology lesson, another priest interrupted to say there was a disturbance in the church. An old lady had brought in a girl who was cursing and screaming and drooling in front of the tabernacle. The superior immediately left to see what was happening. Later he returned and surprised the students with the observation that he thought the girl was possessed, so he had taken her to see the exorcist of the diocese. As Father Carmine recalls, the classroom erupted into laughter, and he thought to himself, *This is ridiculous, something from the Middle Ages. Nobody believes in possession anymore, do they?*

A few days later, the superior approached Father Carmine and another seminarian to ask whether they would be interested in participating in the exorcism. Father Carmine agreed, and the experience changed his life. "I saw horrible, horrible things," he says. At one point during the exorcism, as the girl thrashed and screamed, her normally closed eyes popped open and she turned and looked at him. "In her eyes I could see the hate, such pure hate that it hurt me very deeply." During the exorcism, he and his fellow seminarian also felt mysterious blows on their shins, as if someone standing in front of them had kicked them, yet no one was near.

Eventually, toward the end of the exorcism, the girl began vomiting huge quantities of human sperm, accompanied by a nauseating stench that nearly forced Father Carmine out of the room. "I was scared to death, shocked," he says. "I realized that demons do exist, that the Devil is not that puppet with the horns that we see in comic books and laugh about. I had to reverse all my theological concepts, which up until that point were very superficial. I became aware that we are all under the threat of this enemy."

After he was ordained in 1981, he spent some time in a mission in Bolivia before returning to Rome, where he began to study exorcism under Father Giacobbe, a disciple of Father Candido. Father Carmine remembers Father Candido's specifications for an exorcist's qualities. "He has to try to live an evangelical, virtuous life, a life of prayer; he has to have knowledge, meaning that he has to study theology, the Bible; and thirdly he has to have experience." Father Candido also stressed the role that an exorcist should play with respect to the ministry. "He is exhorted to be as generous as possible in helping the poor people who suffer because this is a ministry of assistance, of help for those who suffer." Taking this advice to heart, Father Carmine began performing exorcisms in 1987.

AFTER MASS ON SUNDAY, Father Gary stepped out of the tranquillity that was the Casa and merged with the throngs of people heading down Via Vincenzo dei Lucchesi and toward the Trevi Fountain. Sundays are busy days for foot traffic in Rome, when people who live on the periphery make their way down toward the city's more famous piazzas to join the never-ending stream of tourists. And rather than ones and twos, most traveled in large clumps, creating havoc on the narrow streets amid snarling traffic, much to the consternation of taxi drivers who never hesitate to let their frustrations be known.

Moving on toward Via della Stamperia, he steeled himself against a gust of wind that funneled down the tunnel-like street. On Via del Tritone he turned to his right and began walking up the hill in the direction of Piazza Barberini. A large group of people stood around on the sidewalk near a series of bus signs, and he took his place among them. He wasn't sure how long it would take him to get out to the Basilica di San Lorenzo Fuori le Mura (Saint Lawrence outside the Walls), but he'd given himself forty-five minutes just to be on the safe side.

———

THE BASILICA OF SAN LORENZO has a long association with death. Built on the site of Christian catacombs from the third century and adjacent to the sprawling citylike Verano Cemetery, the basilica houses the bones of three saints—Saint Lawrence, Saint Stephen, Saint Justin—as well as those of Pope Pius IX. From the outside, when compared to its siblings, such as Saint John Lateran or Saint Paul outside the Walls, San Lorenzo has a very simple, almost missionlike quality—a red-brick structure with white, columnlike teeth that slopes backward into the crypts and mausoleums. The church is extremely old—one section was built by Pope Pelagius II in the sixth century, while the second, including its simple porchlike facade, was built in the thirteenth century by Pope Honorius III. And unlike the encroaching suburbs of Rome, it appears that little about the building has changed over the years.

At one point, the basilica was surrounded by fields and vineyards, located along one of Rome's ancient roads, the Via Tiburtina, used by the wealthy Romans to escape the city for their country villas.

Walking down from the bus stop, Father Gary found himself in a relatively peaceful part of town. The basilica was set back from the street a little, located across an expanse of asphalt shaded by clusters of towering cypress and umbrella pines. Several flower stalls dotted the parking lot outside the arching gates of the cemetery, their owners sitting on cheap wooden chairs reading newspapers. Since he was fifteen minutes early, he wandered toward the basilica.

Built on two different axes, the medieval interior of the basilica with its tiers of arches and wooden roof almost appeared to have been carved out of the earth. As he meandered up and down the nave, Father Gary found the place to be too cold and dark, the air too musty and stale for his taste.

At ten o'clock, he walked across the small courtyard that separated the basilica from the friary. He pushed the tiny buzzer located next to the double doors and stood for a moment studying the two lion's head knockers that decorated the door, wondering about Father Carmine. He was grateful for being allowed the rare opportunity of seeing an exorcist in his working environment.

After a few minutes, the door opened and a barrel-chested man of medium height in the traditional friar garb appeared. He wore his hair short, and his three-inch beard was streaked with gray. Though his blue eyes were perhaps his most striking feature. Only narrow slits, they were sandwiched between a pair of ruddy cheeks and thin, dark eyebrows that arched playfully near the ends, giving him a jocular, almost mischievous appearance that made him seem much younger than his fifty-three years. After scrutinizing Father Gary for a few long seconds, a light seemed to turn on behind his eyes and his expression softened. "Ahhh, Padre Gary," he said, *"Bene, bene."* And then in heavily accented English, "Welcome."

Stepping through the door, Father Gary entered a small reception room full of mismatched furniture; various framed religious photographs, including those of the previous five popes; and a three-foot statue of Mary on a pedestal near the doorway to Father Carmine's office. Two windows covered by incongruous lace curtains completed the picture of a room originally used for something else. Father Carmine hadn't yet taken down his Christmas decorations. A large, intricate Nativity set, adorned with blinking lights, occupied a corner. The room's only living inhabitant was a rather large, mangy tabby cat that lay completely still, curled up on one of the chairs. *"Malato"* (not well), Father Carmine said, indicating the cat. Father Gary, who wasn't a cat person, kept his distance.

"Come, come." Father Carmine motioned, and led the way into

his office, which had the same eclectic ambiance. A large, cluttered wooden desk took up most of the small room, while a faded floral print love seat and a few worn office swivel chairs constituted the room's only other furniture. The walls were practically covered with all manner of religious items (some apparently handmade) and photos he had collected over his years as a missionary in South America.

Father Carmine took a seat behind his desk and Father Gary sat opposite. He handed the letter from his bishop to Father Carmine, who studied it, passing his right hand down his cheeks until his thumb and forefinger met at the tip of his beard. *"Bene, bene,"* he said. "The bishops are finally starting to get it," he said in Italian. As the two talked for about a half hour, Father Gary again told a little about himself. He could tell that Father Carmine did not speak much English, but would slip an English word in here or there. More importantly, though, he understood English pretty well, which meant Father Gary could at least express himself. Father Gary tried to speak some Italian, and though he often made mistakes, he'd learned enough to communicate the basics. *"Sì, sì, io capisco,"* pronounced in halting little jumps followed by a long flourish, was a frequent crutch. Yes, yes, I understand.

Father Gary liked the Capuchin immediately and felt he was in good hands. He always looked Father Gary in the eye as he spoke, and his gaze was unwavering as if he were searching for something, testing. Later, Father Gary would learn that most exorcists study people's eyes, as they are the "windows to the soul." In fact, one of Father Carmine's criteria for discerning possession is when the victim is unable to look the exorcist in the eyes.

Father Carmine's description of how he performed the *Ritual*— even and calm—made a big impression on Father Gary.

At one point, Father Carmine pointed to a small wood-paneled room attached to his office, really no bigger than a walk-in closet. "I perform the blessings in there," he said. Father Gary tried to make out what he could from where he was sitting and saw a few metal chairs and nothing much else.

After he seemed satisfied, Father Carmine brought the conversation to a close. *"Va bene,"* he said. "Why don't you come back tomorrow afternoon at five and we'll get started on the hardest cases first."

Father Gary's fieldwork had begun.

CHAPTER EIGHT

tHe fIrsT nIgHt

Midway on our life's journey, I found myself
In dark woods, the right road lost. To tell
About those woods is hard—so tangled and
    rough
And savage that thinking of it now, I feel
The old fear stirring: death is hardly more
    bitter.

—*Dante,* The Inferno

For the remainder of the afternoon, Father Gary couldn't stop wondering what he might see at San Lorenzo the following day. Because Father Carmine had given no indication of what to expect, he pictured the worst—images like Father Daniel's experience of the woman's jaw unhinging and moving over to the side of her face.

All he had to go on was an audio clip he'd listened to on Father Daniel's MP3 player, a recording of Father Daniel confronting a woman who had interrupted mass by shouting at the congregation. Thinking the woman might be possessed, he'd taken her and her companion into a side room to try to calm the woman down. At that point he turned on his recorder. To Father Gary, the voice on the audio clip sounded nothing like a woman's. Deep, raspy, guttural—a cornered animal came to mind. *"Devi dire di no!"* You have to say no! the voice screamed over and over, followed by periods of wailing and moaning that didn't sound human. *"Devi dire di no!"* The voice howled again, this time followed by Father Daniel's *"Basta! In nome di Gesù Cristo ti ordino di smettere."* In the name of Jesus Christ, I order you to stop.

Recalling that voice, Father Gary imagined what it must have been like to be in that room, to realize that you were in the presence of pure evil. Father Daniel had told him how frightened he'd been at the time. Father Gary pictured himself listening to such a hateful diatribe in the room Father Carmine used, which was so small that he'd be practically on top of the person. If the person went crazy and started attacking, he'd be right in the thick of it.

That night, after his evening prayers he spent a few extra minutes asking God for the strength to overcome whatever lay ahead.

ON MONDAY AFTERNOON, Father Gary again stood among the crowds on Via del Tritone waiting for a bus. He was wearing his black clerics and carried a small bag containing the purple stole he would wear during the ritual, as well as the small red *Ritual* book itself. He'd purchased it a couple of weeks before at a bookstore on Via della Conciliazione. Even though he was out of practice with his Latin, he planned to follow along anyway.

Sitting on the bus as it lurched through the narrow streets, he wondered how this experience would change him.

He arrived at San Lorenzo around five in the evening, just as the sun was starting to set. Traffic was heavy on Via Tiburtina, and all the rubber tires traversing the cobblestones created a high-pitched whine that seemed to stalk him like an angry swarm of insects as he walked down to the basilica.

A small group of people stood outside the closed door to Father Carmine's office. They represented a broad spectrum—an older lady in her sixties, dressed conservatively; a man in his late thirties; two young thirty-something women wearing brand-new Nike sneakers and fashionable clothes; and a serious-looking couple in their fifties. Some chatted, while one man stood off on his own, his arms crossed tightly across his chest.

As Father Gary approached, a few looked in his direction, eyeing him suspiciously. The younger woman with shoulder-length blond hair refused to even look at him.

Taking his place among them, he wondered who they might be. He looked for signs of "trauma," anything that might indicate these people were suffering from demonic possession, but found nothing. He knew from Father Daniel that exorcists sometimes did simple blessings. Perhaps the more serious cases hadn't arrived yet.

A few minutes later, the door swung inward to reveal Father Carmine, who barely gave the group a glance before shuffling back inside. One by one, and with an after-you attitude, the group filed inside and took up positions around the waiting room, unwrapping coats and scarves. The door to Father Carmine's office was ajar, so Father Gary gently pushed his way inside, and said, *"Buona sera."* Father Carmine returned the greeting and asked if he was ready.

"*Sì,*" Father Gary replied.

"Good," Father Carmine said. "*Allora, cominciamo.*" Okay, let's begin.

Father Gary took off his coat, slipped on his purple stole, then entered the small room off the office, which contained a wooden end table near the door and four metal chairs, two against one wall and two shoved into the corner. Thinking it would be best to make himself as unobtrusive as possible, Father Gary took a seat in the corner, still only a few feet from the other two chairs. The room, which seemed even smaller from the inside, was an odd setting for an exorcism. Like most European rooms, it had a very high ceiling. The upper walls were crisscrossed by exposed pipe while the lower walls were covered by a fake wood paneling about six feet high. Each wall held some form of sacred image—a framed picture of Padre Pio along with a hand-woven rug depicting Mary and the baby Jesus on one wall, a purple stole (belonging to Father Candido) encased in glass on another wall, and a black-and-white picture of Christ crowned with thorns directly above the two empty chairs. To his immediate right, the room's only window, which he could reach if he were to stand on his tiptoes, was latched shut.

From his seat, he could just make out the contents of a little wooden box resting on the end table near the door: a picture of Saint Francis, a rosary, various medallions, a roll of paper towels, a wooden crucifix, and a squeeze bottle of holy water—essentially, the tools of Father Carmine's trade.

As he waited, Father Gary glanced at the two empty chairs against the wall. Just above their backs, a patch of wood paneling was rubbed and scraped raw, as if someone, or something, had clawed it.

Seconds later Father Carmine, now wearing a thin, wrinkled purple stole, entered the room carrying a plastic shopping bag that he hung on the back of the door handle. Satisfied that everything was ready, he ducked out to the waiting room.

Father Gary eyed the bag, wondering why they would need it. A few seconds later, Father Carmine returned with the man in his late thirties who wore a V-necked sweater and collared shirt.

Father Gary could tell the man was unnerved by his presence, so he tried to put him at ease. "Hello," he said, holding out his hand. "*Mi chiamo* don Gary Thomas. *Vengo dalla* California."

The man smiled as he shook Father Gary's hand. "Oh, California! *È un piacere.*" It's a pleasure to meet you.

The man sat down and Father Carmine stood directly in front of him. Father Gary, perplexed by the man's cordiality, took his seat and opened the *Ritual* book.

"*In nómine Patris et Fílii et Spíritus Sancti.*" In the name of the Father, the Son and the Holy Spirit, Father Carmine said as he blessed the man with a few drops of holy water from the squeeze bottle. Following this, he placed his hand on the man's head and immediately began praying the deprecatory prayer of the *Ritual* from memory, skipping a good chunk of the book that Father Gary had opened on his lap. "*Deus, humáni géneris cónditor atque defénsor . . .*" God, creator and defender of the human race, Father Carmine began, "look down on this your servant, whom you formed in your own image and now call to be a partaker in your glory." Father Carmine spoke with an even, almost soft tone, the Latin blending into a shushing sound.

Occasionally, as he prayed, he would turn to Father Gary and point to a spot in the *Ritual*. Father Gary tried his best to follow along, though he was distracted by trying to gauge the man's reaction.

Initially, the man sat perfectly still, his eyes clenched tight as Father Carmine recited the prayers. After a few minutes, however, he began to cough—at first just a bit, but then the coughing got worse and worse. He began to move his head from side to side as if trying to dislodge Father Carmine's hand. Then he began trying to push Father Carmine away—not violently, but as if he were drunk and didn't have complete control of his motor skills.

Father Carmine, meanwhile, used his free hand to keep the man's flailing arms away. He continued praying the *Ritual* without skipping a beat, occasionally accentuating a word from the prayer. As he intoned, "*Ipse Christus tibi ímperat,*" Christ commands you, the word *ímperat*, commands, was spoken louder, though still not shouted.

While he watched, Father Gary prayed a few Hail Marys and Our Fathers silently.

The man's cough continued to get worse, until he was hacking as if something was stuck in his throat.

Father Carmine then took his free hand and pushed on the man's sternum, causing him to let out a belching sound.

To Father Gary it sounded more like air escaping than a belch caused by food—"Uhhhhhhhh. Huuuuhhhhhhh."

The man continued belching for a few minutes then suddenly stood up and, with tightly clenched eyes, pushed past Father Carmine toward the door.

Father Carmine immediately spun him around and expertly plopped him back down into the chair. He continued the *Ritual* for several minutes until he abruptly stopped and tapped the man's forehead with his index finger, at the same time roughing up his hair in the manner of an older brother razzing a younger sibling.

As he did this, the man stopped fidgeting and opened his eyes. He sat for a moment, rubbing his eyes, taking a few deep breaths.

"Come stai, giovanotto?" How are you, young man? Father Carmine asked him while patting his shoulders.

The man, now fully aware, looked up at him and nodded. *"Bene,"* he replied.

It took a moment for Father Gary to realize that the exorcism was over. From start to finish, the whole episode had lasted about twenty minutes.

As Father Carmine led the man out into his office, Father Gary stayed behind in the room. The exorcism certainly hadn't gone as he had expected. He'd seen none of the symptoms talked about in his exorcism class nor the dramatic reactions Father Daniel had described. Instead this guy only coughed and belched. Father Gary hated to admit it, but he felt underwhelmed.

Next, a conservatively dressed blond woman in her fifties entered, accompanied by her husband, who wore a slightly rumpled suit. Again, Father Gary introduced himself and sat back down in the corner. Father Carmine asked the woman a few questions in Italian, and Father Gary caught something about "not being able to receive the Eucharist." She began to cry and Father Carmine consoled her, *"No, no, non ti devi preoccupare."* No, no, you don't have to worry.

Father Gary took note that Father Carmine blessed both the woman and her husband, a gesture he found touching. *It's not only about the woman*, he thought, appreciating the pastoral significance of it and making a mental note to do the same when the time came for him to perform an exorcism.

As before, Father Carmine invoked the Holy Spirit by putting his hand on the woman's head and then skipped straight through the *Ritual* to the exorcism prayers. This time, the woman went completely rigid and didn't move a muscle.

Midway through the exorcism the phone rang in Father Carmine's office, and to Father Gary's surprise, Father Carmine interrupted the exorcism to walk out and answer it. As he did so, the woman remained where she was, though the rigidity seemed to leave her. She seemed unfazed that Father Carmine had taken a phone call, while Father Gary wondered whether his mentor was taking the woman's situation seriously.

After a few minutes, Father Carmine came back in, picking up where he left off. Once he resumed the prayers, the woman immediately went rigid again. The exorcism continued for another fifteen minutes.

Afterward, Father Carmine blessed a six-pack of bottled water that the couple had brought, waving his hand in the sign of the cross. As they walked out, Father Carmine, perhaps sensing Father Gary's confusion, felt compelled to explain: *"Lei è posseduta da un demone muto,"* he said, struggling to find the right word in English. "Cannot speak," he said. "A very powerful demon."

"A mute demon?" Father Gary asked. Father Carmine nodded.

Father Gary had heard about mute demons through the course. Father Daniel had weighed in on them, too. He wondered, though, how an exorcist could tell whether a person was really possessed by such a demon. Before he had time to question Father Carmine further, the Capuchin was ushering in a couple in their forties. This time the exorcism lasted about ten minutes, and the only noticeable reaction was the man's continual yawning. As with the two previous cases, Father Carmine tapped the man's forehead with his index finger, which Father Gary took to mean that the exorcism was finished.

The fourth person was another woman in her late fifties, with short curly reddish hair that was noticeably thinning. She entered with her husband and a ten-year-old boy who appeared to be her grandson. They all sat and Father Carmine began bantering with the boy, asking about school and reminding him to behave. Father Gary could tell that Father Carmine had become almost like a parish priest, checking in with people, listening to their problems. After a few minutes, Father Carmine blessed the family, sprinkling them with holy water, and then the boy and the husband left. Alone with the woman, Father Carmine asked her how she was doing. "The headaches," she answered in Italian, holding her head. Her voice became choked and she dabbed at tears with a handkerchief. "Terrible, terrible," she said. Father Carmine nodded.

The woman sat with her head bowed and her arms in her lap as Father Carmine prayed the *Ritual* over her. Tears continued to stream down her cheeks and she grimaced occasionally, a little squeak of pain escaping from her clenched mouth as if she had stomach cramps.

After this case, Father Carmine took a ten-minute break, and he and Father Gary sat down in the office. Early on, Father Gary had decided he would not ask unnecessary questions or disturb Father Carmine's rhythm during the exorcisms. He didn't know Father Carmine all that well yet, and he wanted to make a favorable impression so he could keep coming back. Now, however, as they paused, he couldn't resist. "How do you know these people are possessed?"

Father Carmine quickly explained his "technique of discernment"— he noticed things through little "signs." Most of these people, he said, had already been through several hospitals and had seen numerous doctors, none of which helped. "This last woman," he said, "has terrible headaches, the kind that don't go away. They completely block her. No matter how many aspirins she takes, it doesn't help. You understand?"

"*Sì, sì,*" Father Gary agreed, but he still wasn't sure how to be absolutely certain. The course had stressed that an exorcist should be skeptical in the beginning, and while he trusted that Father Carmine knew what he was doing, it bothered Father Gary that the "signs" weren't as apparent to him as they were to Father Carmine. Wary of being disrespectful, he held his tongue.

At 6:45 they took a short break and went to the basilica for evening prayer. Around fifteen people, including two other friars, crowded into the Cappella di San Tarcisio just off the sacristy. Among those praying, Father Gary recognized some of the people he'd seen in Father Carmine's waiting room. Apparently he would have to rethink his concept of what it meant to be possessed. Weren't demons supposed to stop people from worshiping?

They returned to Father Carmine's office and resumed the exorcisms. None of the reactions extended beyond coughing and yawning. One woman coughed so much that she brought up some foam. Father Carmine gave her one of the paper towels to wipe her mouth, then he threw it in the plastic trash bag he had attached to the door. At least Father Gary got an answer to the question about the bag's purpose.

Toward the end of the evening, Father Gary could see that the strain of so many exorcisms was starting to affect Father Carmine. Drenched and aching from being on his feet for hours, he shifted continuously and hooked his left hand into his rope belt behind his back while he prayed. Father Gary knew he must be exhausted.

Finally, at eight o'clock, Father Carmine turned to Father Gary and announced with a heavy voice, "We're finished."

He could see that Father Carmine was drained; still he couldn't resist. "*Un momento,*" he said to Father Carmine. "*Una domanda?*" A question.

Father Carmine turned to look at him, his eyes lidded and heavy.

"Come back tomorrow afternoon at three-thirty," he said with a nod. "We can talk a little then."

When Father Gary stepped outside, the streets were practically deserted. A handful of antiquated streetlights cast a dull glow over him as he walked briskly to the bus stop on the opposite side of Via Tiburtina. Once on the bus, he realized that instead of providing answers, the evening had only raised more doubts. The people had certainly appeared to be troubled, but whether the cause was demonic, he couldn't say. None had displayed the classic symptoms of demonic possession. He knew that Italy had socialized medicine, that its population was 83 percent Catholic—maybe seeing a priest was easier for people than seeing a counselor, he hypothesized. And wouldn't a priest locked in battle against a demon let the answering machine pick up the phone?

He had to trust that Father Carmine had the experience to diagnose these people; after all, he'd been an exorcist for more than eighteen years. Still, something about the experiences troubled Father Gary. He felt let down that he hadn't found the definitive proof that he sought.

CHAPTER NINE

DISCERNMENT

Every man has close by him two angels, the
one an angel of holiness, the other an angel
of perversion . . . And how then, O Lord,
shall I recognize the workings of these two
since they both dwell within me?

—The Shepherd, *by Hermas*

In mid-January, even before participating in his first exorcism, Father Gary had been asked by the director of pastoral formation at the NAC, forty-seven-year-old Father Steve Bigler, to give a talk to the seminarians about discernment. While not an exorcist himself, Father Bigler had taken the exorcism course the year before and wanted his seminarians to have more practical exposure. He thought of Father Gary, whom he knew from their time together the previous fall at the NAC.

The concept that most terrified Father Gary about exorcism was discernment—the possibility that he might get it wrong. He knew that several mental illnesses could mask themselves as demonic possession. Performing exorcisms on people with severe mental disease would most likely harm them, "fixing" them in this state. He was extremely wary of doing anything that might add to a person's pain by making an existing condition worse.

When Father Bigler contacted him, Father Gary immediately warmed to the idea of imparting some of his knowledge to the seminarians. In fact, early on, once he began to sink his teeth into the course material, he'd realized that while he might never be called upon to actually perform an exorcism, he could still be a resource for priests in the parish who had questions. He had seen how callous some priests could be in unfamiliar situations, turning people away who sought comfort for problems such as depression.

He gave his presentation on a Saturday afternoon in one of the NAC's small gathering rooms, with the seminarians arranged around a horseshoe-shaped table. Attending the talk had been optional, so only eight seminarians showed up, along with two spiritual directors and the director of spiritual formation, Father Mike Tomaseck. All found the subject intriguing.

Father Gary's portion of the talk focused on the teachings of the Church with respect to the Devil. To help the seminarians with the concept of discernment, he passed around a list of questions they might ask a person who claimed to be possessed, telling the seminarians that "these are just food for thought."

The questions ranged from the obvious ("Please describe the experience that led you to believe that you are being affected by a presence of evil.") to the less obvious ("How would you describe your own personal self-discipline?"). At the bottom of the page, Father Gary had written a small "end note," explaining how the questions had been derived from the course material and how, in his opinion, "many of the lectures that have been presented do not only apply specifically to the demonic but to experiences leading up to demonic possession or other kinds of harassment and evil manifestations."

Afterward, despite the low turnout, he was pleased with how his talk went. His main goal was to give the seminarians "some equipment in their pastoral bag" that could help them "minister and serve people, rather than tell them they were crazy." From the course he had picked up the phrase "the exorcist must be the ultimate skeptic," and he never got tired of saying it.

***

IN ADOPTING THIS PRUDENT APPROACH, Father Gary was following recognized protocol. The guidelines set forth in the *Ritual* clearly state that "the exorcist should not proceed to celebrate the rite of exorcism unless he has discovered to his moral certainty that the one to be exorcized is in actual fact possessed by demonic power." In order to do this, the exorcist "must above all exercise necessary and extreme circumspection and prudence . . . He must not be too ready to believe that someone beset by some illness, especially mental illness, is a victim of demonic possession [nor] should he immediately believe that possession is present as soon as someone asserts that he or she is in a special way tempted by the Devil, abandoned, or indeed tormented, for people can be deceived by their own imagination."

The discernment of spirits is far more than just an educated guess, and is not to be confused with "intuition." Instead, according to Sicilian exorcist Father Matteo La Grua, discernment is one of the gifts that God gives to the faithful. It is like a "holy light" that comes from God and that allows those who receive it "to see how God is present in things." The Bible lists discernment as one of the nine spiritual manifestations (or fruits of the Holy Spirit), mentioned by Paul (1 Corinthians 12:8–10).

The practice of discerning spirits has a long history in the Christian tradition. For the mystics, such as Saint Ignatius of Loyola, it was a way to understand the impulses of the soul, which, he claimed, were influenced by either good angels (who desired the soul to be filled with "faith, hope, love and all interior joy that invites and attracts to what is heavenly") or by demons (who strive to impede our spiritual advancement with temptations of sin and desperation). And while it may sound simple, it's not, because in their cunning, demons often disguise their attacks, sometimes even appearing as "angels of light." The best way to differentiate between them, said Saint Ignatius, is to look at the end result of the action. If the message will lead to selfishness, hate, violence, and such, then its origin is Satan and should be resisted; however, if the end result is for good, then the source is God.

The *Ritual* gives three signs that indicate the possible presence of a demon: abnormal strength, the ability to speak or understand a previously unknown language, and the knowledge of hidden things. Yet even when these things are present, the *Ritual* still cautions the exorcist about proceeding. "These signs can offer some indication, but since [they] are not necessarily [caused by the Devil], attention should be paid to other factors, especially in the realm of the moral and the spiritual, which can in a different way be evidence of diabolic intrusion." The most common of these is an aversion to the sacred—for example, the inability to pray or say the name of Jesus or Mary, to go to mass, or to receive communion. And when the two are put together (the signs and the aversion to the sacred), an exorcist may suspect he is dealing with a possession.

People seek exorcists for several reasons. The person (or someone who knows the person) simply attributes various problems to the intervention of the Devil. "When a person comes, there are many, many people who say, 'Father, I have the demon inside me, give me an exorcism!' Usually they don't need it," says Father Carmine. "Generally, they are people who are a little unbalanced or maybe scared by some books or a movie. This is a very delicate issue. You have to divulge but without being judgmental."

By far, say exorcists, the vast majority of people who come to see them fit into this category, and they spend much of their time convincing people that nothing is wrong with them. Unfortunately, this is not always easy. Many exorcists lament the damage done by well-meaning but overzealous people who convince others that they are possessed when this is really not the case. One exorcist from a diocese in the Midwest was visited by a parishioner convinced that her daughter's problems were caused by an evil spirit. She'd gone to see a "ghost whisperer" who told the woman that indeed her daughter was suffering from a curse that could be removed for $1,000. Upon hearing that there was an exorcist in the diocese, the woman took her daughter to see the priest. After an initial interview, the exorcist uncovered a history of mental illness in the family, so he advised the woman to take her daughter to a psychiatrist, telling her that it was highly unlikely that her daughter was suffering from a demonic attack. The mother, however, was unconvinced and returned to the ghost whisperer and paid to have the curse removed.

Numerous mental illnesses can also be mistaken for demonic possession. For this reason, exorcists should insist on a full psychiatric evaluation before proceeding. More often than not, the person has already seen several doctors without relief. Based on this failure of medical intervention, if a demonic presence is suspected, the exorcist might believe he has grounds to proceed. Typically, though, an exorcist will have a team of individuals (a psychiatrist, psychologist, and perhaps a neurologist) whom he trusts to help him with discernment. Not just any psychiatrist will do, however; collaboration is possible only when the medical or psychiatric expert is open to the possibility of demonic possession or obsession. Their being Catholic (or Christian) is also a plus.

Dr. Richard Gallagher is an academic psychiatrist in the New York area who has worked with exorcists in the discernment process. A devout Catholic, Dr. Gallagher believes in demonic possession, which doesn't mean that he seeks it out. "The role of the psychiatrist is to make sure that these phenomena don't have a natural explanation before jumping to a preternatural or supernatural one. There are many individuals for one reason or another in life that become psychotic briefly; they are delusional, they may well hallucinate and they are prone to think that God, the Devil, a spirit, aliens, are communicating with them and they really believe it."

Over the past fifteen years, Dr. Gallagher has identified a handful of cases that he claims have shown clear signs of demonic possession. In one such case, he was working with a demonized person who was clairvoyant. One night while Dr. Gallagher was at home with his wife, his cats suddenly went crazy and began tearing at each other. The following day, when he went to see the patient, she asked if he liked the joke she played on his cats the night before.

"I am an experienced psychiatrist," says Dr. Gallagher. "Obviously I have seen multiple personality disorders, but these cases never include the paranormal." Instead, claims Dr. Gallagher, instances of demonic possession are more straightforward than cases involving mental illness. For instance, a person who has a "severe personality disorder" and who simply thinks that he has evil inside him won't typically have his voice completely change or experience total amnesia after a session, he says. "In fact, it is indicative of the full possession syndrome that the individual affected never remembers what the demon says while it is speaking during an exorcism." And if it is a case of just an overactive imagination, according to Dr. Gallagher, an experienced psychiatrist should be able to tell the difference. "If you have the paranormal there is no way you can believe that it is not coming from somewhere. Even if you don't believe in the Devil, you have to say that there is some explanation beyond the natural here."

People also come to see an exorcist because they are thirsting for attention (the fakers), a category also known as pseudo-possession. Exorcists say the difference between pseudo-possession and the real thing is fairly obvious. People who are faking generally will depict the evil spirit in the most banal and superficial of ways, while in a real possession, the evil spirit will correspond to the Devil as he is known in the New Testament.

Some exorcists have also devised little tricks to help them weed out the pseudo-possessions. Exorcists will use regular water instead of holy water, or even read Latin prose out of a text instead of reciting a prayer to see whether the person responds. Since in either case a demon should not react because the objects are not sacred, if the person does say, for example, "That water is burning me!" then the exorcist knows the possession is fake.

Only in extremely rare instances, say exorcists, is a person indeed suffering from some form of demonic attack.

―――――――――

"THE FIRST THING THE EXORCIST MUST DO," says Father Carmine, "is to listen to the person." The person almost always suffers from some degree of oppressive guilt or despair, so it's necessary "to comfort the person and cheer him up, which you do by giving a little homily about the faith."

During the first interview, the priest will usually ask victims about their lives and when their problems started. The exorcist may suspect possession if it comes out that the person was dabbling in the occult or had visited magicians or card readers.

Any physical symptoms are carefully examined. "I can draw conclusions from a certain behavior that makes me suspicious," explains Father Carmine. "For instance, when someone doesn't want to enter my office, when they have a look of hate, or when they don't look at my face—little attitudes that with experience make me think, Ouch, ouch, ouch . . ."

People don't usually attribute their problems to a demon. Instead, they typically go to several doctors and come away with a number of diagnoses. Somehow, often at the prodding of a friend or loved one, they end up on the doorstep of an exorcist. "This is one characteristic of a true possession; people seldom think they are possessed but attribute their problems to some other cause," asserts Father Bamonte.

Two areas most commonly affected by evil influences are the head and stomach, resulting in terrible pains accompanied by the desire to vomit. Victims may also feel intense pain in other parts of their body, such as the kidneys or joints. The pain will then migrate, perhaps affecting their arm or neck the following day. Medicine has no effect whatsoever. According to Father Amorth, "one of the determining factors in the recognition of diabolic possession is the inefficacy of medicines, while blessings prove very efficacious." The person may also experience temporary numbness, or excessive hair loss.

Beyond these physical symptoms, any manner of strange phenomena can accompany a possession. In addition to the intense aversion to the sacred, victims may have terrible nightmares, "so terrible that they don't even want to go to sleep," says Father Carmine. Hearing voices and seeing visions, or having urges to commit terrible acts such as murder or suicide, are common afflictions. They may have sudden mood changes, often feeling a deep depression. They believe they can also sense evil in people or know other people's sins.

The presence of foul odors is another indicator, including the smell of sulfur filling the room. During one exorcism while Father Carmine was still apprenticing, the stench of rotting garbage became so strong that he had to leave the room. Yet another indicator is the temperature in the room dropping.

During the interview, if the exorcist suspects something, he may conduct a simple blessing, such as, "Let's pray that the Holy Spirit can come upon us to guide us through this process." Father Bamonte likes to ask the person to praise Jesus Christ: "Let's get on our knees and praise the glory of Jesus Christ" or "the Blessed Mother." If there is a demon present, it will almost always refuse to do so, he says. An exorcist may also pray surreptitiously in his mind while he listens to the victim's story.

In order to determine whether a girl was possessed, Father Nanni once said a prayer in his mind in French. The second he did this, even though the girl was sitting about ten feet away and with her back to him, her head spun around and her eyes rolled up, revealing the whites. Looking directly at him, she sneered in Italian, "It is useless that you pray in that language because we know them all."

In conjunction with the other symptoms, if the exorcist sees a negative reaction to a blessing or mental prayer during the interview process, he usually has enough evidence of possession to begin an exorcism.

Since some demons are stronger than others, meaning they can resist a simple prayer, some exorcists claim that the only way to unmask the demon is by performing an exorcism. Because of the suggestive nature of exorcism, however, the majority of exorcists frown upon the practice of using the rite itself as a diagnostic tool. "That is not the purpose of the *Ritual*," says Father Dermine. "Most demons will manifest with a simple prayer. There is no need to pray the whole *Ritual*."

In the most difficult cases, say exorcists, the person may be suffering from both mental illness and demonic possession, or the demon may be masking his presence by creating symptoms that mimic mental illness. This is especially true in cases of obsession, in which the demon attacks the victim's mind. Father Bamonte writes, "There are cases in which [obsession] has an exclusively pathological origin; other cases in which the origin is due to an extraordinary action of the demon; and still others where the extraordinary action of the demon amplifies, in an abnormal manner, little obsessive thoughts and compulsive behaviors that can be normal when they happen only once in a while, are quick, and most of all controllable, but that become all of a sudden invasive, insistent, and continuous under this action, heavily disturbing the psyche of the person."

A good rule of thumb, say exorcists, is that if the cause is natural, then the patient's condition will not improve dramatically with prayer. If the cause is demonic, however, a person's condition should improve after an exorcism. Since the difference between what is natural and what is demonic is such a delicate distinction, most exorcists continue to have the victim seek the help of a doctor even while undergoing an exorcism.

FOR MANY PEOPLE, of course, the idea that a person can become possessed by a demon is beyond ridiculous. Instead, a whole host of mental illnesses as well as other "natural" psychological motivators including "goal-oriented behavior" are seen as explanations of the symptoms.

Schizophrenia is typically associated with hearing voices, sometimes accompanied by hallucinations and paranoid delusions. Sometimes people imagine their TV is speaking to them, or a UFO is transmitting signals to them. A person brought up in a strict religious environment might easily characterize these "voices" as demonic.

Likewise, when suffering from *somatization disorder* (what used to be called hysteria), people will typically manifest various physical ailments—such as nausea, depression, even hearing loss—with no identifiable physical cause. The subconscious can convince the conscious brain that there is some kind of disability when there isn't.

People with *bipolar disease* can suffer from paranoid delusions or their moods can fluctuate, sometimes violently.

Those with *obsessive compulsive disorder* (OCD) feel tormented by obsessive thoughts or compulsions that compel them to act in ways they know may be irrational.

Historically, *epilepsy*, which in Greek means "to seize and carry off," has been associated with spirit possession, as has *Gilles de la Tourette's syndrome*, a disease characterized by uncontrollable tics, movements, or speech. We now know it to be a neurological disorder caused by abnormal electrical activity in the brain. Similarly, *mi-*

graines are thought to be responsible for some of the visual auras and auditory hallucinations that may have caused accusations of possession or beatific visions in the past.

Disassociation is perhaps the most common way in which a person might feel "possessed." In simple terms, disassociation refers to a variety of behaviors that stem from "a lack of integration of psychological processes that normally should be integrated." These behaviors can run the gamut from "zoning out" while driving the car, to feelings of being located outside the physical body, such as in out-of-body experiences.

"Basically, what it really comes down to is our conscious experiences as an act of construction," says Dr. Barry L. Beyerstein, a professor of psychology and a member of the Brain Behavior Laboratory at Simon Fraser University. "It doesn't just happen. Our sensory processes scan the world around us, and in order to make sense out of it, the brain has to assimilate it into a model of reality. And as we grow up we get so good at doing this that we don't even realize that we're constructing this, because it really is a state of the brain where we're trying to put together a feeling of being in a three-dimensional world."

The problem emerges when this "system" breaks down. "Ordinarily this is all so seamless that everything jives with everything else; but every once in a while (thanks to a number of things such as weird migraine states or exhaustion or mental disorders like schizophrenia), the ability of the brain to make a coherent model of the world can be disrupted. And when that happens, people are apt to feel as if something odd is going on, i.e., some external entity must have usurped control of their thoughts or actions." At the heart of the issue, says Dr. Beyerstein, is the fact that most of us underestimate just how much of our own behavior is dependent on these "nonconscious mechanisms."

Originally from Vancouver, British Columbia, Dr. Beyerstein received his Ph.D. in experimental and biological psychology from the University of California at Berkeley in the late 1960s. "[This field of study] is sort of an interface between neuroscience, which studies the physiology and anatomy and chemistry and electrophysiology of the brain, and psychology," applying this toward discovering how the brain produces consciousness. Dr. Beyerstein is also on the board of the Committee for Skeptical Inquiry (CSI), a sort of skeptical think tank created to debunk stories about the paranormal (ESP, UFOs, ghosts, and spirit possession).

"I've yet to see anything that contradicts any well-established law of science or dents my belief that the mind is equal to a state of the brain in ways that I would dearly love to understand," he says with a good-natured chuckle. However, Dr. Beyerstein is quick to point out that this doesn't negate the reality of these experiences. "We're not saying that people aren't having these experiences, just that the onus of proof is on the claimant, and that they should have evidence that can't be explained by prosaic means."

Many scientists think that Dissociative Identity Disorder (DID)—what used to be called Multiple Personality Disorder (MPD)—offers the best explanation for demonic possession. DID is characterized by an individual claiming to have one or more "alters" that control behavior, with distinct voices and different names, personality characteristics, even handwriting. Memory and other aspects of the person's consciousness are said to be split among the different personalities that occur spontaneously. However, the disease is fairly controversial, and psychotherapists are divided on how to treat it.

DID can be diagnosed in one of two ways. One approach, which has come to be known as the traditional disease view, theorizes that DID "is an etiologically distinct condition that is best conceptualized as a defensive response to childhood trauma, particularly sexual and physical abuse."

The other approach, known as the sociocognitive model, "conceptualizes DID as a syndrome that consists of rule-governed and goal-directed displays of multiple role enactments that have been created, legitimized, and maintained by societal reinforcements." In other words, people *act* as if they have different personalities in them. "I think most cognitive scientists would tell you that people don't in fact house different personalities with separate streams of information processing, separate memories," says Dr. Steven Jay Lynn, a professor of psychology at the State University of New York at Binghamton who has done extensive work on disassociation and hypnotic states. "Rather, people come to think of themselves in this way, oftentimes by things they've read about, learned about, or because their therapist has suggested it (either very explicitly through hypnosis or leading questions or subtly through implicit suggestions) and that the sense of oneself, as being divided, is really shaped and created by these cultural forces." According to proponents of this view, the media and to a large extent the cultural mores of the society that the patient comes from also play a big role in helping to perpetuate the condition.

One of the most relevant aspects of the sociocognitive view of exorcism is "role playing," in which either the exorcist or the possessed person learns to enact experiences by participating in numerous rituals over time. Anthropologists have seen ample evidence of this. In Puerto Rico, for instance, *espiritistas* (spirit mediums) are chosen in childhood and often apprentice with a more experienced healer. These experiences teach them the behaviors of the various possessing spirits. Nicholas Spanos, author of *Multiple Identities and False Memories: A Sociocognitive Perspective*, offers a number of social issues that help explain why the belief in spirit possession has persisted over the years. "The notion provided a culturally consistent explanation for various physical disorders and for otherwise inexplicable propriety norm violations. When coupled with exorcism procedures, the role provided a way to reintegrate deviants into the community, served as a device for proselytizing, and in numerous ways bolstered the religious and moral values of the community." In certain contexts, demonic possession can also give marginalized individuals a means to improve their social status. Anthropologists, for instance, have documented that women in certain East African tribes use possession as a way of empowering themselves.

In the context of the different societies, the "goal-directed nature" of demonic possession can also change depending on the social cues that the victim receives. According to Spanos, the Catholic exorcism, in which the demon is addressed, "produces strongly cued demon self-enactments as a central component of the demonic role." Another example would be the person screaming that his skin is burning when the exorcist sprinkles him with holy water.

The prayer of exorcism itself is admittedly a highly suggestive one, according to Father Gramolazzo. It's not hard to see the correlation between a priest wielding a crucifix while saying, "I command you, foul serpent, to depart!" and an accommodating person undulating in the manner of a serpent. Numerous studies have shown that through suggestive methods, people can be convinced that they have experienced events that never took place. In one such study conducted in Italy, people were made to believe falsely that they had witnessed a demonic possession or had somehow taken part in an exorcism.

Dr. Giuliana A. L. Mazzoni is a professor of psychology at the University of Hull in the United Kingdom who conducted a study in the late 1990s on how memory and suggestivity can play a role in shaping our beliefs, even when those beliefs are considered "implausible." In the experiment, performed on university students, Dr. Mazzoni and her fellow researchers proposed a "three-step model" for developing false memories: "First, the event must be perceived as plausible. Second, individuals must acquire the autobiographical belief that it is likely to have happened to them. Third, individuals must interpret their thoughts and fantasies about the event as memories." To do this, she and her team instructed people to read some articles about the reality of possession and how often it occurs. Then, they asked the subjects a series of questions about their fears, which the researchers purposefully "interpreted" as evidence that the subjects had witnessed a possession. Then, in the last session, participants rated the plausibility of witnessing a possession and stated whether they had seen one themselves.

"One of the crucial aspects of the manipulation was that the people had to believe that these experiences were happening in their own culture," says Dr. Mazzoni. "If they read reports about shamans or cases of possession in the ancient world, they were less apt to believe in it. If you can interpret people's fears in terms of being due to a specific experience, then you can get people to believe that they actually had that experience. Twenty-five percent came out pretty convinced. The others also increased their beliefs."

When it comes to the world of exorcism, it's not hard to see how the theory about suggestivity could also be applied to an exorcist, who might influence a person's opinions by, say, providing a book about exorcism for the person to read. As Dr. Beyerstein observes, "When people go to see an exorcist, there is a role to be played; and they assume the role or they don't agree to be part of it." All of this points to the potential pitfalls of a priest, untrained in medicine and without the help of a trained professional, diagnosing whether or not a person's mental illness is caused by the presence of a demon.

While all these conditions could be mistaken for similar traits symptomatic of possession, they do not explain the more dramatic symptoms related to possession, such as the paranormal or "poltergeist-type" manifestations. After all, it's one thing to be praying over a person who screams or claims to see visions; it's quite another to watch her levitate four feet off the ground, or be able to identify hidden objects sealed in a bag. "These phenomena definitely create a big question mark," says Dr. Mazzoni. "Perhaps in fifty years we'll be able to understand why these things happen, but at the moment we can't."

CHAPTER TEN

CROSSING OVER

Hell hath no limits, nor is circumscrib'd
In one selfe place: but where we are is hell.
And where hell is there we must ever be.
And to be short, when all the world dissolves,
And every creature shall be purifi'd,
All places shall be hell that are not heaven.
                            —*Christopher Marlowe,*
                            Doctor Faustus

On Tuesday afternoon, Father Gary once again found himself in the small room next to Father Carmine's office. In a repeat of the previous night's events, the waiting room was overflowing with people, some even walking in off the street for impromptu blessings like those performed at the Scala Santa. *Jesus, Mary, and Joseph and good Saint Ann*, he thought, *where do all these people come from?* He knew from the course that belief in the occult was rampant in Italy, and perhaps here was the proof.

Again, he was surprised by the relative "normalcy" of the folks as they entered the tiny room, pausing to take his hand and sometimes even offering gracious smiles as he stumbled through his greeting in Italian. None of them "looked" possessed. Once again, physical reactions included coughing and yawning. A few people tried to push Father Carmine away, while still others cried when he touched them on the back of the neck or on their knees with his crucifix. A couple of times people would dry-heave or bring up some "froth" that they, or the person with them, would wipe away with a handkerchief.

Sometimes Father Carmine would pray the whole *Ritual*, sometimes only a simple blessing, and sometimes one of the exorcism prayers. Father Gary wondered how Father Carmine made this distinction. Were there levels of possession, or a set of criteria? Then there was his habit of tapping people on the forehead with his index finger at the end of each exorcism. Sometimes he would also push his finger into their foreheads or pat their foreheads a few times with his palm as if giving them a high-five. In each case, they would open their eyes and take a few deep breaths to collect themselves, and the exorcism would be over. Was this a signal of some kind?

After some exorcisms, the person would break down, sobbing. One woman in her sixties turned to Father Gary with a look as if to say, "It's not my fault." After they'd seen around five people and were taking a quick break, Father Carmine explained, "They feel somehow they brought this upon themselves. They are deeply, deeply ashamed."

At the Casa later that night, Father Gary reflected on what he'd seen. In that cramped little room out at San Lorenzo, nothing had gone according to script. He wondered why Father Daniel seemed to be seeing more dramatic cases at the Scala Santa. Just recently the Franciscan had told him about a woman who vomited seven black two-inch-long nails—six of which had dissolved into a dark liquid but the seventh he kept. Father Gary had also expected to see longer, more drawn-out exorcisms, not fifteen minutes of a person sitting in a chair yawning. Did they send the harder cases to certain exorcists?

Father Carmine had told him to return the following afternoon, and he hoped to get answers to a few questions then.

BY THE TIME HE ARRIVED at San Lorenzo, as usual a small crowd had gathered outside the door. All the faces were new, however, and an image of a never-ending stream of people popped into his mind. A few turned to acknowledge him with a nod, but most kept to themselves. Nobody talked. Father Gary noticed a pair of women wearing the navy blue habits of religious sisters, with matching down jackets. One was young, perhaps in her mid-twenties, with short curly black hair and hard, tense features (her name would later be revealed as Sister Janica). Her kind-faced companion was in her late fifties. The older sister gave him a polite smile, but Sister Janica refused to look at him. There was something about her that he couldn't put his finger on—in some deep way she seemed very troubled.

The group waited patiently for another ten minutes until Father Carmine opened the door at around 3:40, looking groggy, having just awakened from his afternoon *riposo*.

As everyone filed in, Father Gary went into the office. *"Ciao, Father Carmine, come stai?"* How are you?

"Bene," Father Carmine answered, but he seemed in a dark mood.

Realizing the toll of day-in-and-day-out work like this, Father Gary pulled out his carefully folded purple stole and draped it around his neck. He entered the now-familiar room, almost as if he were punching a time clock on the factory floor.

A few minutes later Father Carmine entered, followed by the two nuns. As she had outside, the older woman smiled at Father Gary when he introduced himself, while Sister Janica averted her gaze and sat down in the chair, not even bothering to take his hand.

Father Carmine, who usually chatted for a second or two with the person before beginning the *Ritual*, wasted no time. Picking up the squeeze bottle filled with holy water, he blessed both women. The older woman made the sign of the cross, while Sister Janica grimaced, clenching her eyes tightly as the drops of water splashed over her head. So far, nobody had reacted so strongly to the holy water.

As he had done with the others, Father Carmine put his hand on top of the nun's head. He then invoked the protection of Saint Michael the Archangel, revered by Christians as the leader of God's army, which was something new. Then, without so much as a pause, he jumped right into the *Ritual*.

"*Deus, humáni géneris cónditor atque defénsor, réspice super hunc fámulum tuam, quam ad tuam imáginem formásti et ad tuæ vocas glóriæ consortium*" [God, creator and defender of the human race, look down on this your servant, whom you formed in your own image and now call to be a partaker in your glory], he said, beginning the deprecatory prayer. "*Vetus adversárius eam dire torquet, acri ópprimit vi, sævo terróre contúrbat. Mitte super eam Spíritum Sanctum tuum, qui eam in lucta confírmet, in tribulatióne supplicáre dóceat et poténti sua protectióne múniat.*" [The old adversary twists her torturously, oppresses her with violent force, and disturbs her with savage terror. Send upon her your Holy Spirit, who strengthens her in the struggle, who teaches her to pray in tribulation, and who fortifies her with his powerful protection.]

Within a minute, Sister Janica began to whine and shake her head. She halfheartedly tried to push Father Carmine's hand away.

To Father Gary, it seemed as if Father Carmine's hand had suddenly been plugged into an electric socket and a current was shooting through it, animating the nun.

"*Exáudi, sancte Pater, gémitum supplicántis Ecclésiæ: ne síveris filiam tuam a patre mendácii possidéri; fámulam, quam Christus suo sánguine redémit, diáboli captivitáte detinéri; templum Spíritus tui ab immúndo inhabitári spíritu.*" [Hear, Holy Father, the groanings of your supplicant Church: do not suffer your daughter to be possessed by the father of lies; do not suffer your servant, whom Christ by his blood has redeemed, to be detained in captivity of the devil; do not suffer this temple of your Spirit to be inhabited by this unclean spirit.]

Sister Janica began banging the back of her head against the wall, gently at first but then with increasing intensity, until the picture of Christ hanging on the hook above her head began to rattle. Father Gary edged forward on his seat, worrying that she might hurt herself. Her companion, however, slipped an arm behind Sister Janica's head to protect it and a struggle ensued. Father Gary wondered whether he might have to intervene, but for some reason remained riveted to his chair, looking between his copy of the *Ritual* and the strange rocking figure. He prayed silently that God would come to her aid.

As Father Carmine continued with the prayers, a low guttural growl began to emanate from Sister Janica. Father Gary studied her, trying to determine its source. The sound seemed to be coming from deep inside her, from her stomach. It sounded like the noise a dog makes when it's getting ready to bite someone. From his reading he did know that it was possible for a demon to attack an exorcist during the *Ritual*. In one such instance a demonized person had ripped a bedspring from a bed and stabbed the exorcist with it. He had no idea what he would do if something violent like that occurred.

"*Exáudi, Deus, humánæ salútis amátor, oratiónem Apostolórum tuórum Petri et Pauli et ómnium Sanctórum, qui tua grátia victóres extitérunt Malígni,*" Father Carmine intoned. [Hear, God, lover of human salvation, the prayer of your Apostles Peter and Paul and of all the saints, who by your grace emerged as victors over the Evil One.]

All at once, Sister Janica lashed out at Father Carmine, trying to knock his hand off her. As she struggled, her companion tried her best to keep Sister Janica from hitting Father Carmine.

"No, no, NO!" Sister Janica shouted, followed by an ear-piercing *"Basta!"*

Father Gary's eyes were now fixed on the nun, whose eyes remained tightly clenched. Again he wondered whether he might have to jump in and restrain her. If things got worse, he didn't think that Father Carmine and the companion could do enough to stop her.

"Líbera hanc fámulam tuam ab omni aliéna potestáte et incólumen custódi ut tranquíllæ devotióni restitúta, te corde díligat et opéribus desérviat, te gloríficet láudibus et magníficent vita." [Free this your servant, from every foreign power and keep her safe, so that restored to peaceful devotion, she may love you with her heart and may serve you zealously with her works, may glorify you with praises and may magnify you with her life.]

Sister Janica let out a low, torturous moan. It didn't sound human.

Father Gary studied her again, aware that a change had come over her. What was it? He couldn't put his finger on it. It didn't seem like she was there anymore.

Without pause, Father Carmine moved on to the imperative formula. *"Adiúro te, Satan, hostis humánæ salútis: agnósce institíam et bonitátem Dei Patris, qui supérbiam et invidíam tuam iusto iudício damnávit,"* he said, accentuating the word *Adiúro*. [I adjure you, Satan, enemy of human salvation: know the justice and goodness of God the Father, who damns your pride and envy with His just judgment.]

Once again Sister Janica screamed, an otherworldly tone that unnerved Father Gary. Then he heard it, a deep rasping guttural sound that made the hairs on the back of his neck stand on end. It was the "voice."

"Shut up, you stupid priest!" The furious voice screamed in Italian at Father Carmine. "You dirty sack of shit!" followed by more howling and groaning. Sister Janica was breathing heavily now, her face contorted into a mask of rage.

Father Carmine paid no attention to this tirade; in fact, it didn't seem to faze him at all. *"Adiúro te, Satan, princeps huius mundi: agnósce poténtiam et virtútem Iesu Christi, qui te in desérto vicit, in horto superávit, spoliávit in cruce."* [I adjure you, Satan, prince of this world, know the power and strength of Jesus Christ, who defeated you in the desert, overcame you in the garden, vanquished you on the cross.]

Sister Janica screamed again. Her head shook violently. *"Zitto!"* the gruff voice shouted over and over, trying to drown out Father Carmine. "Shut up! Shut up! Shut up! You have no power over meeeeeeeee!" A high-pitched wail was immediately followed by a deep bass groan. Father Gary had never heard such range in a human voice. Beyond the tone, there was also a certain quality to it: It seemed infused with a kind of superiority while at the same time caged—like a trapped animal striking out.

"Adiúro te, Satan, decéptor humáni géneris: agnósce Spíritum veritátis et grátiæ, qui tuas repéllit insídias tuáque confúndit mendácia: exi ab hoc plásmate Dei." [I adjure you, Satan, deceiver of the human race, know the Spirit of truth and of grace, who drives off your snares and confounds your lies, depart from this creature of God.]

"Fuck off!" the voice shouted, followed by a string of blasphemies and more curses in Italian. Father Gary recoiled from the viciousness.

Sister Janica suddenly stood up and Father Carmine pushed her back down into the chair, never taking his hand from the top of her head. He said something to her, and she hissed and spit at him. He turned to Father Gary. "I am trying to ask the demon his name," he said in English.

It took a second for the words to register. Father Gary knew that the *Ritual* specifically prohibits the exorcist from talking to the demon, except in the case of trying to find out his name. It seemed to have something to do with how the person could become liberated.

"No, no, no," the rasping, guttural voice kept repeating, followed by loud screaming. Like a doctor examining a patient, Father

Carmine lifted Sister Janica's eyelid. Her eyeball had rolled completely up into her head. He then tilted her head to the side, poured a few drops of holy water into each ear, and slightly pinched the lobe with his finger as if pressing the liquid into her skin.

The nun immediately went into a fit, screaming and flailing so fiercely that she threw herself onto the floor, where she flopped around like a fish, grunting and growling.

Father Gary sat stunned. She hadn't fallen hard, but he was worried that she might have hurt herself. Before he had time to react, Father Carmine and Sister Janica's companion took hold of her and she sprang up off the floor almost like a bouncing ball, as if her body weighed nothing, and she was placed back in the chair.

Father Carmine continued without pause. The room was extremely hot and Father Carmine's forehead was dripping with sweat. *"Recéde ergo, Satan, in nómine Patris et Fílii et Spíritus Sancti."* [Depart, therefore, Satan, in the name of the Father and of the Son and of the Holy Spirit.]

A loud screech pierced the room, followed again by that hideous, guttural voice as Sister Janica railed against Father Carmine, grunting and hissing at him between clenched teeth. Finally, after a particularly vicious struggle, the voice said: *"Chi è lui?! Che sta facendo qui?!"*

Again Father Carmine turned to Father Gary, saying in English, "The demon just asked me who you are and what you are doing here. I told him that you were here to learn to do what I am doing."

Father Gary's heart jumped into his throat. He looked at Sister Janica as she writhed in agony in the chair, her eyes clenched tight. *Okay*, he thought, *why is the demon asking about me?* He couldn't keep his mind from racing, wondering if somehow he'd been marked by this demon.

The exorcism continued for another thirty minutes, as Father Carmine followed the *Revised Ritual* with the older *Ritual*, and then brought back a few Psalms and prayers from the *Revised Ritual*. It was the longest and most extensive exorcism that Father Gary had seen Father Carmine perform, and he could tell he was pulling out all the stops, using every tool at his disposal to try to help Sister Janica. The room had become incredibly stuffy, and Father Gary saw that both Sister Janica and Father Carmine were wrung out. Finally, when it seemed like the exorcism might go on for the whole night, Father Carmine smacked her lightly on the forehead, and after a few seconds she gradually came to, her eyes blinking open.

For a moment the room was still. Sister Janica looked as if she might fall out of the chair from fatigue; her black hair was matted with sweat and she panted like a marathon runner after a race.

Father Gary was at a loss for words. His experience this evening had completely changed his understanding of what happened during an exorcism. Was it over? Had the demon been cast out?

Father Carmine broke the spell. "I'm going to hear her confession now."

Father Gary and Sister Janica's companion stood up and went out into the office to give them some privacy. Later, Father Gary would come to understand the significance of this gesture in the context of liberation. Now that the demon had been temporarily weakened by the exorcism, Sister Janica could truly confess her sins, something the demon would never have allowed her to do otherwise. For now, however, Father Gary saw the gesture as being more pastoral. Here again was an example of how being an exorcist meant more than just sprinkling holy water onto someone and saying a prayer. It was also about bringing the sacraments back into people's lives.

Father Gary and the older woman said nothing as they waited out in the office. He now had the proof he had been searching for—there was no doubt in his mind that what he'd witnessed was a demon. The pain she had undergone had been so intense. As if to underscore how dramatic this case was, he heard a thumping sound as Sister Janica once again started to bang her head against the wall. He turned to the older woman, who looked down at her hands in resignation.

Five minutes later, the door opened and Father Carmine and Sister Janica emerged. She was still a little dazed from her ordeal, so Father Carmine had her rest on his office sofa, into which she sank gratefully.

Father Gary would have preferred to take a moment to digest

what he had just seen and to ask Father Carmine a few questions, but that did not seem appropriate with the women still in the room. Besides, Father Carmine had already opened his office door and was motioning in two young women in their thirties. As they entered the small room, Father Gary followed them. It was time for the next exorcism to begin.

Father Gary realized that exorcism could indeed be a lot more explosive than the first two days had suggested. He sat more alertly as Father Carmine began the *Ritual* this time. As it turned out, the exorcism was similar to those he'd watched the other two nights. As Father Carmine prayed, he touched various parts of one of the women's bodies with the crucifix—her knee, her elbow, her back. Here again was something that the course hadn't talked about. When he touched the back of her neck, she covered her ears and howled in pain. Father Carmine left the crucifix there for a few seconds while he kept his other hand on her forehead and prayed. The exorcism lasted the standard twenty minutes.

After they were finished, Father Carmine went into his office to see how Sister Janica was doing, while Father Gary stayed behind inside the small room. He could hear the two speaking but couldn't quite make out what they were saying. Once his Italian improved, he would realize that the conversation was quite banal—Father Carmine was scheduling her next appointment.

Father Carmine saw three more people after that: a young man dressed in painter's overalls who screamed "Ahhhhhhhh!" loudly over and over as if his feet were being roasted over hot coals; an older woman who went completely rigid; and a housewife in her forties who groaned, whined, and coughed.

Afterward, with about fifteen minutes to kill before evening prayer, Father Gary took the opportunity to ask a few questions. Sister Janica was still very much on his mind. "I have never seen anything so dramatic in all my life," he said to Father Carmine.

Father Carmine nodded, his face looking perhaps more wan than usual as he confirmed that Sister Janica was indeed a nun.

"How could a nun become possessed?" Father Gary asked.

"It is very sad," Father Carmine sighed. "It involves the whole family. She is from Austria and her father used to perform satanic rituals in the house; some were performed on her when she was a child."

Father Gary was astonished, but even more surprised when Father Carmine told him that she had been coming to see him for nine years.

"Nine years?" Father Gary repeated with incredulity.

Father Carmine nodded. "She is incapable of functioning. It is a terrible thing."

The streets were dark and cold when Father Gary stepped out from the friary and headed up the driveway that bordered the cemetery. His mind was racing. What he had seen that night had completely reversed his opinion on the reality of demonic possession. It wasn't something that only happened in the history books, but was a living, breathing reality in the twenty-first century.

He couldn't get the voice of the demon out of his head, the unnatural way it sounded. He thought back to when the demon had questioned Father Carmine about his presence in the room. He wasn't one to be overly sensitive, but for a split second he couldn't help but wonder, "Is there a demon following me home?"

He wondered if Father Carmine was ever afraid. He had never seen the Capuchin lose his cool, or seem to doubt himself, which was reassuring. In the end, Father Gary knew he had to trust that God would protect him.

ALL THROUGH THE BUS RIDE HOME he sat deep in thought. He was beginning to see how what he'd witnessed that night would ripple into the rest of his life. He wondered how many people had such an evil force operating in their lives. Probably more than anyone realized. After just one week of participating in exorcisms, he was amazed that so many of his ideas about what constituted demonic possession had been reversed. Apparently it didn't have to be an all or nothing affair; there were obviously different levels. What constituted those levels or even why they existed would be questions to ask Father Carmine.

Walking through the crowded streets of downtown, he moved like a ghost—savoring the human interaction yet somehow removed from it. He decided to stop in a *pasticceria* near the Trevi Fountain to buy some *cornetti* for the following morning. Just the simple act of buying a pastry helped to bring back a sense of normalcy. The bar was filled with the aromas of sweetened dough and fresh espresso. Unable to resist, he opened the bag and started eating one of the *cornetti* on the spot.

While the night's events had revealed several important things to him, perhaps what mattered most was his realization that if called upon he would be able to perform an exorcism himself. Maybe it was the calm way that Father Carmine had gone about praying the *Ritual*, or the pastoral flourishes he brought into the process. It certainly didn't hurt that he had seen some pretty terrible things himself as an embalmer, which had prepared him in a way. Beyond the spectacle, what had touched him most was the victims' profound suffering. And while he knew what it was like to suffer, this suffering was like nothing he had seen before; it went beyond simple pain, much deeper. If he could do anything in his power to help these people, he felt it was his duty. "These people suffer so much," he thought. "May God help us."

CHAPTER ELEVEN

THE FALL

The problems or crises which arise, due to no fault of our own, are part of the human condition we call mystery and related to our own vulnerability, our mortality.
—*Father Gary Thomas,* Town Crier, *1996*

One of Father Gary's idols, the late Joseph Cardinal Bernardin—who died of cancer in 1997—wrote, "Whenever we are with people who suffer, it frequently becomes evident that there is very little we can do to help them other than be present to them, walk with them as the Lord walks with us." For Father Gary, such feelings of powerlessness had manifested in the form of guilt. As he helped others overcome tragedy—whether administering last rites in a hospital or comforting a spouse dealing with a nasty divorce—he was well aware that he'd gotten off relatively scot-free. While he certainly didn't wish horrible things upon himself, he couldn't help but wonder, *Why hasn't anything happened to me?*

IN THE SUMMER OF 1997, Father Gary was pastor at Saint Nicholas Parish, a position he'd held since being promoted from associate pastor in 1993. Initially, he'd started out with high hopes for the parish. Saint Nicholas was a quaint 250-seat church located a few blocks from the upscale boutiques and coffeehouses of downtown Los Altos. There was a real sense of community here; it was the kind of town where he could get to know each and every one of his parishioners. A few things needed fixing; but on the whole, with the right leadership, the parish had the potential to be a good Christian community. In addition, he relished the challenge of dealing with important leaders (one of the founders of Adobe was a parishioner), and he hoped his actions would foster an environment in which prayer and the Eucharist would inspire them to make the right decisions.

After four years, though, his vision hadn't panned out. Try as he might to engage some of his parishioners, apathy seemed to prevail. Was he setting his expectations too high? Perhaps. After all, not everybody has enough time for work and family as it is, let alone time to volunteer at the church. Los Altos being smack-dab in the middle of Silicon Valley and the technological rat race didn't help either. Perhaps he was frustrated at the materialistic society in general, which forces people to dedicate so much time and energy to work in the first place. He also took responsibility. Why hadn't he been able to motivate his parishioners? Was he doing enough? These were questions that bothered him during the spring and summer of 1997.

AROUND THE SAME TIME, Jim Michaletti, a former parishioner of Father Gary's, was undergoing similar soul-searching. Originally from Palo Alto, Jim and his wife had moved to a town in the foothills of Yosemite called Twain Harte, where Jim worked as a teacher in a school for troubled teens. Father Gary had vacation time, so the two decided to get together and turn to the Lord for help.

They went for a hike with Jim's two golden retrievers (Buck and Spitz) to a place called Three Pools, which was near the Lion's Lake Reservoir. The day was incredibly hot, and Jim carried a backpack with a Bible and two water bottles. On the way out, they hiked up a dry riverbed, which snaked through the South Fork Stanislaus River Canyon. Here and there the ground was broken by rocks and boulders, some as big as small cars. While not treacherous, the hike could be tricky. At one point, while making his way over a large rock, Father Gary slipped and sprained his ankle.

As a result, on their way back, Jim decided they should take a different path. A little deer trail bordered the riverbed, and it seemed easier to negotiate. After a few minutes of paralleling the riverbed, however, the trail rose steeply until eventually the two were walking along the edge of a sixty-foot cliff. When they came to a section of the trail where some rocks were covered by moss, Jim's dog Buck slipped and tumbled over the edge, disappearing from view.

Imagining his dog twisted and dead among the rocks below, Jim peered over the edge, but was unable to see anything. "I've got to go down and see if Buck is alive," he called, tossing the backpack to Father Gary. "Stay here with Spitz and keep him away from the cliff. And watch out for that rock." He pointed to the moss-covered rock.

Jim then hurried down the nearby cliff, scrambling and half sliding until he reached the bottom. When he finally made it over to Buck, the dog was miraculously still alive—sitting up on a patch of dirt between two clumps of jagged rocks. Had he landed a couple feet in either direction, he would have been killed. Instead, his only injury was a badly broken leg.

Relieved, Jim started back up. However, as he scaled the steep incline hand over fist, he heard Father Gary shout, "Oh God!" followed by the sickening thud as his body hit the ground a few moments later.

From where he was, Jim couldn't see where Father Gary had fallen, but there was no question in his mind that his friend had just died. *Oh my God*, he thought, *I have just killed a priest.*

When Jim finally reached him, Father Gary was lying on his back, just a few feet from Buck. Like the dog, he'd narrowly missed the jagged rocks, but his face was covered with blood and he wasn't moving.

Expecting the worst, Jim was surprised to see that Father Gary was still alive, but just barely. His face was cut and one eye was basically a pool of blood, his kneecap appeared to be shattered, and it was impossible to know whether he had any internal injuries.

"Father, can you hear me? It's me, Jim!" he shouted.

Father Gary moaned.

Jim reached out and Father Gary gripped his hand tightly, which Jim took as a good sign. Trying to establish how cognizant he was, he asked him to recite the Lord's Prayer in Latin.

"Pater noster, qui es in caelis, sanctificetur nomen tuum. . . ." Father Gary began weakly, continuing until he finished the prayer.

Jim was relieved. No obvious brain damage, but his friend's breathing was very shallow. At that point, Jim faced a difficult decision. Should he stay with Father Gary or run for help? Going for help would mean going back down the riverbed—over the rocks and boulders—

for about a mile and a half before he'd reach South Fork Bridge, where he could hope to flag down somebody with a cell phone. If not, he'd have to hoof it into town, another five miles down a dirt road. Father Gary might not last that long. He agonized over the decision for a few seconds before realizing he had no choice. He bent down and gave Father Gary a little blessing on his forehead. Then he turned and ran.

Sprinting over the uneven ground, he screamed for help. It was like one of those nightmares when his legs couldn't carry him fast enough. While he ran, he prayed: "Lord, please keep watch over him, please keep him alive."

Finally he reached the bridge and was able to flag down two old men in a beat-up pickup truck. Neither had a cell phone. "A man is going to die!" he screamed. "We have to get help." Perhaps alarmed by Jim's appearance—in his rush to get to the bridge, he had somehow lost his shirt—the men balked. With his adrenaline pumping, Jim reached out and throttled one. "Get in your car right now and let's go!" They acquiesced and, once they'd all piled in, drove off. Much to Jim's dismay, however, the old heap would go only about twenty miles per hour. About a mile down the road, they passed an SUV heading in the opposite direction that Jim was able to flag down. Luckily this couple had a cell phone. After describing what had happened, he left them calling 911 while he took off back in Father Gary's direction, hoping his friend would be alive when he got there.

When Jim finally reached the cliff, he saw that an amazing thing had happened during his absence. Three hikers who'd heard his calls for help had come to investigate. As Jim came sprinting up, he saw one, who turned out to be a nurse, bending over Father Gary and talking to him.

The nurse had mopped Father Gary's face using Jim's discarded shirt and had kept him alert by talking to him. However, Father Gary was going in and out of consciousness and his vital signs were low. "He could go at any time," she warned Jim. Still, their only option was to wait for help. Moving him would risk further damage.

Over the next two hours, Jim and the nurse stayed with Father Gary, praying with him, consoling him and each other.

Finally, rescue personnel—including paramedics, members of the Tuolumne County Sheriff's Search and Rescue Team, and a few Stanislaus National Forest Rangers—began arriving. After doing what they could to stabilize Father Gary, the paramedics called in a helicopter, only to learn that all were out doing rescues in Yosemite. They would have to wait for a helicopter to fly up from Lemoore Naval Air Station near Fresno, nearly a hundred miles away.

After an hour or so, the stillness was broken by the loud thump-thumping of a helicopter approaching from the south. The Navy had sent a large CH-46 Sea Night with twin rotors. By then it was late afternoon, about four hours after Father Gary had fallen. For Jim, the sound of the approaching helicopter was extremely comforting. *If Father can just hold on*, he thought.

After circling for several minutes, the crewman was lowered in a metal basket. Father Gary was placed inside and the crewman hooked the line up while the helicopter thundered overhead, the massive twin rotors shaking the trees violently with their downdraft. While this was going on, Jim remembers the crewman saying more than once, "We're losing him!" as Father Gary's blood pressure dipped dangerously low. When everything was set, the crewman got on top of the basket to secure it, and the helicopter lifted them into the sky, whipping through the air like a child's toy.

As the helicopter disappeared from view, Jim and the other rescuers exchanged hugs. Gathering up their gear, they made their way down to South Fork Bridge. Jim's dog Buck was hoisted onto a stretcher (the one intended for Father Gary) and carried along as well, while Spitz followed on foot. When they reached the road, Jim was confronted by an amazing sight: The bridge was packed with every kind of rescue vehicle imaginable, including about ten fire trucks. In addition, a large earth mover had been employed in an attempt to carve out a road through the riverbed, though after fifty yards, this idea had apparently been abandoned.

Meanwhile Father Gary was flown to a nearby abandoned golf course and dropped down on the ninth green, where a Life Flight helicopter was waiting to fly him to Memorial Medical Center in Modesto. Nobody on board thought he was going to make it.

IN MODESTO, the doctors immediately went to work performing a series of operations on Father Gary, the first of which lasted about fourteen hours. His injuries were extensive: The accident had fractured the c6 and c7 vertebrae in his neck, caved in a part of his skull, shattered his right wrist (this injury wouldn't be discovered until later), damaged the carpal tunnel, severed his orbital nerve, broken his kneecap, and turned his right elbow to dust. In addition, his face was severely lacerated and bruised and would require over a hundred stitches. The big question was brain damage; his head injury was serious and the surgeons wouldn't know the extent of the damage until they opened his skull.

After surgery the doctors had good news. The brain membrane was intact, so there would be no brain damage. He also wouldn't be paralyzed, since he'd broken only two of the three bones in his neck (breaking all three can lead to paralysis). This relative stroke of luck was attributed to his probably falling directly onto the water bottles in the backpack, which somehow cushioned the blow. The only real doubt was whether he'd be able to use his elbow again. They had scoped it out twice, cleaning out shattered bone, but the damage was extensive.

FOR THE FOLLOWING TWO DAYS Father Gary remained heavily sedated and in the ICU. He underwent another eleven-hour operation. And while he was conscious, the shock of the accident combined with the drugs clouded his mind. Doctors assured his parents that he would eventually come out of the fog.

The whole time his parents, his friends, and numerous priests kept a vigil over him. In addition, prayer services were held throughout the diocese as word got around about Father Gary's terrible accident.

On the fourth day, much to everyone's relief, Father Gary came around, waking up in the ICU wearing a neck brace, a cast on his arm, and bandages on his knee. Seeing his mother standing over him, he posed the obvious question: "What happened?"

"Don't you remember?" she said.

In truth he didn't. The last thing he recalled was Jim handing him the backpack. "What am I doing here?" he said.

She broke it to him. "You fell off a cliff."

He struggled to understand. "What day is it?" She told him it was Saturday.

"I have two weddings to do today," he responded.

The doctor smiled. "That's great! He remembers."

After spending ten days at Modesto, he was transferred to Sequoia for twenty days of rehab.

After yet another operation in August to repair his wrist, he went to stay with his folks, battered and bruised and barely able to function. After losing about a third of the mobility in his right hand, he couldn't do even simple tasks such as buttoning his shirt.

Taking a leave of absence, he spent the next eight months recuperating at his parents' house in San Mateo, going to Stanford for rehab twice a week and doing an additional six hours of therapy every day at home—back exercises, knee exercises, and neck exercises. Some part of his body always needed to be addressed.

Almost immediately, the effect of post-traumatic stress began to take its toll. At times, the pain was unbearable. Unable to bathe or go to the bathroom by himself, he felt uncomfortable with his own body and stripped of all dignity. His hair had been shaved for the surgery on his skull and coupled with that there were the bruises and numerous facial lacerations. He barely recognized himself in a mirror, which proved an apt metaphor for how he felt about life in general.

In addition to his other injuries, the fractured skull caused a constant sensation of vertigo, necessitating that he walk with a cane. Beyond this, he began to obsess about the cause of the accident, and about when, if ever, he would feel whole again. At the hospital Jim had half jokingly called him "Lazarus" because he seemed to have been raised from the dead. But now that he was in so much pain, he began to question his faith, wondering why God had allowed him to survive at all. Now he was the one who needed tending, and he understood the plight of many parishioners in an entirely new way. *Physical pain doesn't hold a candle to depression,* he thought.

Going back to work—which he did in November 1997, at first easing in one day a week—helped him stop obsessing. By January 1998, he increased his work schedule to three days a week, and by April, just nine months after his accident, he was back to full time.

At first, it wasn't easy going. He still walked with a cane, had a shaved scalp and a face disfigured with scars. He was very self-conscious about his appearance. There were days when he would tell the staff, "Bear with me today. I am really depressed, and it's not you." At times his depression got so bad that he contemplated suicide. Over and over he would ask the same question: Why did God save me on those rocks? Why didn't He let me die? In the end, the only thing that pulled him through was his reluctance to leave the world that way. Thinking about his parents quickly put an end to his suicidal thoughts—he would never burden them with that grief.

He began taking medication and went to a trauma clinician—recommended by one of his parishioners—who helped him find relief through a technique known as EMDR (eye movement desensitization and reprocessing). He also went to healing masses at Saint Joseph's in Capitola. Already a big believer in the sacrament of the sick (in which the priest prays for the person to be healed in "body, soul, and in spirit"), he found the masses helpful not only for the blessings they bestowed, but also because they helped him reconnect with the healing ministry of Christ and with the power of prayer.

In August 1998, he went to a neurologist, Dr. Susan Hansen, also his parishioner, to find out why his vertigo hadn't gone away. In the process of doing an MRI, Dr. Hansen inadvertently answered the question that had been tormenting Father Gary. She surmised that Father Gary's heart murmur must have caused his heart to throw a clot, in turn leading to him having a slight stroke before the fall. The stroke would have caused him to be disoriented, and as a result, he had probably just walked off the cliff. (The MRI also exposed the fact that Father Gary has a dangerously enlarged heart, and if that condition had gone undetected for much longer he could have suffered a major heart attack.)

The second he heard the news he felt healed. He was elated as he shared this revelation with his parents and Jim. "I don't know why I am so damn excited," he confessed. But the realization that he hadn't done anything wrong was a huge relief.

In January 1999, nearly two years after his accident, he underwent one last operation to chisel down the bone growth in his elbow, which enabled him to have full movement of his arm again. He was finally healed—spiritually and physically.

Because of this accident, Father Gary comprehended the depths of suffering following a traumatic event and could respond in a uniquely empathetic way to people who were convalescing or depressed. He also saw the importance of prayer in the healing process. As a result of the benefit he'd gained from the healing masses he'd attended, he planned on conducting a weekly healing mass at Saint Nicholas. Perhaps the most important thing he took away from his accident was that it helped him to understand the concept that "suffering was the cross," which ultimately brought him closer to God. He could see now that "suffering was a part of life," and that "nobody escapes this world unscathed."

CHAPTER TWELVE

SUFFERING
OF THE SOUL

This ministry is very hard, but I thank God because it has allowed me to grow very much. Being in touch with people who are suffering can be an advantage, because they can somehow teach you a lot about patience and a real Christian life. In this way I feel privileged, even if it is very hard to be so in touch with the world of suffering.

—*Father Carmine De Filippis*

What you are saying is worthless!" the guttural voice growled at Father Carmine.

The Capuchin stood with his right hand on Sister Janica's forehead while in his left he held his crucifix against the back of her neck. She howled in pain.

Father Gary, sitting a few feet away, kept his eyes trained on the nun's face. He'd seen a number of exorcisms in the two weeks since her last visit—including several dramatic ones in which he heard the gruff, demonic voice speak—but he was still struck by the violence of Sister Janica's reaction to the prayer.

"I am stronger!" the deep voice bellowed. Sister Janica took several strained breaths that sounded more like screeches, "Heeeeeeeee! Heeeeeeeee! Heeeeeeeeee!" She bared her teeth.

"Adiúro te, maledícte draco, in nómine Dómini nostri Iesu Christi eradicáre et effugáre ab hoc plásmate Dei," recited Father Carmine. [I adjure you, accursed dragon, in the name of our Lord Jesus Christ, to eradicate yourself and depart from this creature of God.]

Again the voice exploded: "Really! Who do you think you are? You can't make me do anything! We are many!"

Father Carmine continued, undeterred, *"Ipse Christus tibi ímperat, qui te de supérnis cælórum in inferióra terræ demérgi præcépit."* [Christ himself commands you who enjoined you to be cast down from the heights of heaven into the lower parts of the earth.] Again he repeated *ímperat* a few times, accentuating it as he did, "Ímmmm-paaa-rat. Ímmmm-paaa-rat."

Sister Janica screamed, "You think so?"

"Illum métue, qui in Isaac immolátus est, in Ioseph venúmdatus, in agno occísus, in hómine crucifixus, deínde inférni triumphátor fuit. Da locum Christo, in quo nihil invenísti de opéribus tuis," intoned Father Carmine calmly. [Fear that one, who was sacrificed in place of Isaac, who was sold in place of Joseph, who was killed in place of the lamb, who was

crucified in place of man, and then was triumphant over hell. Give place to Christ, in whom you have found nothing of your works.]

Sister Janica's demeanor suddenly shifted from snarling and prideful to whimpering and whining. *"Basta,"* she begged, in an almost inaudible whisper. "Stop. Please stop." She began to cry and curl up into a fetal position in the chair.

Father Carmine paid no attention to this change in tactics. *"Humiliáre sub poténti manu Dei."* [Be humbled under the powerful hand of God.] He repeated the word *humiliáre,* drawing it out in a slightly deeper tone, "humiliaaaaare."

"Basta!" the voice screamed, once again becoming enraged. "Don't you know who you are talking to?"

Father Carmine put a few drops of holy water on his fingers and pinched the bridge of her nose. She immediately thrashed wildly, shoving at Father Carmine and slamming herself backward into the wall repeatedly. Her companion and Father Carmine tried to hold her, but she was too strong.

Unable to stand on the sidelines any longer, Father Gary tossed his *Ritual* book aside and jumped into the fray. He worried that she was going to hurt herself or possibly even Father Carmine. He threw himself between the chair and the wall. Sister Janica pushed back with such incredible strength that all he could do was keep her from pounding a hole in the wall with her head.

For nearly twenty minutes, he struggled to hold her back. When it was over, everyone was exhausted. When Father Gary glanced down at the metal chair, he was surprised to see the back legs were completely bent out of shape.

AFTER HIS THIRD WEEK, Father Gary had begun to recognize some of the Latin words of the *Ritual* and was generally only a few lines behind Father Carmine, keeping one eye on the page and another on the reactions of the victim. Usually, Father Carmine prayed fifteen to twenty minutes per person, but this varied—some got a simple blessing, while the more stubborn cases, such as Sister Janica, might go on for the better part of an hour.

Since there is no time limit specified in the *Ritual*, Father Gary wanted to know how Father Carmine knew when to stop. In the beginning he'd just assumed that an exorcist followed the prescribed prayers all the way to the end—including the litany, the Gospel readings, and the actual exorcism prayers. Instead, the reality proved very different.

"When the situation is bad, when you are dealing with a possession, in those cases you cannot pray for just fifteen or twenty minutes. It's not enough," Father Carmine would later tell him. "It also depends on how much time you have or the person has, as well as on their ability to resist the prayer."

"But how can you tell when they have reached that point?" Father Gary wondered.

"You know it, you see it," Father Carmine assured him, "and you see that the person can't take it anymore; they are in pain, worn out."

Most of the people Father Carmine saw had what Father Gary would characterize as "minor reactions," such as coughing or yawning. However, he did see some more dramatic cases. One of these involved a wholesome-looking brother and sister, both in their mid-twenties, whom Father Carmine exorcised together. During the *Ritual* the woman howled and groaned, her eyes rolling back into her head, while the brother made noises similar to a moose. Each had dry heaves and spit up frothy foam. Their mother, who had accompanied them, used her handkerchief to carefully wipe off the spittle. The sight of her lovingly caring for her children, who had been reduced to a subhuman level, moved Father Gary tremendously.

When he asked Father Carmine about this case, the Capuchin responded that while it is rare, people can be hit with the same curse, and they can then be prayed over simultaneously. There was also the issue of time. On the night that he saw them, the waiting room was once again filled to capacity.

Another case, involving a career woman in her forties, proved to be violent as well. Father Gary suspected something immediately when the woman—who appeared to have stepped out of a boardroom—entered and eyed him suspiciously. Following her into the room, Father Carmine wasted no time, sprinkling her with holy water almost before she sat down. The woman reacted instantaneously. She grabbed the wooden chair and swung it at Father Carmine, smashing it against the wall. Father Gary, along with the woman's companion, were forced to jump in to keep her from trying it again.

In yet a third case, a mild-mannered housewife who had baked a cake for Father Carmine was transformed into a grunting beast, swearing at Father Carmine and saying in Latin, "We will never leave her!" only to smile politely at everyone when the exorcism was over fifteen minutes later.

The diverse reactions amazed Father Gary. He was learning that every demon has his own "personality," even to the point that an exorcist can recognize him. Father Carmine told him that demons apparently vary their reactions from one exorcist to the other, so that if two exorcists pray over the same person at different times, they will see different responses. Or exorcists may experience the same exorcisms differently. Father Gary would have such a thing happen to him a few weeks later when he was witnessing an exorcism along with an American exorcist from Indianapolis. During the exorcism, Father Gary had the overwhelming sensation that the room was suffocatingly hot, while the priest from Indianapolis smelled a terrible "overpowering" stench.

Occasionally, Father Carmine would turn to him and fill him in on the history of the case. "This person has been coming to me for three years and is afflicted by a curse," or "this person has trouble studying, thanks to the demon." Though few and far between, these little snapshots allowed Father Gary to piece together the tattered lives of some of the people who sought Father Carmine's help. Most, he learned, had either been involved in the occult or were victims of a curse.

EVER SINCE THE LESSON delineating the causes of possession, Father Gary had pondered how to accurately assess whether a person was suffering from a curse. To him, the symptoms bordered on superstition.

One woman complained to Father Carmine that her marriage had failed because of a curse. As Father Gary watched, however, it was clear to him that Father Carmine didn't believe her; and instead of praying the *Ritual*, he'd performed a simple blessing and admonished her not to believe in such notions.

Later Father Carmine explained that such cases are common and warned, "You must never believe when a person says to you 'I have a curse on me,' In the majority of the cases, it's not true. Especially if another person told them that they were cursed, never, never give credence to this other person's words. The people who have a real problem will never tell you that the cause is demonic. Usually it is the last thing they think about." And even if Father Gary suspected a curse at work, Father Carmine cautioned him to proceed slowly and prudently. "If you think the person might be cursed or have a problem, simply do a quick blessing over them. Tell them to calm down, that you are going to say a simple blessing, or pray the *Ritual* under your breath so they don't hear. If you told the person, 'Yes, it's true, you've got a curse on you and now I am going to exorcise you,' you could do huge damage to their psyche."

Hoping for more clarity, Father Gary asked Father Daniel how to discern the presence of a curse, and Father Daniel described a scenario involving one: A young couple is engaged but the man's parents are against the match. The in-laws invite the woman over for dinner and give her something to eat, perhaps a piece of cake (sometimes bones are ground up into a powder and baked in the cake, as are bits of dried blood or other substances). Soon after she eats the cake, she begins to feel pain in her stomach or suffer from a severe headache. These "symptoms" always correlate with either seeing her fiancé—for example, going out on a date or planning the wedding—or with going to church (because the agent of the curse is demonic). Armed with such a story, Father Daniel told Father Gary that if the exorcist prays a blessing over the person and she reacts negatively, it is highly likely that she is afflicted.

In the lore of exorcism, perhaps nothing is as infamous (because it is so spectacular) as the victim vomiting strange objects or copious amounts of fluid, sometimes even blood. Most of us remember Linda Blair's projectile vomit in the film *The Exorcist,* and Father Carmine had a case wherein a woman vomited buckets of sperm. Such action typically signifies a curse; the person has eaten cursed food that he or she needs to eject. Vomiting objects such as finely woven hair or beads, and even blood clots, is a common indication of a curse as well. Or, in the case of a voodoo doll, the victim might vomit up a nail.

Note that exorcists believe these objects don't necessarily come from the person's stomach, but instead materialize in the mouth. In this way, such people are not harmed physically even though they appear to vomit sharp objects such as pieces of glass or needles. According to Father Nanni, spirits can modify the state of matter, even to the point of provoking "materializations." "A person can vomit an object, but he doesn't have it inside from a material point of view. It is there spiritually, but for the person he feels it inside, a wasp stinging, or a scorpion stinging, the pain of a nail, and then he vomits and the object materializes outside the mouth."

Other exorcists have seen things that defy explanation, such as pools of mysterious black liquid appearing on the floor, or live animals—including crabs or scorpions—vomited up. Father Carmine once saw a woman vomit a small black toad that was alive. When he went to catch it, it fizzled away into black saliva.

Psychotic patients swallow strange objects and expel them routinely. For this reason, the exorcist has to take these phenomena in context with other manifestations rather than simply depend on vomiting as proof of a possession.

If the curse were carried out indirectly, say exorcists, it often turns out that objects from home, such as pillows, when blessed and torn open, reveal strange objects as well—perhaps pieces of metal or bones wrapped in twine, braided hair. When they find these objects, exorcists usually say another blessing and burn them. Some objects, however, do not burn right away and need to be blessed repeatedly before they finally ignite.

Just as surprising to Father Gary, however, were the times Father Carmine was unable to discern the cause of possession. In one such case involving a devout woman in her early thirties, she was neither a victim of the occult nor a curse. In the end he surmised that her possession must be for the "expiation of sin."

BEYOND THE DIFFERENT REACTIONS of the victims, Father Gary thought that something about the relationship between the demon and the *Ritual* itself was peculiar. It seemed as if the demon were somehow "stimulated" by the prayers. When Father Carmine began the prayers, he and the victim entered into their own little world, as if surrounded by a bubble. Then, at the end of each exorcism, Father Carmine would either tap the person's forehead with his finger, or give a little pat, at which point the bubble would burst. Father Daniel would later explain to Father Gary that when Father Carmine tapped people, he was essentially bringing them out of a trance.

Rather than being a continuous thing, demonic possession alternates between periods of calm and "moments of crisis," when the demon manifests its presence—that is, takes over the person's body and speaks and acts through it. Between crisis moments, however, during periods of calm, it is possible for a victim to carry on as if nothing is out of the ordinary.

Typically, in hearing the word *possession*, one imagines an evil spirit as dwelling "inside" a person. The Bible says: "When the unclean spirit has gone out of a person, it wanders through waterless regions looking for a resting place, but finds none. Then it says, 'I will return to my house from which I came.' When it comes, it finds it empty, swept, and put in order. Then it goes and brings along seven other spirits more evil than itself, and they enter and live there" (Matthew 12:43–45). While the primary purpose of this verse is to show that once liberated, demons may return, it nonetheless illustrates the popular concept that demons reside inside a person, almost as if the body were a physical home. However, as Thomas Aquinas points out, pure spirits do not occupy space. Therefore when a demon "possesses" a person, he is merely acting on that person. According to Father Nanni, "During a possession the demon is not present; it is connected like a pipe, and so he sends inputs into that person that the person can perceive." Typically these "inputs" can be a variety of things that the person can experience, such as voices or noises, or even thoughts. "In this way, [the demon] tries to solicit the permission of our free will to evil, with the purpose of causing and reinforcing in us a growing dependence on him." The goal is always the same: to drive the person to desperation and isolation, to make him a willing "slave" to the demon and sin.

"In the moment of the crisis, however, the demon is not only connected but he comes, he is there; and the prayer of exorcism forces him to be present because it provokes him and forces him to reveal himself," says Father Nanni. "The majority of people can resolve their crisis state with a prayer of thirty to forty minutes. I say 'resolve' but I mean temporarily. When the state of crisis begins, you keep performing the exorcism until the demon gets tired and detaches himself, and so the person comes back."

During an exorcism the demon suffers and causes suffering. "Every exorcism is like hitting the demon with a bat. He suffers greatly; at the same time he also causes pain and weakness to the person he possesses. He even admits that he is better off in hell than during an exorcism," relates Father Amorth.

Just how a spiritual being might feel pain by being touched with material sacred objects is somewhat of a mystery. "There is some kind of relationship between the matter and the spirit. When they enter into a human body they are not in one place but all over the body. It is as if they somehow penetrate into the matter and so they also suffer the consequences of it. Saint Augustine talks about spirits as having some kind of matter to them; Saint Paul talks about spirits of the air, and the air is ethereal but it is still matter. However we can't say for sure," Father Nanni admits.

For the Church, these sacred objects (holy water, blessed oil, a crucifix) possess a kind of "power" because they carry the blessing of the Church. "Of course the object itself has no power; rather the power lies in that of Christ Himself which has been placed upon the particular object," writes Spanish exorcist Father José Antonio Fortea.

Most exorcists are affected by the intense suffering that they see during their ministries. As Father Amorth wrote, "The strongest and most lasting impression, for a beginner-exorcist, is coming in contact with a world where suffering of the soul—more than of the body—is the norm."

Father Gary was particularly moved by just how personal this pain could be. Not only did it touch the individuals, but it affected the lives of their family, loved ones, and friends as well.

FROM THE TIME SHE WAS A LITTLE GIRL, Anna, now thirty-five, felt that something was not completely right:

I had problems but I didn't know they were connected. When I was a little girl I heard noises that people around me couldn't hear, like the ticking of a watch. It bothered me a lot, and I used to cry and ask my mom what it was, but she would only tell me that she couldn't hear anything. So I started to think I was going crazy. I could also sense a presence in my room, and so I used to hide myself under the covers. My mom thought I was just "acting out," but I was very scared.

Around the age of seven or eight, I started to feel a choking sensation when I was lying down in bed and I had to stand up just so that I could breathe. Several times I almost choked to death and my mom had to pull my tongue out. I went to many doctors who told me I was perfectly fine, that all these things were just a kid's fantasies.

When I turned twelve, I became very interested in sex. My interest was very extreme, exaggerated. It was wrong, of course, but back then I didn't know. When I was fourteen I started to have intercourse, also in a very dirty way. For me it was normal, but at the same time I had an immense amount of suffering going on inside. I had very low self-esteem and as a result I began to suffer from anorexia and even thought about committing suicide many times. I felt terrible and became addicted to some drops that were supposed to help me sleep.

Meanwhile on the outside I always looked fine. I always had perfect makeup on, and I was well dressed. When I started working, all my salary went to buying clothes, drinks, going out to the clubs.

When I became addicted to the drops I was sixteen and my mom started to pray for me, but I found that out only later on. As a result, whenever I saw her I felt this intense hatred for her; I mean I really hated her. Now I know why, but back then I didn't know anything. Another thing was that whenever I saw Pope John Paul II on TV, I used to run away or turn the channel immediately. And I never so much as put a foot inside a church, which was strange because even as a little girl I loved to attend mass.

This went on for some time until finally, when I was twenty-eight, a friend told me, "Let's go to Saint John Lateran to get a blessing." I was bad at the time. I couldn't sleep without the drops. I was anorexic. I was bulimic. I also had this weird sensation of a hand pressing on the small of my back, as if somebody kept his hand on me the whole time. A few days before going for the blessing, I started to say, "No, I'm not going. Why should I go? I'm totally fine; all I need is to meet a guy and then I'll be fine." Instead my friend made me go.

When I got to the church my head was pounding. I couldn't understand what people were telling me. I didn't have any reactions until I got in front of the priest, and then I burst into tears, sobbing and crying so much that I wasn't able to stop. The priest just let me go on. Afterward, when I went home, I was no longer addicted to the drops—from one day to the next—and the weird sensation of the hand on my back disappeared. Even after this reaction, I didn't change my lifestyle at all until the day that I went to confess my sins. When the priest blessed me, I fell on the floor and started to scream, after which I didn't remember anything. The priest told my girlfriend to take me to Father Tommaso at the Scala Santa. I went and he blessed me and nothing weird happened. Later I met Father Alberto from Saint Anastasia, and he helped me to return to a spiritual path, to praying and belonging to a community of prayer.

When I started praying again, I began to feel a little better on the inside, but outside I got worse and worse. During the night sometimes all of a sudden I could not move, as if something was blocking me. I cried a lot during this time and I said to myself that I must be crazy. I told Father Alberto and he said, "When this happens, start to pray." It was very hard for me to pray because in those moments I couldn't remember the words of the prayers. At the beginning I remember saying simply, "Help, help, help, Mary, Mary, Mary!" Then I started with the Hail Mary, and gradually those episodes went away.

One day Father Alberto prayed Psalm 90 over me and I began to vomit and feel really bad. As I was doing it I kept thinking, "Why am I vomiting?" I felt like I was choking but I didn't know why. I also saw a strange vision of some kind of ritual in which people were chanting. Father Alberto told me that maybe I needed an exorcism. I said to myself, "Who me? I'm fine." I told myself that I was just doing all this so that I could get attention.

About this time I met my husband and things got really bad, especially when we blessed the engagement rings. In that moment I lost consciousness and the demon manifested for the first time and told my husband that if he were to marry me I would kill him.

From that point on, I started to feel really sick. I had problems with my ovaries, problems with my stomach, headaches. The worst thing that ever happened to me physically was that one morning I *woke up with one side of my body totally numb. I went to the hospital and they diagnosed me with multiple sclerosis.*

I had two major problems: first my arm and then my leg. They were totally numb; I didn't feel them anymore. The doctors were not very optimistic. I would have lost the use of my limbs sooner or later, but instead I followed the treatment of cortisone together with the blessings and in my case the illness froze completely. Slowly it is going away. The doctors want me to continue with the cortisone, but I would prefer not to do it—especially now that I put myself in the hands of the Lord. But I have to say that Father Alberto always tells me to do it because he says that the Lord put science in the hands of man.

Around this time I began seeing Father Francesco [Bamonte], and my husband came with me to the exorcisms. All this time I continued to doubt myself, to doubt that I needed an exorcism. I still thought I was making everything up to get attention. Father Francesco did a little test.

In order to prove that she wasn't imagining everything, Father Bamonte brought in a plastic shopping bag with an object sealed inside. He ordered the demon in the name of Jesus Christ to reveal what the object was. At first the demon resisted, but eventually, as Father Bamonte insisted, the demon correctly identified the object: a pair of gloves that belonged to Padre Pio.

That scared me a little, but I knew then that I wasn't crazy, so I understood and I felt calm. I said to myself, "Okay, now we are going to get rid of him."

After we got married we went on a pilgrimage for our honeymoon to various churches and holy sites around Italy, traveling to Saint Gemma in Lucca, a person I felt particularly close to since I read about her life. At the time I had been told that I couldn't become pregnant and so I asked for her intercession. As soon as I left Saint Gemma's tomb, I started to feel really bad. I was folded in two with pain in my ovaries and uterus. I was hospitalized and diagnosed with a cyst of five centimeters. When I got to Rome, it had grown to ten centimeters. I was supposed to have surgery but slowly it started to become smaller and smaller on its own, something I also attribute to the prayers of the community (I was a member of a prayer group then and we always helped each other). I also think that the prayers of my mother helped a lot as well. Anyway, I followed the therapy prescribed by the hospital and two months later I got pregnant, and now I have a wonderful eight-month-old baby.

When I got married I thought I would have been liberated, but it didn't happen. During the exorcisms the demon began to lash out at my husband. I said terrible things to him there, and it happened even at home.

I remember one night I sat down with my husband to have dinner. My husband blessed the food and after that I don't remember what happened. I woke up on the bed with my arms locked in front of me and my husband standing nearby, out of breath, looking slightly shocked. When I asked him what had happened, at first he didn't want to tell me. While he had been blessing the food, the demon had manifested and told him, "Pay attention because now you are going to choke. I know you are scared of me. You pretend you're not, but I know you are." At one point the demon told my husband, "You make me so mad because I can't touch you! I'm not allowed to touch you."

Another time, my husband and I were watching a movie on TV one night about Pope John Paul II, and at one point I broke down in tears. My husband tried to console me, saying, "Don't cry, John Paul II is in the sky and he prays for you." But then I turned on him and started to say bad words because it wasn't me. It was the demon.

Thank God my husband knew how to handle it. He didn't answer; he started to pray.

Throughout this time I kept having obsessive thoughts. Every time I had to come to see Father Francesco, I had this thought in my mind like "Where are you going? Now you are going to tell the priest a bunch of lies, you are going to look in his eyes and you are going to lie to him," and in my mind I told him the most terrible things.

I felt this constant heaviness on me. Like a weight. It was a chore *to do anything. I couldn't clean, I couldn't wash my baby because it took too much of an effort. I was exhausted. Father Francesco prayed over me and I began to get better. Slowly I felt the weight lifting.*

After the exorcisms I feel tired, but I can see things clearer and the pain goes away. Father Francesco has made me understand that I wasn't crazy. I wouldn't have believed that I was possessed, but the exorcisms have helped me to understand it. I would never have imagined that things like this could happen but now I know. All I can say is that if the Lord created exorcists, there must be a reason for it. Satan exists and works on people without their knowing it. If I hadn't had people praying for me probably I wouldn't be here now.

———

ANNA WAS EVENTUALLY LIBERATED in November 2006 (her liberation was recounted in the prologue) and remains free of the symptoms. Father Bamonte believes that her possession was probably caused by a satanic ritual performed four generations ago by members of her family who sought to gain power by sacrificing an infant to a demon (this was the ritual that Anna herself said she saw when Father Alberto prayed over her). And though he was never able to verify the claim, according to Father Bamonte, during the exorcisms, the demon would often hum the singsong chant used by the participants of this ritual. The chant sounded like a jingle used in a TV commercial for a popular aperitif. When the commercial came on TV, Anna would feel compelled to quickly change the channel without realizing why.

———

ONE DAY AFTER PERFORMING EXORCISMS, Father Gary decided to stay in San Lorenzo and have dinner with Father Carmine. While he considered Father Carmine to be a "holy man," there was no denying that there was a distance between them. Much of it was cultural, and because of the language barrier as well. But there was something else, too—a sort of professional wariness that comes from two people meeting to perform an arduous task under unpleasant circumstances.

They ate inside a horseshoe-shaped dining hall that offered little in the way of decorations beyond the scuffs and dings that come from long continuous use. The meal was staggered in two shifts, with Father Gary and Father Carmine sharing the space with about eight other friars. Since he was the superior, Father Carmine sat at the head of the table, while Father Gary took a place near the end, next to a layman in his seventies, who lived at the convent and taught English as a second language. As Father Gary talked and enjoyed dinner with the layman, he noticed that Father Carmine's demeanor here was very different from what he displayed at his office. He appeared much more relaxed and conversed with the other priests as he presided over the meal. Because the juxtaposition was so striking, Father Gary realized that it must have been hard for Father Carmine and his fellow exorcists to maintain any sense of equilibrium.

What Father Gary didn't realize was that, even though Father Carmine knew it needed to be done, he didn't like training new exorcists. "Yes, apprenticeships are necessary," Father Carmine would say later. "In order to become an exorcist, you need to apprentice, to see and have experience; but you can't say it is an enjoyable thing. I prefer to teach beautiful things, good and holy things, things of God. Personally I thank God for this 'job' because it puts me in touch with a supernatural world and so my faith grows as a result. However, that does not make it a beautiful job."

CHAPTER THIRTEEN

A PASTORAL APPROACH

"We can do only our best, and then we must
leave the final decision up to God."
—*Father Candido Amantini,*
as quoted in An Exorcist Tells His Story,
by Father Gabriele Amorth

By February Father Gary had settled into a comfortable routine. After morning mass he would usually do some reading, either up in his room or in the NAC library. Then in the evenings on Monday through Thursday, he would see exorcisms at San Lorenzo until dinner. On Thursday morning he would head out to the Regina Apostolorum and then in the afternoon over to his class on the history of spirituality at the Angelicum.

About this time, an American exorcist, Father Vince Lampert, from the diocese of Indianapolis, got in touch. In Rome to participate in the continuing education program at the NAC, Father Vince had recently been nominated exorcist and figured that it would be a good idea to participate in a few exorcisms while he was in town. Like Father Gary, when his archbishop had appointed him exorcist, he'd told him that "he had no idea what he was asking [him] to do."

A slender, thoughtful man whose unedited bluntness comes off as a bit gruff, Father Vince is nonetheless very personable and quick to laugh at a good joke. Meeting one night for dinner in a trattoria near Saint Peter's, the two priests immediately hit it off. As they got to know each other, Father Vince filled Father Gary in about the circumstances that led to his nomination and his concern (like most American exorcists) that he had no training and wasn't sure where he should begin.

Father Gary, for his part, was candid about his own background. He had checked with Father Carmine about bringing Father Vince along, but he wanted to prepare him—remembering his own feelings of disappointment alternating with shock.

As he listened, Father Vince's favorable impression of Father Gary grew. This was not a priest that was out to bag demons and make a name for himself, but somebody who leveled with him and told him that some of the victim's reactions were downright "odd."

The two decided they would meet the following Monday at the Casa first and then together go to San Lorenzo on the bus.

Like any novice, Father Gary included, Father Vince had been growing more and more anxious about what he might see in his first exorcism. He'd spent the previous day readying himself in the only way he knew how, going to confession and spending extra time in prayer. He had purposefully tried to steer clear of films like *The Exorcism of Emily Rose* (some priests at the NAC had watched it one night) because he didn't want to be prejudiced. Before he left the NAC that afternoon, he told a few fellow priests where he was going; they replied that they would pray for him.

On the bus, his apprehension grew. Father Gary filled him in on the protocol and what he might expect to see, displaying a demeanor that helped calm his nerves. When they arrived at San Lorenzo, the usual crowd had already gathered in the courtyard. And as they waited, Father Gary gave Father Vince what little history he could on the various people.

After the first night, the two stopped to have a coffee and decompress. That night had been a particularly violent one. A woman in her early forties with sharp, attractive features and shoulder-length black hair had shaken so violently that Father Vince had seen her levitate five inches off the chair, at which point Father Carmine had simply pushed her back down with the palm of his hand. Father Gary, who was momentarily engrossed in the *Ritual* book at the time, had missed it.

Father Vince had several questions. As he was wont to do, Father Carmine had pinched the bridge of the woman's nose, which Father Vince found strange. Father Gary chuckled, telling him that he'd had that same question himself. (Father Carmine would later explain that he pinched the nose because the demon enters through the person's senses.)

Both Father Gary and Father Vince, thinking ahead to the day when the fate of a person's spiritual well-being would rest in their hands, were keen to learn practical tips. Since the *Ritual* is imprecise on how an exorcism should be performed, their chief concerns were avoiding mistakes. Father Gary, for one, had read that if the exorcist went about it wrong, he could actually open himself up spiritually to an attack. One author had even gone so far as to suggest that if the exorcist touched the person during an exorcism, the demon could enter into him.

Father Carmine scoffed at this. "Absolutely not. It's not a disease," he would later say. However, there were dangers. Father Carmine was adamant about not engaging the demon.

"Whenever the demon talks, you should never listen to him. You should never ask questions to the demon in order to know something hidden; this is a very serious mistake. A priest is not to ask the demon anything that you don't already know the answer to [for instance, "Why did you try to put yourself above God when you know He is all-powerful?"]. Never ask questions so that the demon could be considered a source of information, never! First of all because he is a liar and so what he says can very well be a lie, and second because you can't give him the honor of being your source of information."

The *Ritual* does permit the exorcist to ask the demon his name, which in the ancient Hebrew tradition is believed to give one a kind of power over another, also evidenced by the ancient practice that prohibited writing or pronouncing the name of God.

The foundation of asking for the demon's name comes from the Bible, where Jesus asked the name of the Gerasene demoniac (Mark 5:9). Early exorcists considered it worthy and codified it in the old 1614 *Roman Ritual*, which allows the exorcist to ask "the number and name of the spirits inhabiting the person, the time when they entered into him and the cause."

"One of the first things that he struggles to avoid is to confess his name, because to do so is some sort of half defeat for him," says Father Amorth.

A demon's name delineates the type of spirit it may be. Sometimes the names are purely functional, such as "anger" or "lust"; at other times they are recognizable names from the Bible, like Beelzebub or Asmodeus.

Even exorcists admit that there is a lot of mystery to it. For instance, if the demon Asmodeus is present in two or more people that an exorcist sees (actually, it's more than that), why doesn't the demon recognize the exorcist? Shouldn't he be able to say to the exorcist, "Hi, remember me? We met this morning." In actuality, sometimes it does happen that an exorcist will pray over a person, even in another part of the world, and have the demon say, "We fought each other five years ago in Jerusalem"—referring to an exorcism that the victim knows nothing about. However, this is rare, and the average exorcist (especially in Italy) may see Asmodeus three times in the same week without so much as a "Here we go again!" But according to one Italian exorcist, the actual name isn't that important. It may signify "the army" of that particular evil spirit. In other words, a demon saying "Asmodeus" is like a World War II American G.I. saying "I'm a Marine" or "I'm under Eisenhower." "All that matters is that they give you a name, any name, so long as they respond to it," says the exorcist.

For this reason, many exorcists actually prefer not to talk to the demon at all. Father Dermine, for example, doesn't even ask for the name. "I don't ask anything because I don't believe them. I know this may sound disappointing, but demons are such big liars that I just continue with the prayer almost as if they weren't there."

It can also happen that a demon will sometimes give a person's name, such as "Adam." A great debate exists among exorcists about whether or not the soul of a deceased person can cause a possession. The more theologically inclined exorcists say no (when a person dies, the soul goes straight to heaven, hell, or purgatory), while those who have spent some time in places like Africa (where the belief is widespread) say yes, it is possible. Father Nanni once prayed over a person who claimed to be the soul of a dead Mafia boss. After months of refusing to give any other name, Father Nanni did a little checking and discovered that the person in question never existed. On this occasion, the demon finally relented and confessed that he'd been trying to fool the exorcist all along.

In addition to the moments when Father Carmine was able to answer a few of their questions, Father Gary and Father Vince made it a

habit to have a coffee or try to grab a bite afterward. Through Father
Gary's knowledge of the personal histories of the victims and Father
Vince's understanding of Italian (since he was fluent in Spanish, he
could make out more Italian than Father Gary could), the two would
compare notes. During one of their late-night repasts, Father Gary
explained to Father Vince something that had taken him weeks to figure out—why Father Carmine touched people on certain parts of
their body with the crucifix. He was searching for the points that had
been "hit" by a curse. "People will often be dedicated in certain rituals and cursed objects will be placed on the back of their neck."

They also discussed actions they felt wouldn't fly in the States,
like Father Carmine slapping people at the end of the exorcism. They
talked at length about the fact that the majority of bishops in America knew little about the reality of exorcism. Both agreed that bishops needed to be better informed.

As he continued to participate in exorcisms, Father Gary
came to realize that while they could be grueling affairs, perhaps the
most arduous aspect was the endless repetition. Father Carmine ran
San Lorenzo as though it were an outpatient clinic. He would pray
over people for fifteen to twenty minutes, and then, after scheduling
a follow-up appointment, they would go about their day. From talking to Father Daniel, he knew that many of the other exorcists in
Rome had similar approaches.

Later, Father Gary would discover that each exorcist has his own
system, in part because almost all had other duties to perform besides being an exorcist. Father Carmine, for example, was the superior at San Lorenzo and was busy with running the day-to-day
operations of the basilica and parish, which meant he could schedule
people only three to four days a week, usually in the evenings. So
Father Carmine tended to lump the more severe cases on certain
days and see fewer of them, perhaps five rather than ten. However,

people also showed up unannounced looking for a quick blessing. One day a trash collector parked her miniature sanitation truck outside in the courtyard, stomped in wearing her bright green reflective striped uniform, and asked the assembled throng whether Father Carmine was taking walk-in visits. As it turned out, he was not.

Then Father Gary considered the more entrenched cases, such as Sister Janica. The second time he had seen her, she seemed worse than before. On top of that, he reminded himself that she'd been coming to Father Carmine for nine years. Didn't the prayers of exorcism work?

People, Father Gary realized, are under a huge misapprehension that exorcism is a one-shot deal; that once an exorcist begins the *Ritual*, it is a fight to the finish that can last for days on end—until only one is left standing. An American exorcist in Scranton, Pennsylvania, coined the phrase "drive-through exorcisms" to describe this won-and-done approach that the media and Hollywood films have made popular. Not surprisingly, this misconception is held by many who visit exorcists, most of whom go looking for a quick fix.

"People don't understand what we do," says Father Gramolazzo. "People come to see us expecting to be healed right away. They think, 'I have a headache because of the demon,' 'My job isn't going well because of the demon.' People are not properly informed."

Instead, as Father Gramolazzo explains, exorcism is more akin to a journey, with the exorcist acting as a kind of "spiritual director" helping the victim to "rediscover the grace of God" through prayer and the sacraments. This is one of the reasons why exorcists believe God allows people to become possessed in the first place. "This message is extremely important," insists Father Gramolazzo. "This is why it takes so long for people to become liberated. It is a journey of faith for the person, the family, and for the parish."

Getting people to see it this way is not always easy for the exorcist. "Half the battle is to change their whole purpose so they don't see it in the light of getting rid of a problem, but see it in the light of being more fully converted or being converted at all," says English exorcist Father Jeremy Davies. "That's the whole aim. It's what I'm always telling people week by week. And that's the most important thing—the exorcism is secondary to that."

Simply put, the prayers of the exorcism weaken the power that the demon has over the person. The healing, however, cannot happen without the full participation of the individual. Victims of possession are exhorted to go to weekly confession, to recite the rosary daily, and above all to receive the Eucharist. "I always say that the exorcism is ten percent of the cure; the remaining ninety percent is the responsibility of the individual. What does this mean? It means that there is a need for much prayer, frequent reception of the sacraments, living a life according to the Gospel, using sacramentals [exorcised water, oil, and salt]," writes Father Amorth.

"I have people that I've been exorcising for twenty years," says Father Amorth. "Saint Alfonso de' Liguori says a very exact phrase, 'You don't always get to the liberation; you always get to some kind of relief.' This means that those people who in the past used to throw themselves on the floor just for a blessing, screaming and yelling, after years of exorcisms are calm; they can live their professional life and their careers. But every once in a while, they feel a little disturbance and so they come, people who in the past used to come every day or once a week, after a few years of exorcism they may come once every two months or every six months. What I mean is that they have a progressive improvement."

ON THE NINTH OF FEBRUARY, Father Gary climbed up the beige marble stairs and into the classroom at the Regina Apostolorum for the last time. While the second half of the course hadn't matched the quality of the first half in his mind, he was definitely looking forward to this last lecture, a roundtable discussion lead by three exorcists—Father Bamonte, Father Nanni, Father Amorth—and a fourth priest, Father Alberto, who ran a spiritual listening center called the "centro ascolto."

Bringing in the exorcists to talk about their ministries was a compromise for the course organizers. Originally, they had contacted the International Association of Exorcists (IAE) and asked for an exorcist to actually perform an exorcism in the classroom. Father Gramolazzo had told them, however, that while the IAE thought the course was a good idea, exorcism wasn't a spectator sport. Putting a victim on the spot like that would only add to the suffering and cheapen the whole affair.

Father Gary was very impressed by the three exorcists as they filed into the classroom. The trio appearing together at a lecture was akin to an all-star lineup addressing a group of Little Leaguers. Like Father Bamonte, Father Amorth wore a long black cassock that lent him an air of piety. Bald and wearing glasses, at eighty years old he walked with a slight stoop and took his time climbing the three steps that led up to the podium. He was hardly the larger-than-life figure that the media portrayed him to be, and instead exuded a more jovial and avuncular quality. Thankfully, despite the presence of such luminaries, the media wasn't obtrusive.

After opening prayers, Father Amorth spoke for forty-five minutes in a gravelly yet steady voice, his eyes fixed on a far corner of the room. The theme was familiar to those who followed his public appearances and read his numerous books: Exorcism goes to the heart of what it means to be a Christian and is something that every priest should take more seriously. This went double, of course, for the bishops whose job it was to appoint exorcists. In interviews, Father Amorth had even gone so far as to say that any bishop who doesn't appoint an exorcist is committing a mortal sin.

Fifteen minutes into the lecture, the little voice in Father Gary's ear suddenly went silent, as his translator mysteriously went missing. Annoyed, but not necessarily surprised, Father Gary spent the next thirty minutes straining to piece together the remainder of Father Amorth's talk. His Italian was much better than it had been on the first day of the course, but he still struggled. At the break he went back to find out what was going on, wondering if this great opportunity was going to be squandered as well. As it turned out, the first translator had tracked down a young seminarian to replace him, and Father Gary was spared from having to scour the halls.

After the break, Father Nanni spoke for half an hour about the crucial role of cooperation between the exorcist and his bishop, ensuring that only officially appointed exorcists performed the *Ritual*. In other words, just because someone had taken the course didn't mean that he could begin praying over people on his own. Since Father Gary was an official exorcist, this was a moot point, though it did remind him that he would need to work closely with his bishop once he got back.

Father Bamonte then discussed the importance of an exorcist having a team approach, stressing the need to have a close working relationship with a therapist or a psychologist. As he listened, Father Gary was struck again by the fact that Father Carmine didn't have such colleagues. Most victims brought a companion; but still, on certain occasions, Father Carmine would have been all alone but for Father Gary—something Father Gary vowed he'd never do, if only just for "legal" considerations.

For Father Gary, Father Alberto, who ran the *centro ascolto*, proved to be the most engaging speaker. The listening center was basically a spiritual center, staffed by two priests, two nuns, a therapist, and an attached prayer group. It was a place for people with spiritual or psychological problems that they attributed to spiritual issues. The concept was similar to that in a book Father Gary had bought: *Stumbling Blocks or Stepping Stones: Spiritual Answers to Psychological Questions* by Benedict J. Groeschel. Father Gary was inspired by Father Alberto's emphasis on the continual need for people to practice the sacraments—especially confession—and to bring prayer back into their lives, which he said people were filling with a lot of other activities. And while not necessarily terrible, these "distractions," as Father Alberto put it, were still exposing people to the wrong kinds of influences. First and foremost he wanted to create venues where people could pray. He'd set up a permanent chapel inside the Basilica of Saint Anastasia for Eucharistic adoration (a Catholic tradition of meditating in front of the exposed Blessed Sacrament). Of course Eucharistic adoration wasn't novel, but Father Gary liked the idea of people needing more "quiet time" with God. He also appreciated Father Alberto's intention of getting back to the traditions of the Church. These approaches would also benefit him as an exorcist. While it might be hard to talk to people about demons, he could certainly tell them about the benefits of praying, and he would be practicing "preventive medicine," as Father Kevin Joyce recommended.

After Father Alberto finished, Father Gary was delighted that there was an entire hour just for questions and answers. The session was so absorbing he could have sat there listening for much longer.

Father Amorth's response to one question made Father Gary chuckle: "Everybody who is considering doing this needs to be apprenticed." After all that trouble he went through to be able to apprentice! Knowing there are 185 dioceses in the United States alone—which meant that many exorcists would have to be trained and apprenticed—it was impossible for him to conceive that "six guys who are over here breaking their backs" could all of a sudden tutor 185 priests. But if they didn't, who would?

Father Gary left that final day of the course feeling reinvigorated about his calling as an exorcist. Not only had the course given him the grounding he needed, but it had reinforced his desire to help people. He could see now that rather than just being on the fringe, there was also a strong pastoral element to exorcism.

CHAPTER FOURTEEN

WINDOWS TO
THE SOUL

The commander triumphs in victory; yet he could not have conquered if he had not fought; and the greater the peril of the battle, the more the joy of the triumph.

— *Saint Augustine,* Confessions

As the evening dragged on, Father Gary noticed a shift in Father Carmine's demeanor. By 6:45, after the Capuchin had exorcised about nine people, his once upright posture stooped heavily, braced against the wall by his left hand. Despite the freezing rain outside, his brown robe clung to him, heavily matted with sweat. Father Gary had no idea how his mentor maintained his stamina day in and day out.

By the end of February, Father Gary had seen more than forty exorcisms, including some in which the reaction was so explosive that both he and Father Vince had helped subdue the person. One case involved a small, bent-looking nun in her full habit, probably in her fifties but seeming much older, who had changed so completely during the *Ritual* that he no longer recognized her. He also saw Sister Janica a third and fourth time, each exorcism seemingly more violent than the previous one.

It came as no surprise when he learned that the repetitive nature of exorcism can be challenging for an exorcist. "For me," says Father Carmine, "the hardest thing is that the liberation never happens right away. Sometimes you need years and years, and this methodical perseverance is not only very tiring, but the demon takes advantage of it in order to try to insinuate the poison of doubt, as if to say, 'You are wasting your life and you are deceiving people.'"

Exorcists also have to deal with the real threat of suicide. Father Daniel had told Father Gary of a time during an exorcism when he had to tackle a woman who tried to jump out the third-story window.

In Italy, where every exorcist has a cell phone, it is common for an exorcist to receive several messages a day saying things like "Today I am finally going to end it all!" or "I can't go on without your help!" As Father Amorth relates in his book, *An Exorcist Tells His Story*, a woman seeing Father Candido threw herself out the window between exorcism sessions. Faced with a daily environment that is this rife with suffering and desperation, many exorcists feel overburdened.

Father Gary began to notice that the exorcisms were starting to affect him as well. Even though he hated to admit it, he began to feel that he was in a rut. He realized Father Carmine saw many of the same people over and over again and neither their condition, nor the way he prayed over them, changed much. With the exception of the more dramatic cases, there was nothing new for Father Gary to see. Besides, he was just a passive observer; perhaps his attitude would change once he started his own ministry and felt the import of being in charge.

The big surprise was that while he found himself distracted sometimes during a ritual, he noticed that the exorcisms were affecting him outside of San Lorenzo as well—and not in a good way.

FATHER GARY WAS AWARE that exorcists were prime targets for attacks by the Devil. Both the exorcism course and the numerous books he'd read had all pointed this out, some in lurid detail. "He need only enter into the stream of our own inclinations, when we treat lightly things that lead us astray; he has only to press against that which already totters, to hold back that which seeks to rise. His influence spreads like a poisonous gas, which we inhale without knowing it," wrote the Dominican theologian Antonin-Gilbert Sertillanges.

Christian tradition has long held that the more a person's life reaches upward toward God, the fiercer the Devil attacks. Numerous saints have suffered as a result of their devotions, including Saint Paul, Teresa of Avila, Padre Pio, and Gemma Galgani.

In his book *The Dark Night of the Soul*, Saint John of the Cross describes how God maintains a certain "equality" among all things, so that we may attain grace comparable to our station. Just as a heavyweight prizefighter wouldn't break a sweat beating up on an amateur, so too would a saint's devotion ring hollow unless it were properly tested. The graces that we receive through prayer and the gifts given us by the good angels do not escape the notice of Satan, says John of the Cross, "partly so that he may do that which he can against them according to the measure of justice and that thus he may not be able to allege with truth that no opportunity is given him for conquering the soul, as he said concerning Job."

It is for this reason that Saint Peter warns early Christians, "Discipline yourselves, keep alert. Like a roaring lion your adversary the devil prowls around, looking for someone to devour. Resist him, steadfast in your faith, for you know that your brothers and sisters in all the world are undergoing the same kinds of suffering" (1 Peter 5:8–9).

Father Gary had decided to quit drinking over a decade before because of the effect it had on him. He wasn't a big drinker at the time, but he noticed that if he even drank a glass or two of wine with dinner, he would feel the edges of his self-control starting to slip. Upon arriving in Italy, however, a place synonymous with wine and three-hour meals, he'd decided to relax that stricture a little. The Casa often served wine with lunch (as was the custom), and now and again he allowed himself to enjoy a glass. And while things had been fine for the first half of his stay in Rome, once he'd started participating in exorcisms it was as if somebody, or something, had hooked his libido up to a satellite dish and images were streaming in.

Sexual temptation is one of the main dangers an exorcist faces. "We have to be very careful sometimes of the people we exorcize because they can really arouse some desires in the exorcist," says Father Dermine. Some of the women who sought help from Father Carmine were quite attractive, and during the exorcisms a few would actually try to tear their clothes off, or rub themselves. The surprising thing was that Father Gary's temptations came not during the exorcisms but afterward, while he was riding on the bus or walking the streets of Rome. Unable to overcome them on his own, he went down to the chapel in the Casa, or over to the little Church of Santa Rita, which was right around the corner, and prayed silently for God to give him strength. When the thoughts didn't go away, even after intense prayer, he began to get upset with himself. Had he opened a door that had allowed a demon to attack him?

WHILE EXORCISTS ADMIT that their ministry can sometimes be a heavy burden, it would be a mistake, they say, to overstate the power of the Devil. As Father Amorth writes, "A priest who is afraid of the Devil is like a shepherd who is afraid of a wolf. It is a groundless fear." "The Devil," says Amorth, is already "doing us as much harm as he possibly can."

And so rather than fear him, exorcists say, it is better to emulate saints such as Teresa of Avila, who proclaimed, "If this Lord is powerful, as I see that He is and I know that He is, and if the devils are His slaves (and there is no doubt about this because it's a matter of faith), what evil can they do to me since I am a servant of this Lord and King? Why shouldn't I have the fortitude to engage in combat with all of hell?"

While exorcists don't have a patron saint, many feel a strong devotion to Mary. In the traditions of the Catholic Church, Mary holds a particular place of honor: "Throughout her life and until her son died on the cross, Mary's faith never wavered. She never ceased to believe in the fulfillment of God's word. And so the Church venerates in Mary the purest realization of faith." And because of this acceptance of God, Mary represents a parallel arc that is the exact opposite of the Devil's. "God made [Satan] magnificent in his nature and he corrupted himself; God made Mary humble in her nature (a human being and, as such, inferior to the angels) and she sanctified herself," writes Father José Antonio Fortea. The Bible cites this hostility between Satan and Mary. In talking to the serpent who tempted Adam and Eve in the Garden of Eden, God says, "I will put enmity between you and the woman, and between your offspring and hers, he will strike your head, and you will strike his heel," (Genesis 3:15). Thus many statues of Mary depict her crushing a serpent beneath her feet.

Many exorcists invoke Mary during the *Ritual*. "The demon is so terrified of her that he will never pronounce her name. He'll say 'that woman' or 'she destroys me,'" says Father Amorth.

"The Marian prayer, especially the rosary, is a very powerful weapon in the fight against Satan," explains Father Bamonte. "That is why [Mary] insists so much that we pray the rosary; the rosary is a prayer that really whips the demon into a frenzy." On numerous occasions, Father Bamonte has beseeched Mary for help only to have the person he is praying over say, "She is here!" or "You can't imagine what I would do to you if she weren't stopping me!"

———

AFTER WEEKS OF DEALING with the temptations, Father Gary concluded they had to be demonic in nature; there was just no other way to explain their intensity. The realization helped. The course had warned him about such a possibility, so rather than let it intimidate him, he took it in the greater context of the spiritual path that all Christians undertake. As Saint Paul said, "God is faithful, and he will not let you be tested beyond your strength, but with the testing he will also provide the way out so that you may be able to endure it" (1 Corinthians 10:13). As such, even though he was a target, he knew God would eventually provide him with the means to overcome it.

It also helped to have the support of family and colleagues. He talked a lot of his problems out, calling his parents at least once a week. He also opened up to a circle of priests at the Casa whom he had either known before coming to Rome or who had an interest in exorcism. He especially liked talking to the seminarians at the NAC because he felt they might one day find themselves in a similar situation.

A few of the priests at the Casa were curious enough to want to participate in exorcisms. Some had even had past experiences of their own—praying spontaneous prayers of deliverance over people—and were eager to confirm that what they had seen was real.

Father Gary even made a believer out of Sister Rebecca when he stopped to chat with her at the library, telling her about his experiences out at San Lorenzo.

Other distractions helped take his mind off the events at San Lorenzo and his increasing internal struggles. He had always been a huge fan of classical music, finding it uplifting and inspiring. In fact, his parents had played some of his favorite composers, such as Strauss and Bach, while he was incoherent in the hospital after his accident. So on weekends he went to nearby churches such as San Ignazio, San Marcello, and the Dodici Apostoli as often as he could to listen to the free concerts. Once he saw a performance of Rachmaninov at the performing arts center, and on different occasion, he dragged another priest from the Casa out to Saint Paul's Basilica in the pouring rain to listen to a Vatican-sponsored concert. And while he appreciated such outings, he found it a pleasure just to walk the narrow cobblestone streets. He got a kick out of seeing the restaurants busy even after midnight.

A few parties at the Casa also helped, including the Feast of Our Lady of Guadalupe, which he thought brought many of the priests out of their shells. He took it upon himself to organize the Saint Patrick's Day celebration, asking one of the Irish priests to make Irish coffee and decking out the refectory in green. He even enlisted the help of a real Irish fiddler to come and play for a couple of hours, all of which made the party a huge hit.

For Father Gary, being a priest was all about human interaction. He found it ironic when a parishioner who was going through marital problems told him he was lucky that he didn't have to worry about such stuff. (The irony is that, as a pastor, he had around a thousand families to look after.) "People assume that as a priest I don't have any problems, but I do. We all do," says Father Gary. "Yes, it's true that I don't have some of the problems other people have, such as dealing with the stress of raising a family; but it's also true that I come home to an empty house every night." He loved to get out and be among people and continually looked for ways to include them. For him, community was paramount, belonging to a family that comes together to celebrate Christ's love.

SINCE THAT FIRST DAY in January when Father Carmine accepted him as an apprentice, Father Gary had felt a "monster disconnect" with the victims when the *Ritual* began, despite the cramped space and the bizarre intimacies. All that changed during an exorcism one Saturday in late February.

As usual, Father Carmine had given him no idea of what to expect. When he'd stepped into the office at ten that morning, he was surprised to see Father Daniel, of all people, waiting. "So how'd you get involved in all of this?" Father Gary asked and got a brief sketch of the case before them: The woman was from southern Italy, and because her diocese had no exorcist, she traveled to Rome for exorcisms. Father Daniel happened to be a friend of the priest who often accompanied her.

Father Gary would have liked to hear more, but in walked three people—a Franciscan in his mid-forties with close-cropped hair and a neatly trimmed beard, followed by a plain-looking couple in their early sixties. Wearing a rumpled suit, the man kept his eyes lowered as he entered, while the woman, Giovanna, her hair short and slightly disheveled, had a hard, calcified look about her, as if the weight of some unseen burden was slowly grinding her to dust. She immediately caught Father Gary's attention because she looked "very disturbed" and eyed him warily.

Without wasting time, Father Carmine took Giovanna into the small room and everyone followed—Father Carmine and the two Franciscans in their brown robes, Father Gary in his black clerics. All four priests had on their stoles. The second Father Carmine closed the door, the mood in the room plummeted, becoming very subdued. Giovanna sat down in the chair, and even though the *Ritual* hadn't begun, she began to twitch nervously. Everyone's eyes were fixed on her, and Father Gary could tell immediately that something was unique about this case—he felt a strong sense of foreboding in her presence.

Father Carmine tossed some holy water from his squeeze bottle in her direction, saying, *"In nómine Patris et Fílii et Spíritus Sancti."* [In the name of the Father, and of the Son, and of the Holy Spirit.]

Giovanna immediately let fly a bloodcurdling scream that gave Father Gary the chills. She quickly stood and scooped up the metal chair with one hand, wielding it over her head like a club while Father Daniel, the family priest, and her husband quickly jumped in to stop her from hurting anyone. Wrestling her back down into the chair, Father Carmine didn't hesitate in placing his hand on top of her head and invoking the Holy Spirit, even as she kicked and fought against the hands that held her back.

After a prayer to Saint Michael the Archangel, Father Carmine skipped straight through to the exorcism prayers: *"Deus, humáni géneris cónditor atque defénsor, réspice super hunc fámulam tuam, quam ad tuam imáginem formásti et ad tuæ vocas glóriæ consírtium . . ."* he said. [God, Creator and defender of the human race, look down on this your servant whom you formed in your own image and now call to be a partaker in your glory . . .]

The demon wasted no time in manifesting. "You have no power over me!" he growled at Father Carmine in the guttural voice.

"Exáudi, Deus, humánæ salútis amátor, oratiónem Apostolórum tuórum Petri et Pauli et ómnium Sanctórum, qui tua grátia victóres existérunt Malígni: líbera hunc fámulum tuam ab omni aliéna potestáte et incólumen custódi, ut traquillæ devotióni restitúta, te corde díligat et opéribus desérviat, te gloríficet láudibus et magníficet vita," Father Carmine prayed. [Hear, God, lover of human salvation, the prayer of your apostles Peter and Paul and of all the saints, who by your grace emerged as victors over the Evil one: free this, your servant, from every foreign power and keep her safe, so that restored to peaceful

devotion, she may love you with her heart and may serve you zeal-ously with her works, may glorify you with praises and may magnify you with her life.]

"You don't really believe those children's stories do you?" the de-mon scoffed. Once again the voice reminded Father Gary of a sound a dog might make were it able to speak. It was a deep, dark evil sound that seemed to come from the depths of the woman's stomach.

"Oooooooooohhhhhhhh," she moaned over and over as she fought back with even more violence, forcing Father Gary to jump in to help restrain her. The family priest grabbed her legs while Father Gary and Father Daniel held her arms; Giovanna's husband wrapped his own arm around her torso even as she growled and spit at Father Carmine.

Father Gary had never seen this strong a reaction. Giovanna's face had transformed, displaying a sneering look of pure hatred, with her eyes remaining open. Usually in the rare instances when the eyes stayed open, people had mild reactions to the prayers. In stronger cases victims typically closed their eyes to avoid looking at the sacred objects in the room. This time, however, not only were Giovanna's eyes open, but she boldly glared at the various people in the room.

"Exorcízo te, vetus hóminis inimíce: recéde ab hoc plásmate Dei. Hoc te iubet Dóminus noster Iesus Christus, cuius humílitas tuam vicit supérbiam, lárgitas tuam prostrávit invídiam, mansuetúdo calcávit sævítiam." [I cast you out, old enemy of man: depart from this servant of God. Our Lord Jesus Christ commands this of you, the humility of whom con-quered your pride, the generosity of whom laid low your envy, the gentleness of whom trampled upon your cruelty.]

Again the voice exploded: "Don't you know that he died on the cross? And you are still following him! We are stronger! We are stronger! We win! We win!"

Father Carmine poured some holy water into her eyes, and she struggled violently to shake free, shouting *"Basta!"* and screaming. He continued, undeterred. *"Obmutésce, pater mendácii, neque impédias hanc fámulam Dei Dóminum benedícere et laudáre. Hoc tibi ímperat Iesus*

Christus, sapiéntia Patris et splendor veritátis, cuius verba spíritus et vita sunt," he intoned. [Be silent, father of lies, and do not hinder this servant of God from blessing and praising the Lord. Jesus Christ commands this of you, the wisdom of the Father and the splendor of truth, the words of whom are spirit and life.] Again he repeated the word *ímperat* (commands) a few times, accentuating it as he did, "Ím-mmm-pe-rat," in an effort to force the demon to acknowledge his inferiority.

Giovanna bared her teeth. Thick globs of mucus and saliva oozed from her mouth and ran down her chin. "Shut up! Do you know who I am?" the deep voice growled. "Don't treat me like a pig! Look what I can do to this old woman, look what I can do!" Again her body shook violently, prompting all four men to jump in again to stop her from hurting herself.

"Non mi toccare!" the demon shouted. Don't touch me! After a few minutes, Giovanna calmed down enough that Father Gary and the others could relax their grip. She continued to drool, making no effort to stop the saliva from dribbling onto her shirt. Already there was a small puddle beneath her feet. The family priest grabbed some paper towels and handed them to Giovanna's husband, who dutifully wiped her mouth.

Father Carmine was just starting another prayer of the *Ritual* when, without warning, she turned toward Father Gary, fixing him with unblinking eyes full of hate. He noticed something incredibly unnatural about her eyes, which appeared somehow thicker than normal, almost like Coke bottles, the irises unusually large and black. Even more striking, however, was that a presence seemed to be missing. Her eyes seemed almost dead, the gaze reminding him of the lifeless eyes of cadavers he had seen on the embalming table.

Trapped in the headlights of that "dead" stare, Father Gary felt suddenly exposed, insignificant, as the eyes bored into him. In this profound moment, he knew he was looking straight into the presence of pure evil. Refusing to be cowed, he quickly recomposed himself and refused to waver. *I'll be damned if I am going to let this demon intimidate me,* he thought. And moments later the demon looked away from Father Gary and fixed his eyes on someone else.

The exorcism continued for over two hours, throughout which Giovanna continued to drool and fight violently while staring at everyone in the room in turn. Father Carmine interspersed Psalms with both the revised and the old *Ritual.* More than a few times, she passed out. Knowing this as a trick the demon will sometimes use to prevent his host from hearing the prayers, Father Carmine simply said a blessing or threw holy water onto her and she sprang right back up. Father Gary jumped in to hold her down on numerous occasions.

As they neared the three-hour mark, Father Gary wondered how much longer they could continue. While all the men in the room were spent, especially Father Carmine, Giovanna showed no signs of slowing down, even though, Father Gary imagined, she had to be exhausted. Finally, when it looked like Father Carmine might pray the *Ritual* for the tenth time, he abruptly stopped and slapped her a few times on the forehead to bring her out of her trance.

It took the woman a full five minutes to recover and even then she seemed rather confused. Because she was unable to stand on her own, Father Daniel and Giovanna's husband carried her out of the room and laid her on Father Carmine's couch. Before long, she began grunting and cursing again.

"Did this do any good at all?" Father Gary asked Father Daniel.

Looking grim, Father Daniel responded that the possession was very entrenched. Giovanna had been undergoing exorcisms for more than forty years, and her case was considered one of the most severe that many of the exorcists in Rome (including Father Amorth and Father Gramolazzo) had seen.

"How did it happen?" Father Gary asked.

Father Daniel explained that Giovanna had been cursed by her mother when she was still in the womb. The mother, a poor woman from a small rural town, had originally tried to terminate the pregnancy on her own; when that failed, she had cursed her own baby.

As they were talking, the woman began to shout once again, letting fly a string of blasphemies, at which point her husband and the family priest took her away. When she'd gone, Father Gary turned to Father Carmine, curious to know why this case had been so violent.

"This is a very powerful demon," Father Carmine said, explaining a little bit about what he meant. It was then that Father Gary learned that, just like the angels, demons have an entire hierarchy to their existence.

THE BIBLE INDICATES that there is a hierarchy of demons. The "ruler of the demons" is mentioned in the Gospel of Matthew (Matthew 9:34), while Jesus referred to this hierarchy when he said "the Devil and his angels" (Matthew. 25:41). Moreover, since the demons were once angels, it seems logical to assume that they were once connected to the angelic hierarchy.

The Bible mentions nine different orders of angels: Seraphim (Isaiah 6:2); Cherubim (Genesis 3:24); Thrones (Colossians 1:16); Dominations (Colossians 1:16, Ephesians 1:21); Virtues (Ephesians 1:21); Powers (Colossians 1:16, Ephesians 6:12); Principalities (Ephesians 6:12); Archangels, and Angels (Romans 8:38). Three Archangels appear in the Bible: Michael (Daniel 10:13, 21; 12:1; Jude 9; Apocalypse 12:7), Gabriel (Daniel 8:16, 9:21), and Raphael (Tobit 3:17). Commonly these nine orders are called "Choirs," since their principal job is to sing the glory of God.

Though many writers have attempted to address this hierarchy, perhaps the most well known is a man who lived about 500 C.E. called Pseudo-Dionysius, so named because he was mistaken by later writers as the convert of Saint Paul, Dionysius the Areopagite (Acts 17:34). A neo-Platonist, Pseudo-Dionysius grouped the nine choirs of angels into three hierarchies: the "Supreme Hierarchy," consisting of the Seraphim, Cherubim, and Thrones; the "Middle Hierarchy," with Dominations, Virtues, and Powers; and the "Lower Hierarchy," made up of the Principalities, Archangels, and Angels. For Pseudo-Dionysius, this hierarchy constituted a sacred order of beings who were arranged in their likeness to God in descending order and who in their duties presided over the government of the world. Each hierarchy acted as a kind of "mirror" that "receives the rays of the supreme Deity which is the source of light . . . and pours it forth again abundantly, in accordance with God's law, upon those below itself."

More than a few theologians have pointed out the rigid and arbitrary nature of this structure. In the Bible, Michael appears as the leader of God's angelic army; and yet here, Archangels are near the bottom of the scale.

When talking about the hierarchy, it's impossible not to see the limits of human reasoning at work. If angels are incorporeal spirits living in a world that we as humans can't even begin to comprehend, then how could we pretend to know their various ranks? Saint Irenaeus had doubts about a structured hierarchy of angels, as did Saint Augustine, who wrote: "That there are in heaven Thrones, Dominations, Principalities and Powers, I firmly believe; that they differ among themselves I have no doubt; but as to saying what they are, and in what way they differ . . . I must admit I do not know."

Today, a majority of Catholic theologians lean toward the hierarchy as proposed by Thomas Aquinas, who adopted the Pseudo-Dionysius model, but used a slightly different distinction between the Choirs—that of varying degrees of intelligence.

According to Aquinas, each angel is a distinct individual constituting a species unto itself. As a result each angel and demon varies slightly from the next, though rather than differing in materialistic ways, spirits vary in the degree of their perfection as spiritual beings—in other words, in their ability to manifest their powers.

Yet, as with any intellectual theory, other factors must be taken into consideration. In a practical sense, this is also true when it comes to demons, exorcists say.

The demons of the highest hierarchy always have biblical names like Satan, Beelzebub, Asmodeus, Zebulun, Zebuin, and Meridiano. As Father Carmine explains, "They are usually followed by many others who are secondary and are the ones who go to possess a person because they have been ordered to by their leader." Satan, of course, as the most powerful demon, is always present to some extent in every possession, but almost never is he "physically" present.

The key to being able to differentiate between the types of demons is by their level of intelligence. "You don't measure the power of the demon by the strength of the person, but by the intelligence of the demon who talks," says Father Gramolazzo. "They will always manifest a profound knowledge of theology." In addition, a stronger demon will always be able to resist the prayers of exorcism longer than a weaker one, and he may be able to pronounce sacred names such as Jesus or Mary, names that a weaker demon will never say. Instead of using names, they will simply say, "He is destroying me," or "She is burning me."

While the hierarchy of the angels is based on love, there is no such concept in "hell," say exorcists. The demons keep their former angelic ranks, but the only thing that unifies them is their hatred for God and man. The demons of the lower ranks obey the stronger ones, not out of obedience but out of fear. "They are like slaves," says Father Nanni.

Exorcists have seen this firsthand when a more powerful demon blocked a weaker demon from leaving a person's body during an exorcism, even though the prayer caused him great pain. This is also evident when there is more than one demon present. The weakest demon will always manifest first. "The strongest tend to hide; in the meantime they send out the smaller ones," says Father Nanni.

Some demons seem to be actively antagonistic toward one another. Father Daniel (who became an exorcist briefly in Rome in 2006) had to schedule two possessed people he was seeing on different days. The instant they saw each other, their demons would manifest and become so violently enraged that they would often come to blows. And yet, even while some apparently despise one another,

other groups seem to be able to work together. A stronger demon—or perhaps the leader of the possessing demon—will often come to the aid of a weaker demon. Most often, this will happen during the *Ritual,* in which the exorcist will discern that he is dealing with a stronger demon, or in between exorcisms, when the character of the demon (and its name) will change from one session to the next.

As for Giovanna, there was no way for Father Gary to know the hierarchy of her demon. He had been too engrossed in reining her in to hear whether Father Carmine had addressed the demon by name. Later, Father Daniel would speculate that the case was one of the rarest of rare instances—an actual Satanic possession.

ON THE WAY HOME FROM SAN LORENZO, the bus was jammed with tourists and Saturday afternoon commuters wearing bulky winter coats. The windows were fogged from breath and body heat and the overhead fans blasting hot air. Father Gary had only been able to get a few feet inside the front door and stood crushed between the driver's compartment and the mass of bodies swaying along with the lurching bus. It was a weird juxtaposition to be surrounded by so much humanity after the events he'd just experienced at San Lorenzo. Replaying the exorcism in his mind, he couldn't get over the way the demon had looked at him. The gaze seemed to penetrate his very soul, as if the demon had been able to read him.

Numerous exorcists have attested that they are constantly watched by the demon. Many, if not all, have had strange moments when their lives have been touched by an evil presence. Father Bamonte remembers an exorcism when a demon somehow knew that he was suffering from rheumatism. "How are your bones feeling this morning?" the demon asked him sarcastically. Father Carmine once had a demon mock a recent trip he had taken, saying, "How stupid you are to think that visiting Lourdes would actually help you," even though he hadn't mentioned to the person he was praying over that he was going.

"The spiritual dimension is adjoining to the material one—[angels and demons] live between us and they see us but we do not see them," explains Father Nanni. "From a biblical perspective, their function is one of catching every mistake we make in order to throw them in our face." It's for this reason that on numerous occasions Satan is referred to as "the accuser," as in this passage from the Bible: "Then I heard a loud voice in heaven proclaiming, 'Now have come the salvation and the power and the kingdom of our God and the authority of his Messiah, for the accuser of our comrades has been thrown down, who accuses them day and night before our God'" (Revelation 12:10).

"This means that the demon is always actively watching people and he gets pleasure when he sees that they are not faithful to God and, as a result, take his side," says Father Nanni. "He wants humankind to rebel against God as well, and this is the one 'accusation' that he can level against an individual at the Last Judgment that has the most weight."

For the next few days the experience of having the demon lock eyes with him would continue to dog Father Gary. He wondered what kind of effect such a direct connection would have on him. After his hiking accident, he'd often wondered if God had saved him for a reason. Over the years since then, when something would happen in his life, he would think, *Well, maybe this is the reason why.* After some time, he stopped worrying about it. However, when he looked back on the series of events that had led him to Rome, there did seem to be a logical sequence at work. His time in the mortuary, his accident, his depression, his belief in healing prayer—had God somehow been grooming him to be an exorcist all along? Ultimately he couldn't say; but he knew that, as a result of those experiences, he would certainly be more motivated to try. And if this was what God wanted him to do, then even if the Devil were somehow watching him, so was God; and that's all that mattered.

CHAPTER FIFTEEN

LibEraTion

The Devil's main trick is to make people think they are unworthy of God's forgiveness. This is the biggest lie that the demon gives us, not making us believe in God's mercy.

—*A charismatic individual who assists Father Bamonte during exorcisms*

Father Daniel and Silvia, a hollow-eyed woman of thirty-seven with thinning hair, sat together on a bench across from the shrine. Silvia, wearing a scarf and heavy jacket to ward off the night air, kept her eyes focused on the statue of Mary while Father Daniel, his dark brown robes partially hidden under a black parka, prayed the rosary softly under his breath. It was nearly midnight and the shrine was deserted. Eyeing his watch, Father Daniel wondered if the demon's promise would turn out to be true. Two months before, the demon had proclaimed his departure for this very night. Father Daniel, who normally didn't put much stock in what demons said, remained skeptical. This time, however, over the course of several exorcisms in Rome, the demon had been very precise, giving not only the date, but the time and place—at the stroke of midnight in Lourdes, France.

Silvia continued to finger her rosary beads as she prayed, rocking slightly. Father Daniel was trying not to get his hopes up. Her possession had been a terribly trying case, lasting more than twelve years (though he had been praying over her for only eight months) and bringing her to the brink of suicide.

As the minute hand ticked closer to midnight, Father Daniel wondered what would signify her liberation. Would the demon depart violently or would she vomit up a talisman? He braced himself. His mind returned to the rosary, and he lost track of the time. They continued to pray for several minutes, when suddenly Silvia let out a deep, guttural sigh, as if some invisible hand were pushing on her abdomen: "Huhhhhhhhhh."

He looked up, studying her. She had a slightly puzzled expression on her face.

He scrutinized her carefully to see if the sigh was a prelude to something more. Silvia sat completely still. Finally she turned, looking a little unsure.

"How do you feel?" he asked.

"Fine," she said, thinking about it.

"Anything else?" he persisted.

She shook her head no.

He waited for her to add something, but she didn't. Remembering, he looked down at his watch and saw that it was only a few minutes after midnight. She was not wearing a watch herself, so she was unaware of the precise time.

"Let's say a prayer of thanksgiving together," he suggested, secretly hoping that this wasn't a nefarious ruse on the part of the demon.

They prayed for several minutes, while Silvia's mood continued to lighten. She wiped away tears as the realization of what had happened dawned on her. The demon was finally gone.

A week later, back in Rome, still hesitant to declare victory, Father Daniel sent her to Father Amorth, who prayed over her. After two sessions in which she showed no reaction, he said another prayer of thanksgiving, sang a hymn, and declared her "healed." Silvia's long ordeal was indeed over.

———

IT CAN TAKE A LONG TIME for a person to become liberated, and Father Gary had yet to see it happen, though Father Carmine had told him about improvements in some of their "regulars." At one point, Sister Janica hadn't been able to even get out of bed. Another young woman who had been unable to study was now going to the university full-time. But for Father Gary, who had only recently met these people, it was hard to gauge any true progress. On one occasion, he thought Sister Janica seemed a little better. After one exorcism toward the end of his stint with Father Carmine, she actually smiled at him and kissed his hand.

Exorcism is not a magic formula. There are three factors, say exorcists, to consider when it comes to liberation: the behavior of the victim, the action of the exorcist, and the permission of God. All three are important, yet obviously to varying degrees. Essentially, liberation comes when the Spirit of God commands the demon to depart. In an exorcism, of course, it is the exorcist who, as a representative of the Catholic Church and by invoking the name of Jesus Christ, does this. And while this action is important, God is still the one doing the heavy lifting. As Father Matteo La Grua states, "Liberation is a gift from God, and God can liberate when He wants and how He wants, even without the intervention of man." The effectiveness of God's presence depends, however, in large part on the cooperation of the victim and to a lesser extent on the faith of the exorcist. A good analogy is a person who burns an ant by focusing sunbeams through a magnifying lens—the sunlight represents the Spirit of God and the lens the person who accepts God's love, focusing it on the ant, which of course is the demon.

In order for any exorcism to work, victims must cooperate with the exorcist. They must renounce the demon and any sins or actions that may have led them to become possessed; they also should pray and return to practicing the sacraments. (Not everybody has to be a Catholic, or convert to become liberated, though some do. Father Amorth says he has exorcized Muslims and Hindus on rare occasions, but mentions that he will pray the *Ritual* using the name of Jesus Christ. "I also ask them to fulfill their spiritual duties. For example, Muslims have the obligation to pray and so I tell them to do so. Otherwise I tell them to be a good person, an honest person who fulfills their professional and moral duties.")

The sacrament of reconciliation, say exorcists, is incredibly important. "Exorcism can drive a demon out of a person's body; confession can drive evil out of a person's soul. Confession not only forgives, but heals our soul and fills it with light," writes Father José Antonio Fortea.

Liberation can be a particularly drawn out process when the person has strayed far from God, or in some cases has joined a satanic cult. Another difficult hurdle to overcome, claim exorcists, is the victim's inability to forgive. "Sincere forgiveness, which includes prayer on that person's behalf and having masses said for the person's conversion, often breaks open a deadlocked situation and helps speed up the healing," writes Father Amorth.

This is a difficult process for the demonized person to undergo, and the demon will attempt to stop it, say exorcists, attacking internally (by convincing the person that he or she is only crazy, not possessed, and so doesn't need an exorcism) or by intervening directly (for instance, causing such fatigue that the victim can't get out of bed). According to Anna, when she was close to liberation, the demon almost convinced her that she was imagining everything, even putting the thought in her mind that Father Bamonte was trying to take advantage of her by recording her exorcism to write about it in a book, for his own benefit. Father Bamonte freed her from this obsession by tricking the demon into guessing the contents of a sealed envelope. When the demon knew what was in the envelope, Anna says her conviction was affirmed. After this incident, Anna's sense of desperation faded and she began to pray with renewed vigor.

Obviously an exorcist needs to have a strong spiritual core. "An exorcist must live an intense life of prayer and not be afraid," says Father Bamonte. "If you don't have a strong spiritual life, if you don't have the protection of your faith, how can you be able to fight? Praying, loving God, not committing sins—those are the weapons an exorcist uses."

Some demons are apparently more difficult to cast out than others. The duration of the possession is the first and most important element that exorcists look at. A person who has been hit in infancy and then doesn't see an exorcist until adulthood is going to have a much harder time getting rid of the demon that has now become almost a part of his or her identity, say exorcists.

The strength of the demon can also be another factor, though the most difficult cases are said always to involve a curse. As Father Carmine explains, "There remains a connection between the victim and the one who caused the curse. In those cases it's difficult because it's about the hatred of other people toward the affected person."

Unlike a natural illness for which treatment usually brings relief, the process is reversed in demonic possession. Once the demon is discovered, he fights hard to resist the prayers of the exorcism. And even though the person suffers, these attacks are, in the big scheme of things, an indication that the victim is headed in the right direction, say exorcists.

"It can happen that when a person who has been possessed for a very long time gets close to God, he can be hit by a series of bad events. I know this may sound strange, but this is a good sign because it means that the demon is losing; that's why it is reacting like that. You don't have to be discouraged; it is a good sign. I always say, 'Don't be scared of the demon, be scared of the sin,'" advises Father Bamonte.

As the exorcist continues to pray the *Ritual*, and to pray for the victim to return to God, the power of the exorcism begins to weaken the demon. There are several signs that indicate the demon is close to leaving. "He is weaker in the voice, in the ability to manifest in the crisis; he leaves sooner every time. When those exorcisms become weaker and weaker, when the possession time gets shorter and the temporary liberations come sooner than before, it means that he is getting weaker. Also, outside of the exorcism the person's life is more normal," Father Nanni says.

At the moment of liberation the demon may offer a "sign" that he is leaving. If the person has been hit by a "spell," then the demon may indicate that liberation will come when a certain object is vomited. It may even be expelled through the anus or secreted through the skin. Exorcists have seen it all. Father Carmine once saw a woman sweat a green mucuslike substance through her skin. Another sign may be the demon saying a prayer, or reciting a hymn.

In certain cases, the exorcist may ask for a sign that is directly connected to the suffering the demon may be causing. Father Daniel claims that he once asked that a woman become pregnant as a sign of liberation, because the demon had been preventing it. Sure enough, he says, a month after the woman's liberation, she became pregnant—something that she had been trying unsuccessfully to do for five years.

An outward sign is generally not necessary. "If the person lives in peace, is no longer disturbed by the demon, can pray, and lives in the grace of God, you know she is liberated," explains Father Nanni. "If you go back to pray and during another exorcism the crisis starts again, then it means only that the liberation was just temporary." As a precaution, many exorcists will continue to pray over people a few times even after they have been liberated.

Once the person has been liberated, the demon will often try to return. Exorcists generally offer a prayer of thanksgiving (Father Davies uses the Gloria, which Catholics recognize from the Sunday liturgy) and ask that the Holy Spirit fill the void left by the departing spirit. In addition, the newly liberated person must continue to live a Christian life and not fall back into the habits or sins that caused the possession in the first place, or else there is a high risk of becoming possessed again, this time worse than before (Matthew 12:43–45).

In 2003, Beatrice, a forty-six-year-old married woman who worked as a biologist in a medical lab, began experiencing odd phenomena—freak accidents, objects moving around the house on their own, a mysterious force that pushed her mother to the ground, breaking her arm. A year later, burn marks began appearing on all her clothing, always in the same place—on the thigh—and always the same size. Thinking she was losing her mind, she eventually found her way to Father Bamonte, who discerned the presence of three demons. After a grueling two-year battle involving weekly exorcisms, Beatrice was finally freed.

The first of December, 2006, a day which seemed like any other, was the day in which God permitted my liberation. To tell you the truth, my mood had been pretty down for a few days because, after a period of relative calm on the part of "that one" [the demon], I went back to the old times, when I used to scream, to be agitated and to attack everybody either verbally or physically. While in the past I was usually conscious, feeling as if I was split between the sensations of my own life and those from the demon (to the point of even fearing that I was hallucinating, or that those were just the manifestation of my psychosis), in the last couple months I entered in a deep state of trance. I could only feel rage and the other atrocious sensations of that monster which manifested; and at the end, I could remember only a few things, almost nothing.

This new situation unfortunately made me think that things, for some mysterious reason, were getting worse. As a matter of fact, even if I continued to trust in God's divine mercy and in the protection of the Blessed Mother, these strong reactions made me think that the demon had somehow regained some strength and that, as a result, the day of my liberation was still very far off. In spite of that, every day I kept giving my life to the Lord and to the Immaculate Virgin.

In the previous session, I had a huge amount of saliva coming out of my mouth, as if I was "expelling out" all the evil that I still had inside, but in the end "that one" seemed to still be there. The day he left, though, was a special day: It was the Friday after the feast of Christ the King, two days after it would have been the first Sunday of Advent and in one week the Feast of the Immaculate Conception would have started (actually my husband and I had already started reciting the novena for two days). It was basically a marvelous coincidence of sacred events. The exorcism started as usual with the prayers following the formula of the rite; the only difference that manifested after a while was a strong reaction by the demon to the words "For Christ, with Christ and in Christ." It seemed as if he had never heard them before. He started to become very agitated, he lost all his usual arrogance and became desperate. He tried to bite the hands of the people who were trying to hold him or to throw away the crucifix that the exorcist had put on my chest and also (with my great sorrow) to spit on it. All of a sudden (I don't remember the sequence of the events; maybe it was when the exorcist invoked Mary), I felt hit by a huge wave of a very bright white light—it was all encompassing, a light that I could perceive and feel as well, and it gave me a sensation of very sweet peace while for the demon it provoked atrocious pain.

Once again I felt like I was splitting, dividing between my own sensations and "his." If I closed my eyes I could see in my mind's eye that we were in a deep shadow and so I knew that the light that was embracing me was a spiritual one. Closing my eyes again, I could also perceive that this same light was stabbing the eyes of the monster like a thousand swords. Meanwhile the monster was screaming, moving like crazy, saying that the veil of Mary (whom he referred to as "that one") was suffocating him and causing him a huge amount of pain, to the point of causing him to go into terrible, indescribable spasms. Toward the end he launched a scream as he never did before and I felt rent in two, as if somebody turned me inside out.

Then all of a sudden there was calm and silence and I opened my eyes, coming out of the trance by myself. Then Father Francesco [Bamonte] blessed me, ending the rite. I had no idea that something out of the ordinary had happened. In fact, as I said, the three days leading up to the exorcism were terrible for me, and all through that time I had felt a growing rage and a huge sense of mental confusion mixed with a lack of hope. I was familiar with all those kinds of emotions, but I never felt them in such an intensive way. It seemed as if my life was about to end. After the exorcism, I started to feel a little better again, and from that moment I started to improve more and more.

During the exorcism two Fridays later I remained conscious; and even though I closed my eyes, when Father Francesco checked them in order to see how my pupils looked, they stayed in the normal position. *From the very beginning of the rite, my mind started to form thoughts in which I denied with all my will any kind of "cooperation" with the demon, I told "him" that with the help and the strength of God, I would never allow him any kind of power over me, something I had never been able to do before.*

When the rite was nearing completion, Father Francesco suggested to his helpers that they open the Bible and read a passage. One of them opened the Bible at random and they read a passage from the Gospel of Luke in which Jesus reads in the synagogue of Nazareth. "When he came to Nazareth, where he had been brought up, he went into the synagogue on the Sabbath day, as was his custom. He stood up to read, and the scroll of the prophet Isaiah was given to him. He unrolled the scroll and found the place where it was written: The Spirit of the Lord is upon me, because he has anointed me to bring good news to the poor. He has sent me to proclaim release to the captives and recovery of sight to the blind, to let the oppressed go free" (Luke 4:16–18). That passage of the Gospel was the marvelous confirmation of what had just happened: the Lord liberated me! While I was crying tears of joy, I started to thank the Lord and the Immaculate Virgin, which I will continue to do for as long as I live.

FOR MANY YEARS, the scientific and medical community scorned the idea that a person could be "healed" through prayers or ritualistic ceremonies like exorcism. Today, however, the ability of certain healing rituals to offer genuine relief is no longer disputed—numerous anthropologists have documented that people have recovered from problems varying from depression, addictive behavior, or anxiety to even more severe ailments, including life-threatening diseases, through such ceremonies. So how does science account for "anomalous healing"?

At the core of these experiences lies the difference between "healing" and "curing." According to Stanley Krippner and Jeanne Achterberg in the book *Varieties of Anomalous Experience: Examining the*

Scientific Evidence, for many indigenous people "healing" means restoring a person's physical, mental, emotional, or spiritual capacities, while "curing" usually refers to overcoming a disease that is primarily biological in nature.

Scientists and doctors have tried a variety of methods in an attempt to explain how anomalous healing experiences may actually work. In looking at spirit possession in Haiti, for example, scholar Steve Mizrach came to the conclusion that voodoo possession can be considered a kind of psychotherapy or "folk therapy." In addition, I. M. Lewis, author of *Ecstatic Religion: A Study of Shamanism and Spirit Possession*, surmised that the "psychologically highly charged atmosphere" of a séance could be effective in treating certain neurotic or psychosomatic disturbances, adding that even in the case of organic illnesses, he thought it might also provide a benefit simply by strengthening the patient's will to recover.

More than a few cognitive scientists have pointed out the potential benefits of an exorcism in treating people with Dissociative Identity Disorder (DID). Dr. Mazzoni, for example, believes the exorcist gives some people a way out by saying that their problems are caused by an outside entity and therefore they are not the cause, which, she says, "allows the patient to make a clean break . . . People get cured of demonic possession because basically the priest becomes the therapist and the priest is the one who is able to take control of the bad part of the person."

In comparing exorcism with the "traditional" approach to treating DID, Dr. Steven Jay Lynn notes that the former may actually be more beneficial. "In a way the exorcist's ritual is a lot clearer, because if the therapist believes that the person cannot be cured until they know all about the underlying personality system, and recover all the memories and have succeeded in integrating all the personalities— the person or patient can go through a tremendous amount of emotional pain in trying to recover memories, especially if they're not real memories. Now, an exorcism is a pretty clear-cut procedure that doesn't really depend on this extensive background of work with the person, so I would think that it may in fact be much more effective in helping people 'get better,' quote-unquote."

Dr. Richard Gallagher, however, says that that's not really the purpose of the *Ritual*. "I wouldn't do it for mental health purposes," he says. "If you are dealing with a suggestive individual or an individual who is deluded into thinking they are being attacked by the demonic I personally think that an exorcism is a bad idea. I am sure that there are some people who argue that an exorcism can be psychologically therapeutic, but again that is not the primary reason that it is being done. It's being done because [the exorcist] thinks there is a genuine demonic entity involved and they need spiritual help."

Interestingly, neuroscience is also beginning to weigh in on this subject as well. Dr. Jeffrey Schwartz, a neuropsychiatrist at the University of California Los Angeles, has discovered a way to treat Obsessive Compulsive Disorder (OCD) that sounds very similar to how exorcism is practiced in certain circles. In looking at the disorder, Dr. Schwartz saw how the plasticity of the brain actually made people's compulsions stronger if they gave in to them, since the neural pathways increased in number when used. Because Dr. Schwartz believes that the brain has the capacity to rewire itself if given the correct set of instructions, he created a four-step program that he said could address the problem naturally. Similar to a religious person giving a demonic name to the compulsion, the first step in Dr. Schwartz's program teaches the patient to say that the problem is the result of the OCD and not the patient herself. According to Dr. Schwartz, reattributing is a particularly effective technique in helping the patient to redirect her attention away from the demoralizing effects of engaging in compulsive behaviors.

These healing rituals may also work because of the placebo effect. Psychologist Dr. Michael E. Hyland, from the University of Plymouth in the United Kingdom, has done extensive research into placebos, which he prefers to call "therapeutic rituals." "I don't like the word *placebo* because, one, it implies that we know what the cause of it is, and the other is that we know the mechanism, and we don't." He first became interested in placebos as a way to "personalize" therapy. "It doesn't really matter what the therapy is, therapies work, that is the one thing you can be sure of," he says. "Now, the question is, why do they work? That is a much more controversial issue."

According to Dr. Hyland, the conventional wisdom on placebo says that it works because of expectancy, but he thinks there might be other mechanisms involved. "It isn't just the expectation that you are going to get better or be healed; there is actually a far more complex process."

Dr. Hyland has come up with something he calls motivational concordance. "Our research suggests that two mechanisms are involved. One is the well-established mechanism of response expectancy. The other is a motivational mechanism where people gain therapeutic benefit by engaging in therapeutic rituals that are concordant with self-defining or self-actualizing goals. That is, when people self-actualize as part of therapy, then this produces therapeutic benefit through a motivational, non-expectancy-dedicated pathway." Put differently, when a person feels as if his needs are being met through therapy, then this can help him to get better by motivating him to get really engaged with the therapy.

Most important, Dr. Hyland's research showed that it doesn't necessarily matter if the person undergoing the ritual believes in it; what really matters is how it "feels" to them. "The ritual is basically concordant with your motivations. So, for example, if we look at prayer as a therapeutic ritual and people know about it, we see those psychological mediated effects, some of which might be expectancy." In other words, spiritual rituals tend to work for spiritual people.

However, Dr. Hyland is quick to point out that it is not entirely clear how and why the placebo effect works. "Even so, I can only explain ten percent of the variance; I can't explain much variance."

One of the theories he looked at in the hopes of going deeper was quantum entanglement, the principle stating that when two particles become entangled, then an observation made on one particle has an instantaneous effect on the behavior of the other particle, no matter where that particle is. If true, quantum entanglement could help to explain how things like healing from a distance, or the power of prayer, actually work. At present, however, Dr. Hyland is not entirely convinced that there is enough evidence to support this theory. "People say since funny things happen in the quantum world they must also happen in the macro world, and that may or may not be true."

For sheer ingenuity, perhaps no one has gone further in trying to debunk the world of the transcendent than Canadian neuroscientist Michael Persinger, who conducted a series of experiments in which he tried to prove that the major components of certain "mystical" experiences, especially Near Death Experiences (NDEs), could be recreated by stimulating the temporal-lobe region of the brain with electric current. In order to do this, Persinger created a magnetic device—which he termed the "God helmet"—that was supposed to be able to simulate the sensations that accompany mystical experiences and NDEs, namely floating outside the body, having a sense of profound meaning, seeing a tunnel of white light, and so on.

As some critics have noted, however, the results of his experiments are far from conclusive, mostly leaving people with a feeling of slight wooziness, and not the coherent and lucid experiences described by those claiming to have had NDEs. Even British author and evolutionary biologist Richard Dawkins, who used the helmet in 2003 and felt nothing more than a shortness of breath and slight twitching in his leg, said he was "very disappointed" by the results.

In addition, some have pointed out the faulty assumptions behind the concept. As Bruce Greyson states in *Varieties of Anomalous Experience: Examining the Scientific Evidence*, "Correlating a brain state with an experience does not necessarily imply that brain states cause the experience; the brain state may alternatively allow access to or simply reflect the experience." As one critic put it, knowing how a television set works doesn't necessarily shed light on the origin of the signal.

Inherent, of course, in the failures of some of these theories, say religious believers, is the problem of trying to weigh and measure that which may not fit into a laboratory, namely spirits. Believers decry the attitude of critics that they say discounts the value of faith and tries to skew the argument toward the scientific (and especially materialist) canon, an argument that might be paraphrased something like this: Since we can prove a possible natural cause for the occurrence of something, then the onus is on you to show us the proof of your "supernatural" cause. This implies that any "proof" of a supernatural cause would have to be scientific in order for it to be considered legitimate or real. But are scientific standards really the only criteria that matter? In his refutation, theologian John Haught describes a concept that he calls "layered explanation," which can be illustrated by answers to the question, Why does a pot of water boil on a stove? One answer is to say that the water is boiling because the H_2O molecules are moving around and making a transition from a liquid state to a gaseous one. Another answer would be that the water is boiling because someone turned the stove on. A third answer could be that it's boiling because a person wants a cup of tea. All are valid answers but offer very different levels of understanding. For a person of faith, the scientific explanation seems valid only to a certain degree.

Perhaps not surprisingly, some doctors and scientists are trying to bridge this supposed gap between science and religion.

In their book, *The Spiritual Brain*, neuroscientist Mario Beauregard and journalist Denyse O'Leary argue against the belief that humans are nothing more than "biological automatons," and that spiritual experiences are simply the result of synapses firing in the brain. Instead, using a variety of scientific analyses, the authors propose a nonmaterialist view of neuroscience in which the mind is separate from the body. For instance, in looking at Dr. Schwartz's study on OCD and the way patients were able to reorder the neural pathways of their brain, Beauregard and O'Leary stipulated that for this to work, there must be some outside agent running the show.

Similarly, in looking at "mystical experiences" (defined by the authors as "the experience of certain mystical contact with a higher truth or a greater power underlying the universe"), Beauregard used brain-scan imagery on a group of Carmelite nuns who were in a deep contemplative state in order to find out which areas of the brain are most active during such states. The scans showed that when these nuns reported having mystical experiences, rather than being isolated in a single area of the brain (the left temporal lobe, for example) the experiences neurally engaged different regions of the brain responsible for a variety of functions, including self-consciousness, emotion, visual and motor imagery, and spiritual perception. To Beauregard and O'Leary, this finding suggests not only that these mystical experiences are as complex and multidimensional as the people who have them claim they are, but also that these experiences are the products of a healthy and functioning brain and not some simple "trick" or defect of the brain.

Dr. Craig Isaacs, a psychiatrist from San Francisco who also happens to be an Anglican priest, is another person trying to bridge the divide. In the course of his work in both areas, Dr. Isaacs has treated numerous patients for mental illness. However, he is convinced that some of the people he has seen are suffering from a demonic possession, and in that case he has prayed prayers of deliverance over them.

According to Dr. Isaacs, the key to distinguishing between the two is in differentiating the source: "Is the ego perceiving something from within the psyche or is it coming from outside the soul?" In other words, is the person imagining that he is speaking to a being (such as a child who has an imaginary friend) or is he really contacting a separate entity, something that Dr. Isaacs refers to as the "wholly other"? In his research, Dr. Isaacs has discovered five qualities that the ego experiences when encountering the wholly other: First, the patient experiences the phenomena as coming from outside himself; second, the experience is numinous; third, the experience is accompanied by numinous fear or awe; fourth, there is unusual clarity associated with the experience; and fifth, when a vision is involved there is almost always some form of luminosity, either a shadow or a beautiful light.

The criteria are not common to psychosis, claims Dr. Isaacs. And depending on the therapist's school of thought, he says, one may address this problem inadequately or not at all.

Dr. Isaacs believes in the concept that a human being consists of a "tripartite nature," composed of body-soul-spirit, an idea that comes from 1 Thessalonians 5:23. This understanding can then be carried over into illness, for if a person is tripartite, then so too would be the various sicknesses that could affect him or her in one or more of these functions.

In this model, sickness of the body is caused by disease, normally cured through medicine, while the second category, sickness of the soul (that is, neurotic and psychotic behaviors) is caused by "a breakdown in one of [the soul's] functions," the cure for which can be psychotherapy or prayers of inner healing. The third category, "sickness of the spirit," is caused by either personal sin or the demonic and can lead to what Dr. Isaacs calls "existential neuroses"—in which the patient may feel "a loss of freedom or the loss of meaning in life." If the cause is sin, then the patient will be helped through repentance and forgiveness; if demonic, then through an exorcism or a prayer of deliverance.

Since all the functions of a human being are interrelated, any illness in one function can affect the others. "Thus, spiritual illness may also be seen to affect the volition of the soul, or an illness of the soul may affect the actions of the body," says Dr. Isaacs.

———

WHILE IT IS CLEAR that advances in science and medicine *have* been able to explain why many people claiming to be possessed by an evil spirit may actually feel a genuine sense of healing after undergoing an exorcism, several questions still remain. Paranormal events—mind reading, levitation, speaking in previously unknown foreign languages—continue to elude scientific explanation. Perhaps one day science will be able to explain why these things happen. Until then, however, it would seem a betrayal of the tenets of scientific curiosity to discount a whole range of experiences affecting the lives of so many people simply because they defy such explanation.

CHAPTER SIXTEEN

ORGANIZING THE MINISTRY

The profession of exorcism has meaning if we as exorcists, through possession and exorcism, prove that God is not only present but stronger. This is a path of faith and I always tell that to the families I meet with in a parish where there is a possessed person. It is through the grace of God that these people can rediscover the evangelical message of our faith.

—*Father Giancarlo Gramolazzo*

In late March, Father Gary's bishop, along with other priests from the diocese of San Francisco and San Jose, came to Rome for the ceremony creating Archbishop Levada as cardinal. And though only in town for a week, the bishop found time to talk with Father Gary about his new assignment. Back in November, when Father Gary was just four months into his sabbatical, his bishop had asked if he would be willing to take over as pastor of Sacred Heart Parish in Saratoga, California. The two sat in the reading room of the Casa one day, discussing the past and Father Gary's desire to bring renewal to the parish.

With that business out of the way, his bishop asked him how the exorcism training was going, no doubt half expecting to hear a few dry remarks about a classroom, lectures, and textbooks. Instead he was shocked when Father Gary told him that he'd seen around fifteen exorcisms that week alone.

"You mean you've actually *seen* an exorcism?" his bishop asked.

"I've seen about sixty," Father Gary said, correcting him.

His bishop listened intently as Father Gary briefly described some of the scenes out at San Lorenzo. He mentioned Father Carmine's—and other Italian exorcists'—complaints that some bishops didn't take them seriously. As he talked, Father Gary was careful to reiterate how grateful he was to have had the opportunity to come to Rome and study. "Without the training, I wouldn't have known the first thing about how to proceed," he told his bishop. It was a natural segue into the practical concerns of getting other American exorcists trained. "If every diocese is supposed to have an exorcist then we have a hell of a lot of work to do." It just wasn't practical to ask priests to come all the way over to Rome for four months to take the course. One positive development came in the form of a conference in the Midwest that he was planning to attend in August. Apparently the coordinators were attempting to organize something modeled on the conferences of the International Association of Exorcists. This seemed like a good place to start.

He and his bishop also needed to establish a protocol for when someone approached him about exorcism. Since he'd need to get his bishop's permission before proceeding, a system had to be worked out. His bishop promised that they would set it in place when Father Gary got back.

In the meantime, Father Gary shared his ideas about the kind of "exorcism team" he wanted to assemble. Because he was still concerned about discernment, he planned to err on the side of caution and vet potential "patients" through either a psychiatrist or a psychologist. The challenge would be to find competent doctors who believed in the possibility of demonic possession but who weren't overzealous about it, something Father Gary realized could be just as harmful as being too skeptical. In addition, he anticipated having a medical doctor and perhaps a historical theologian (something recommended by an exorcist at the Angelicum). Beyond the medical team, he'd enlist Father Kevin (also for his ability to speak Spanish) and a couple of other priests as possible helpers. He didn't think he was going to use a prayer group just yet (something Father Bamonte had recommended). Because Father Carmine had told him how ashamed people could feel, he thought it prudent to avoid distractions or the potential embarrassment that might result from bringing strangers into the room. At the minimum he would do what Father Carmine did, which was to offer up the person's name at mass.

As their meeting came to a close, his bishop told him he was impressed with Father Gary's intentions and reiterated his support.

EVEN BEFORE MEETING WITH HIS BISHOP, Father Gary had been thinking about the day when he would have to perform an exorcism. He already knew—based on his own experience with depression— that he wanted to establish a measured, calm approach that could help put people at ease and create the right kind of environment for healing. He had been turned off by some of the more "fundamental-ist" books he had read attributing just about every problem under the sun—doubt, fear, alcoholism, greed—to a demon. He found that "theologically troubling." As C. S. Lewis so famously said in *The Screwtape Letters*, "There are two equal and opposite errors into which our race can fall about the devils. One is to disbelieve in their existence. The other is to believe, and to feel an excessive and un-healthy interest in them."

For this reason, he planned on starting out small. The first thing he'd probably do would be to ask a series of questions: Do you go to mass? Do you worship or pray? When was the last time you went to confession? If the answers were no, he would most likely get the suf-ferer to start going back to church and the sacraments before he would perform an exorcism. Of course, he would still offer a simple blessing.

But would it be that easy to convince people to follow this cau-tious approach?

He knew from his experiences at Saint Nicholas, where some of his techno-conscious former parishioners had to have the latest piece of gadgetry, that it wasn't going to be easy to ask people to slow down and invest their time in something that may not show immedi-ate results. "We are a culture of instant gratification," he would later say, voicing a criticism that virtually every exorcist shares.

Months later, Father Vince would have a similar experience when he tried to get a woman who came to see him to return to mass. "It is almost like people want to believe in the extreme," says Father Vince. "I am happy to pray with people; but if I tell them that they need to start going back to the Church and taking advantage of the sacra-ments, they look at me like I am crazy for actually suggesting that they practice their faith. And I know if I told them to go out and do the extreme, 'Go stand on your lawn and swing a dead chicken around your head and you will be fine,' they would do that. But just going to mass or confession—they think that is kind of mundane."

There would be other challenges as well, some of them uniquely

American. Whereas Italy is basically a monocultural (predominantly Catholic) society, America is anything but. In Father Gary's estimate, in the diocese of San Jose alone, more than one hundred different languages are spoken. There is a sizable Vietnamese community in town, as well as a large Hispanic population. He would have to know a little about the cultural mores of the various immigrant groups (as well as their traditions) if he was going to become an effective exorcist.

Father Gary didn't pretend to have all the answers. He hoped to be able to share information and get advice from some of the other exorcists in the United States who might have more experience. He had talked to Father Vince as well as to an exorcist he knew in Nebraska about the need to begin networking. The problem was the paucity of exorcists. Father Gary had heard the number was somewhere around fourteen officially appointed exorcists in the entire United States. In addition, as he'd shared with his bishop, some of these exorcists had received no formal training beyond being handed the *Ritual*. Just trying to work out a common approach would present a challenge, never mind battling a demon.

AT THE BEGINNING OF LENT, Father Gary began participating in mass each morning at one of the old titular houses, original house churches used by early Christians when nascent Christianity was still outlawed. Each morning he would get up around 5:30 and set out from the Casa along with about sixty other priests to walk to the one designated for that day of Lent. Typically, the priests would take turns saying mass at the different churches. When it was Father Gary's turn, he said mass in San Martino ai Monti, a tiny church where it was rumored that the Nicene Creed had been read aloud for the first time. The experience offered him a very real reminder of the traditions of the Church and once again helped him to reconnect to the roots of his faith.

During this time he also continued witnessing exorcisms three days a week out at San Lorenzo, along with Father Vince. Almost all the people were repeat cases, and by now Father Gary was an old hand and knew what to expect, though there were still a few surprises. During one exorcism, a woman seemed to come out of the trance on her own and say in a normal voice, "Okay, I'm fine. You can stop praying now." Father Carmine studied her carefully and then threw some holy water onto her, causing the demon to explode with rage.

After the sessions, Father Gary and Father Vince continued to compare notes over a coffee. Father Gary was still frustrated that there wasn't much time to ask questions. The language barrier persisted as well, even for Father Carmine. After one evening of exorcisms, Father Gary suggested that the three of them schedule an hour to sit down and talk and have the English-speaking layman he'd met at dinner translate for them.

A few weeks after meeting with his bishop, Father Gary was asked to give a talk to a group of priests in the continuing education program whom Father Vince had regaled with stories from San Lorenzo. Worried that they might one day have to face off against a demon themselves, they asked Father Gary if he'd be willing to share his knowledge as well.

The talk took place in the common room of the NAC, used by the seminarians as a sort of TV and game room that included a large collection of travel guides. About sixteen priests, most in their mid-fifties, showed up for the talk. Perhaps not surprisingly, all had at least one story to tell, either about a candle that mysteriously blew out while they were giving a blessing in a windowless room, or having run-ins with parishioners who claimed to be cursed. One priest from Amityville, New York, even described an order of nuns in the diocese that he said had begun practicing Wicca.

Father Gary was his usual candid self, tucking his Roman collar into his front shirt pocket and giving the priests his standard stump speech on the topic: Take the person seriously, ask questions, don't rule out the possibility of demonic possession but don't rush to judgment, and always be conscious that the person is suffering deeply. "Evil takes many forms, and I think becoming more aware of it through our own spiritual lives will make us better priests. If we want to be able to guide someone else, we have to be aware of evil while not being paranoid about it. But I think if we are oblivious to it, or our own prayer life doesn't cause us to enter into the deeper mystery of it, then I don't think we are serving our people well."

When the talk was over, everyone clapped.

Afterward, Father Gary and a friend ate at a noisy, packed pizzeria located just off Corso Vittorio Emanuele II. He was happy with how the talk went, but in truth he had something else on his mind. In a little over two weeks, it would be time for him to return to California.

Sitting in the packed pizzeria, with a huge spillover crowd mingling in the street outside, reminded him how much he enjoyed the energy of Rome. And now that his sabbatical was coming to an end, he realized how much he would miss it.

A FEW DAYS LATER, Father Kevin Joyce flew out from San Francisco, and Father Gary went out to the airport to meet him. The two had a great deal to discuss. Father Kevin had been sent a few cases by the bishop during Father Gary's absence and was eager to get Father Gary's opinion. One woman in her early thirties claimed to have balls of energy fly out of her. At times her fiancé didn't even recognize her. A Hispanic man claimed to hear demonic voices and even see demons from time to time. More than a few times Father Kevin had been called out to bless parishioners' houses.

As Father Kevin listened to what Father Gary had to say about these cases, both became so engrossed that they got on the wrong train and found themselves heading into the countryside rather than toward the center of town.

Father Kevin could see right away how passionate and excited Father Gary was about all that he had learned. Impressed with the new confidence and sense of spiritual growth that he observed in his old friend, he described Father Gary as a "changed man," and observed, "I think with this training you will be a real asset to the diocese."

"I hope," Father Gary responded.

Because Father Carmine was out of town for a few days and thus not available to talk with them, Father Gary instead contacted Father Daniel (who was so busy that he could be reached only between nine and ten in the evening) and asked whether he'd come over to the Casa to answer a few questions. The three sat in the break room for two hours talking about exorcism. Father Gary had already discussed many of the topics with the Franciscan, such as the best way to go about blessing houses; but other topics were new, such as how to recognize the presence of a curse, and about the efficacy of using blessed oil, water, and salt, specifically having the possessed person cook with them. In certain cases, Father Daniel even asked people to put a few drops of holy water into the washing machine to purify their clothes, which he said helped.

Father Daniel also discussed practical issues specific to the United States. For example, he suggested that before Father Gary performed an exorcism on anybody, he might want to draft a consent form for everyone to sign. Father Daniel offered another piece of advice that resonated: "Never bless a home without making sure the whole family is present. It's a great opportunity to perform a little catechesis, and that way you can also see if the problem isn't related to the house but instead to the family."

When they were finished, the two agreed to stay in touch. Father Gary thanked the Franciscan and promised to let him know what happened with his ministry when he got back to the States.

On the Thursday before Holy Week, Father Gary and Father Vince went out to San Lorenzo for the last time. Father Carmine had a light load that day and they saw only a couple of people until five that afternoon, when the three sat down in Father Carmine's office and talked for about an hour and a half. Father Carmine had finally arranged for the English-speaking layman at San Lorenzo to act as a translator, so Father Gary had no trouble getting answers to all his questions, such as why Father Carmine put holy water in the person's ears, or where the demon went when it wasn't tormenting the person. There were also unexpected moments of levity. Since the *Ritual* mentions that the exorcist should fast, Father Gary wanted to know whether Father Carmine did this. Once the question had been translated, Father Carmine responded by laughing and patting his protruding belly. "I don't fast from food," he said, smiling. But then he went on to tell Father Gary that he did fast from other things, such as TV and alcohol, and stated, "I have to deal with many humiliations. This is not an easy ministry." Apparently he felt these humiliations were a form of "fasting" as well.

Near the end of the discussion, Father Carmine turned to Father Gary and said, "It's too bad you have to go home now."

Father Gary thanked Father Carmine for being such a kind and generous teacher, saying it would not have been possible to have even contemplated performing the ministry without his invaluable training.

As he and Father Vince were getting ready to go, Father Carmine imparted one final piece of advice: "During the prayers of exorcism, remember that you are never addressing the person in front of you; you are always invoking the power of God. If you start focusing on this presence of evil in front of you as if your own self is dealing with it, you will get yourself into trouble, because that is not what you are doing; it is what God is doing through you."

As a token of his appreciation, Father Gary gave the Capuchin a silver-plated image of Padre Pio and thanked him again.

With that, as Father Gary and Father Carmine shook hands, the Capuchin patted him on the back in a brotherly way. *"Fai il bravo,"* he said just before Father Gary left. Be good.

IN THE DAYS FOLLOWING HIS VISIT with Father Carmine, as he organized his things for his return trip to the States, Father Gary reflected on his time in Rome. Not only had his training opened up his eyes; it also changed the way he approached his priestly ministry. In many ways he felt like Father Daniel, who said that now that he knew the reality of the spirit world, he felt more responsibility to do something to help people. To go back now to the way he was before would be like "turning my back on God."

AT THE START OF APRIL, the city slowly shifted gears as the bundled-up days of winter were replaced by the leafy *passeggiate* of spring. Father Gary had really been looking forward to celebrating Easter in Rome. He appreciated the holiday more so than the overly commercialized Christmas. For him, Easter was always about baptism and perhaps an apt time to start a new chapter in his priestly ministry. Father Kevin, who had been in Assisi on a retreat for a few days, returned in time for the two to participate together in the Triduum—the three-day period of Holy Thursday (the day of the Last Supper), Good Friday (the day Christ was crucified), and Holy Saturday (the night of the Great Paschal Vigil). On Thursday night Father Gary went to the mass of the Lord's Supper and afterward out to dinner with Father Kevin. On Good Friday, he went to the Vatican for a three-hour service and, in a coincidence, ran into Father Carmine, which allowed him another opportunity to say *grazie*. On Holy Saturday night he went up to the NAC for the Easter Vigil, which he found "glorious" and deeply spiritual. It also presented him with a chance to say good-bye to many of the seminarians and priests, some of whom he had grown close to and with whom he intended to maintain friendships.

When he stopped and thought about it, he had never imagined

that his sabbatical would have turned out this way. It had been an incredibly enriching experience. When he'd told some of the seminarians that he was heading home, a few had said how much they wished they could go home, too. "Oh no you don't." He shook his head. "I have had ten months without stress, and now I have to go home to a set of unknowns."

Beyond a new parish, perhaps the biggest of these unknowns was about his own abilities as an exorcist. That demons existed he didn't doubt, but would they respond to him the way that they had responded to Father Carmine? Would the prayers of exorcism work for him? In addition, he worried about the prospect of having to confront a demon on his own. During the exorcisms that he'd witnessed, most of the demons had directed their attention at Father Carmine, and as an observer he had remained relatively isolated from that exchange. But as an exorcist, he would now have to bear the brunt of it himself. Would he be able to do that? There would be no way of knowing until he actually performed an exorcism himself.

When the vigil was over, it was past midnight and still the streets were packed. Alone now, he walked back to the Casa, and even though it was late he felt completely safe. Most of the restaurants and bars were still full, some with people just sitting down. Passing in front of the Pantheon, he followed the crowds heading down Via dei Pastini and toward Via del Corso, comforted by the fact that he knew his way around the city without a map—certainly a far cry from his first four days at the NAC when he'd been anxious about going out on his own. The nights had warmed up considerably over the past few weeks, making it easier for him to take his time. A few people he passed flashed him a polite smile, but most ignored him. To them he was just another part of the backdrop—a black-clad figure on his way to one of the many churches in Rome.

CHAPTER SEVENTEEN

THE EXORCIST

Once when I was a young man, trees were trees, mountains were mountains and rivers were rivers. When I grew up, trees were no longer trees, mountains were no longer mountains and rivers were no longer rivers. But when I became old, trees once again became trees, mountains became mountains and rivers became rivers.

—*Zen poem*

Father Gary began the morning as he always did, by reading the obituaries. It was a habit he'd picked up from his days in the funeral business. Back then, of course, he'd checked the listings for professional reasons—noting which funeral homes were handling the services. Now he did so to see if he recognized any names. He'd lived his whole life inside the confines of the South Bay and Silicon Valley, and during that time he'd gotten to know the community as only a parish priest can, from the minutiae to the milestones—baptisms, weddings, and yes, funerals. Spared the grief of recognizing anyone on that particular day, he moved on to the sports pages, devouring both the *San Jose Mercury News* and the *San Francisco Chronicle*.

After finishing his morning routine, Father Gary walked to the parish offices. As always, there was much to do and never enough time. As he passed the church—which had nearly triple the capacity of his former parish, Saint Nicholas—and the school (K–8), his mind wandered back to Rome. There was a square patch of asphalt with some trees that served as the drop-off area for the kids; perhaps for no other reason than its shape, he'd dubbed it the "piazza."

His first order of business had been to get to know the staff and let them know just how involved he intended to be in the running of the parish. One thing Father Gary had yet to discuss with them was exorcism. At some point he planned to sit down with Father Kevin and go over the specifics of his exorcism team, but for the moment he figured there would be plenty of time before he had to hash it out. Later that morning, however, while he was chatting with the parish administrator in the conference room, his secretary tentatively knocked. Unsure, she paused for a second as if weighing each word carefully. "There is a couple here for an exorcism."

Father Gary froze. *I don't believe this—already!* he thought, then advised her calmly, "Tell them to wait in the front room. I'll be down when I finish up here." After his secretary left, he turned to the parish coordinator, who was eyeing him expectantly. "There are some things I'm going to have to clear up with you. I can't go into it now, but we'll talk later." Wrapping up the meeting, Father Gary pulled himself away and headed downstairs.

The couple was waiting in a small room just off the entrance to the parish office. As he entered the room, they stood up from the couch and he shook their hands. Their ages were hard to guess but he thought perhaps early thirties. The woman, Stephanie, had a very plain appearance and kept her eyes down, while the man, Chris, did most of the talking. As they began to tell their story, Father Gary recognized their case as one that Father Kevin had mentioned in Rome. In fact, the couple had seen Father Kevin but weren't happy with how things were progressing. "I need an exorcism," Stephanie announced.

Chris described how, at odd times of the day and for no apparent reason, Stephanie would suddenly be overcome by what he called "attacks" on her mind (which sounded to Father Gary like mood swings). According to Chris, she would become enraged beyond any rational thought. One such "attack" had left her walking on the side of the road while Chris sat dumbfounded in the car. It wasn't until Chris brought it to her attention that she became aware of what she was doing.

Thinking that the problem might be spiritual in nature, Chris tried a spontaneous deliverance prayer over her and something amazing happened. During the prayer Stephanie felt "hot spots" on various parts of her body—either her forehead or stomach or the back of her neck—and simultaneously felt that entities were leaving her. Chris also confirmed that while praying he'd felt warm balls of energy releasing from her.

Perplexed, Father Gary dug deeper, asking a little about Stephanie's past, specifically if she had any involvement in the occult, and if there was any particular event that had prompted this problem.

The problem had begun the previous March, when an older woman she knew approached her at their church and gave her a hug. This innocuous act, however, suddenly turned into something very bizarre as she heard the woman's voice change into a gruff, demonic-like growl. The episode triggered an unpleasant memory of being abused by her father as a child, during which he also spoke in the same gruff, demonic voice. In addition, there was some strange relationship with a minister from her church, whom she described as being obsessed with her (she'd stopped attending her church because of it).

At that point she'd gone to see Father Kevin who sent her to an internist, who gave her a clean bill of health. She then went to see a clinical psychologist, an agnostic. He told her that she seemed fine and that maybe her problem was "spiritual" in nature.

After this she returned to Father Kevin, who recommended she see a Catholic therapist. That didn't work out because Stephanie had refused to be interviewed without Chris being present, something the psychiatrist wasn't comfortable doing.

In the meantime they'd searched for other priests who might be willing to help them but had been turned away each time. One priest even said, "I hope it's not something I can catch." Sensing that they were desperate and unsure where to go, someone in the vicar's office at the diocesan chancery ultimately directed them to Father Gary.

Father Gary could see that Stephanie was clearly distressed. It upset him to think of the flippant remarks made by priests who turned her away in such a callous manner.

He told her that he'd recently been trained as an exorcist in Rome but that he'd yet to actually perform an exorcism himself. But, he said, "I am willing to meet with you." He cautioned them, however, not to expect quick results. "We're going to have to start addressing this from the bottom up, and it may take some time."

Stephanie was noticeably relieved. Here at last was an exorcist, and an officially appointed one at that, who was willing to help. "Thank you," she said.

Contacting his bishop, Father Gary relayed the details of the story. The bishop told him not to proceed with anything until Stephanie got a full psychiatric evaluation.

Without his team in place, Father Gary scrambled to locate a person who might assist him. Thinking back to his days at Saint

Nicholas, he contacted a female clinical psychologist whom he knew to be very devout, but she felt the case was out of her league. He got in touch with another female clinician who seemed more willing to help. Father Gary then met with her for two hours, and after asking about her perspective on concepts such as demons and Satan, he was satisfied that she was equipped to give a competent analysis.

At first the couple balked at having to see another doctor. But when Father Gary told them, "If you are even going to contemplate this as a possibility, you have to do it," they relented.

In the interim, Father Gary prayed a simple blessing over Stephanie and anointed her with the sacrament of the sick. She showed no reaction during the blessing but claimed to feel better afterward.

After evaluating her the following week, the psychologist could find nothing clinically wrong.

In the meantime, Father Gary consulted with an American exorcist on the East Coast who was associated with the upcoming exorcism conference in August to ask his advice. The exorcist told Father Gary that he had seen symptoms such as Stephanie's many times.

Armed with this information, Father Gary went back to his bishop, who gave him the go-ahead for the exorcism, reminding him to have the couple sign a release form beforehand (an American prerequisite). Father Gary called Stephanie and told her the news. The exorcism was scheduled for the following Saturday.

During the week, Father Gary was too busy with the details of the parish to spend much time on the exorcism. He did take the parish coordinator and his secretary aside and fill them in about his appointment. Now that the cat was technically out of the bag, it was likely that more and more people would be calling (or showing up unannounced), so it would be better if his staff knew. In addition, at Father Kevin's suggestion, he downloaded the 1952 version of the *Roman Ritual* for exorcism off the Internet. Since his Latin was a little rusty, it would be much easier to pray this version because he was allowed to do it in English.

The morning of the exorcism he was anxious. While he had witnessed nearly eighty exorcisms, this would be the first one he'd be performing. Chris would be present and assisting him if he needed a hand.

He decided to conduct the exorcism in one of the unused offices. The room was tasteful and small, without a lot of furniture that might get in the way. Rather than skip straight through to the exorcism prayers as Father Carmine had, he resolved to pray the entire *Ritual* from start to finish. He didn't want to leave anything to chance.

He began the *Ritual*, reciting the litany of the saints in Latin and then moved on to the Gospel reading in English, followed by a brief homily. After the homily, he had both Stephanie and Chris renew their baptismal vows; "Do you renounce Satan? And all his works? . . ." Once that was finished, he began the exorcism prayers, using a wooden crucifix that had been hanging on the wall in his office and touching it to the back of her neck as he did so. "I cast you out, unclean spirit, along with every Satanic power of the enemy, every spectre from hell and all your fell companions . . ." As he prayed, he tried to keep one eye on the page and the other on Stephanie, who sat placidly on the couch, showing no sign of reaction. After the first prayer, he shifted the crucifix, placing it on the top of her head, and began the second prayer. When he was ready to move on to the third prayer, he placed it on her forehead. After he'd finished, he offered them both communion.

The whole exorcism had lasted about an hour, and as far as Father Gary was concerned, the woman had shown no outward reactions to the prayers.

"So what did you feel?" he asked her.

"I felt this heat on my head, but then it went away," she said. "At one point I felt this thing kind of pull out of my stomach and leave."

Afterward he sat in his office and went over the details. The exorcism had turned out to be pretty uneventful. Was there something he'd overlooked? Or was Stephanie faking? Was she perhaps trying to get Chris's attention? His experiences in Rome had taught him to be circumspect; but since this was his first exorcism, he couldn't be sure. As he analyzed it, he remembered that it was possible for demons to hide—maybe that's what had happened. He knew that exorcism wasn't an exact science and that he would become more competent with experience. Beyond that, he wondered anew how Father Carmine had the stamina to see so many people. Just this one exorcism had tired him out, and there were days when Father Carmine had seen twelve people. No wonder he had skipped to the heart of the *Ritual*.

He saw Stephanie and Chris a few more times over the following months, and each time her reaction was the same—she sat perfectly still and afterward described having a burning sensation where he'd touched her with the cross and then the feeling of entities leaving her. He began to wonder why, if a demon was present, he hadn't manifested yet.

In August he flew out to the exorcism conference being held in the Midwest, hoping to get some practical tips about Stephanie's case, as well as to network with other exorcists. At Father Gary's instigation, Father Vince also attended the conference. Father Vince had seen a few people already, though he hadn't prayed the *Ritual* over anybody yet. He had met one woman he believed might be possessed but she'd failed to return after he instructed her to attend mass and confession in conjunction with any formal help he'd provide. She basically huffed out, telling him that if he wouldn't help her right then and there, she'd go somewhere else. He discovered later that she'd gone to a local prayer group that told her that she could be freed only when she had devoted herself to prayer and her rosary beads turned the color of gold.

The conference was run by a group of Charismatic laypeople who sometimes assisted American exorcists in their ministry.

The day started with prayer before breakfast at 7:30, followed by morning lectures until 11:15, then daily mass and lunch. The afternoon consisted of classes from 3:00 to 5:00 followed by an early dinner; then, at 7:00, there was an hour of questions, after which everyone gathered to pray over one another.

On the whole, Father Gary found the conference to be extremely helpful, especially since it allowed him the opportunity to meet other

American exorcists with whom he could compare notes. He found the talk on the sacrament of reconciliation and the spirituality of mercy and the Eucharist as a weapon against evil influences to be very useful. It also jibed with what he'd learned back in Rome— a fundamental job of an exorcist is to bring people back to the sacraments. However, while he was pleased by the direction of the conference, he also felt uncomfortable with some of the people in attendance who tended to see the Devil in every crack and crevasse of life.

Father Vince had a similar impression. As regards to the attendees praying prayers of deliverance over one another, he objected to the notion that it was necessary, explaining that since he thought demonic possession was uncommon he didn't think it required that everyone be delivered of evil spirits. It also turned him off that some of the participants seemed too eager to become exorcists. One priest boasted that he exorcised his rectory at least once a month, including his telephone, because he was concerned that people on the other end of the line might be possessed. Father Vince found this to be a clear example of the American tendency to gravitate toward the extreme.

Overall, Father Gary appreciated the conference and its efforts to train exorcists as had the course in Rome. He thought the organizers might have gotten more interest if they had held it at a Catholic site (it would be the following year) so that more bishops would attend. More than anything, he envisioned a course sanctioned by the National Conference of Catholic Bishops, which would help legitimize the rite of exorcism, something that he felt was desperately needed.

AFTER HE RETURNED FROM THE CONFERENCE, Father Gary prayed over Stephanie again while Chris was present. Wondering if they were getting anywhere, he asked if she really wanted these spirits to leave. When she answered yes, he reminded her that she was going to have to become more proactive and start praying every day. "You can't just rely on me to do all this for you."

As the sessions progressed, however, Chris and Stephanie became more exasperated. Why weren't these prayers "curing" Stephanie the way Chris's numerous books described? While she did report some improvement, Father Gary's exorcisms didn't seem any more effective than what she had experienced when Chris prayed over her.

Feeling that her improvement wasn't happening fast enough, the couple decided to try another exorcist. Father Gary gave them the name of an exorcist in a nearby diocese and wished them well. He still wondered if he had missed something, or hadn't done it right. He still questioned whether the prayers of the *Ritual* would work for him. Despite the fact that Stephanie said she *felt* better, it was hard to gauge. Even in the milder cases that Father Carmine saw, Father Gary detected at least some external reaction to the prayer.

When the couple returned a month later saying that they weren't happy with the other exorcist either, Father Gary knew there was more to the story. It wasn't just him. In fact, he was beginning to feel ambivalent about their case. Knowing from his experiences with Father Carmine that people can get addicted to exorcism, as if it were a kind of "identity," he told them he'd be willing to see them again but they would have to shift gears and slow down. Disappointed, the couple had no choice but to agree.

OVER THE COURSE OF THE FOLLOWING YEAR, Father Gary saw more people, some from as far away as Oregon. A woman in her fifties said that demons were around her all the time; a Filipino man thought that his brother-in-law had put a curse on him; and another man claimed to be haunted by the ghost of a dead relative. A few times he needed Father Kevin to translate for Spanish-speaking victims, and on one occasion another priest helped out when he saw an older woman who spoke only Vietnamese.

In a few of these cases he prayed the *Ritual*, but in the vast majority he simply prayed prayers of deliverance or offered a blessing if he suspected the cause was not demonic. Sometimes, when people wouldn't take no for an answer, he prayed a simple blessing over them while cautioning them to seek help through therapy.

Father Gary would also bless houses. One family in San Jose claimed to have witnessed various odd phenomena, including a ghostly apparition that would sometimes appear at the foot of the children's bed and a room that always seemed to be filled with an icy chill. Despite blessing every room in the house, Father Gary failed to uncover any curses or infestations that would explain the activities.

The fact that so many people were seeking him out came as a big surprise. Even after witnessing so many exorcisms in Rome, he still thought his services would rarely be called upon in America. And because he had been so busy, there'd been little opportunity to carry out some of the ideas he'd formulated in Rome. For instance, he had yet to meet with the youth ministers in the parish and talk to them about the dangers of the occult. However, he had been able to open up a little chapel off the parish offices for daily Eucharistic adoration.

In January 2007, Father Gary e-mailed Father Carmine to let him know how things had been progressing since his return from Rome, mentioning some of the cases he'd seen and his hope that the ministry of exorcism would soon be seen in a more credible light. Having forgotten most of his Italian, he wrote the message in English.

A few weeks later, Father Carmine responded to his e-mail in Italian, delighted to have heard from his former protégé. He was even happier that Father Gary had written in English, saying that it would give him a much-needed opportunity to practice his language skills, a favor he hoped to reciprocate by responding in Italian.

In closing his e-mail, Father Gary had asked the Capuchin how things were in Rome. Was he still seeing lots of people? Father Carmine had responded by saying that the situation was as bad as ever. In some cases, he was getting people sent to him from other countries in Europe. One woman had sought him out from Germany, where there were no exorcists, he said. "You know how tragic the situation is as far as that goes. I believe that we have to pray a lot for the theologians and bishops that they teach a doctrine that is truly and completely Catholic instead of one which is easier and more accommodating. All of humanity suffers because of a doctrine that is incomplete and unbalanced. But we put our faith in the hands of the Madonna. I praise God that there is a priest like you who can help a lot of poor and suffering people. Be simple and strong! And pray for me, because I need it . . . We will remain united in our prayers."

———————————

SEVERAL MONTHS after receiving Father Carmine's e-mail, Father Kevin got in touch with Father Gary about a case he thought he should investigate. The parents of a young Central American woman, Maria, who lived in a nearby diocese, had reached out to him, hoping that their daughter could receive an exorcism. A week later, Father Gary found time during a busy afternoon to sit down with the three.

The sullen and downtrodden appearance of Maria, a twenty-seven-year-old originally from Honduras, immediately alerted him that something might be amiss. The defeated look the parents gave him reminded him of what he'd seen in people accompanying victims whom Father Carmine had prayed over in Rome.

As in the past, he started by asking Maria to tell him her story.

Ever since the age of seventeen, she said, she had been hearing voices and seeing demons, which would always tell her, "You belong to us." Worried, her parents had taken her to see a witch doctor while they were living in Honduras. When he'd performed a ritualistic exorcism, Maria had entered into a trance and flopped around on the ground. After that, the problem seemed to abate for a time. However, recently it had come back again.

Father Gary continued to probe, noting that Maria had no history of drug abuse; and as far as he could surmise, she appeared sane. According to her parents, the witch doctor had told them that the troubles were most likely related to a curse.

Intrigued, Father Gary told the three that while he was willing to help, the best course of action would be for Maria to get a psychiatric evaluation. In the meantime, however, he told them he would be happy to pray a simple blessing over her. (Remembering his training, he also suspected such a blessing might help unmask a demon if there was one.)

Without much fanfare, Father Gary picked up a three-ringed binder that contained some prayers that he had photocopied from various books and downloaded from the Internet. The prayers he liked most were printed in the back of Father Amorth's book, *An Exorcist Tells His Story*. Selecting one of these (originally from the Greek *Ritual*), he extended his hand toward Maria, intoning: *"Kyrie eleison*, God, our Lord, King of ages, All-powerful and All-mighty, you who made everything and who transform everything simply by your will. You who in Babylon changed into dew the flames of the 'seven-times hotter' furnace and protected and saved the three holy children. You are the doctor and the physician of our soul. You are the salvation of those who turn to you."

Almost immediately Maria's body began to twitch, her legs rocking back and forth. As he noticed this, Father Gary tried not to betray what he was thinking: Here was his confirmation.

"We beseech you to make powerless, banish, and drive out every diabolic power, presence, and machination; every evil influence, malefice, or evil eye, and all evil actions aimed against your servant Maria. Where there is envy and malice, give us an abundance of goodness, endurance, victory, and charity. O Lord, you who love mankind, we beg you to reach out your powerful hands and your most high and mighty arms and come to our aid. Help us, who are made in your image; send the angel of peace over us, to protect us body and soul," he prayed.

Maria suddenly screamed. She began thrashing violently on the couch. Then, much to Father Gary's amazement, her facial muscles tensed in such a way that her appearance completely changed, and she took on the visage of an adder. Even her mannerisms seemed to become snakelike. Her eyes, which had become dead black discs, bored into him while her tongue shot in and out like a snake's.

As he beheld this transformation, his heart pounded in his chest. *This is really happening,* he thought. He wasn't hallucinating. He threw some holy water onto Maria and she lunged at him, but was grabbed at the last minute by her parents, who were sitting on either side of her. Deep hatred poured out at him through her black eyes. There was no doubt in his mind that if he had been alone with her, she would have long since attacked him. He was no longer a spectator; it was up to him to see this through to the end.

"May God keep at bay and vanquish every evil power, every poison or malice invoked against us by corrupt and envious people. Then, under the protection of your authority may we sing, in gratitude, 'The Lord is my salvation; whom should I fear?'"

She kicked and strained, trying to break free.

The struggle continued for a few more minutes, until he decided that it was probably better if he didn't push things too much at this early stage. She needed a solemn exorcism, not a simple blessing. It would also allow him a chance to prepare more. For now it was enough to know that the prayers had generated a strong reaction.

Once the blessing was finished, Maria immediately calmed down and her face returned to normal. As she slumped down on the couch to catch her breath, Father Gary left to get a host, thinking that perhaps communion would do her good. When he reentered the room with the Eucharist, however, she nearly jumped out the window, and probably would have if it hadn't been for her parents once again wrestling her back down onto the couch. When she had recovered sufficiently, Father Gary finally gave her the consecrated host, though even as she received it, she was unable to swallow it. Worrying that the demon might be coming back, Father Gary quickly unscrewed the cap from his holy water bottle and handed it to her, saying, "Here, wash it down with this." Finally, the host went down.

When it was over, the mother approached Father Gary to thank him. She told him that while her daughter's reaction to the prayers had been similar to the exorcism in Honduras, this time it was much more intense.

After the family had left, Father Gary sat for a moment in his office to collect his thoughts. He had been through a tremendous change since being nominated exorcist in 2005. And while many of these experiences had touched him deeply—exposing him to a deep level of human suffering that he never knew existed—something particular about this case definitely stood out. Beyond the sensational, a profound element of it gave him hope. He was finally able to put aside his doubts once and for all about whether the *Ritual* would work for him. *These prayers do have power*, he thought. It was a visceral reminder that the age-old conflict between good and evil, sin and salvation, was far from over. Not only did this validate his calling as a priest, and his choice to become an exorcist, but it was a powerful confirmation of one of the deepest mysteries of his faith. Even though evil existed in the world, there was a way to defeat it.

AUTHOR'S NOTE

IN THE FALL OF 2005, when I heard that a Vatican-affiliated university was offering a course entitled "Exorcism and the Prayer of Liberation," I thought it might be a PR stunt. Did the Church still believe in exorcism? It was intriguing that the course would be open to non-priests, with some of the lessons taught by psychologists and criminologists. Living in Italy as a freelance writer and journalist who'd spent time in the Rome bureau of the Associated Press, I knew how hard it could be to crack the wall of secrecy surrounding the Vatican. Add to that the mystery surrounding exorcism, and I saw the class as a rare opportunity. Not knowing what to expect, I thought there was at least an article in it.

At the time, I knew almost nothing about exorcism. Like most people, I immediately thought of Hollywood movies. Yet, while films such as *The Exorcist* were reportedly "based" on true stories, the cinematic packaging and special effects made it hard to separate fact from fiction.

The first day of the course, however, changed any such preconceptions I had about exorcism. Not only was the ultramodern classroom an odd setting to see priests, Franciscan friars, and nuns of various orders listening to lectures on the powers of Satan, but, to my surprise, I found the students themselves to be anything but the "superstitious" or puritanical priests portrayed in popular culture.

When I first met Father Gary, I was immediately impressed by his honesty and transparency. The two of us struck up a friendship based on a strong desire to immerse ourselves in what we were learning.

As I became acquainted with the details of Father Gary's life, the writer in me began to realize that his journey presented a unique window into the world of exorcism. Here was the chance, I thought, to see what it is like to be an exorcist from the perspective of someone just getting started.

In truth, though, the thought of writing about demons and exorcism wasn't at the top of my list—my wife, for one, didn't find the subject all that appealing. I must say that there were days when I wondered whether it might be better for me to leave things alone, lest my own life be invaded by an unseen "spirit."

Despite being raised a Catholic, I was ambivalent about demonic possession. In fact, in the interest of full disclosure, when I began this book I was more of a "cultural Catholic" than a practicing one. Sure I went to mass now and then, on Christmas and Easter; but beyond that, I probably wasn't the best person with whom to discuss the deeper mysteries of the faith. On the contrary, my approach was more journalistic than anything. I wanted to know what the Church actually taught about exorcism. And in the case of Father Gary, I wanted to know what it took for a person to be willing to stand in a room and square off against demons, if in fact there were demons at all.

As a layperson, the first thing that surprised me about exorcism was that not many priests knew anything about it, especially not American priests.

Most if not all American books about exorcism were outdated, many written in the 1970s. In Italy, however, it was a different story, and almost immediately I found myself turning to Italian books, a vast majority of which (such as *Possessioni diaboliche ed esorcismo* by Father Franceso Bamonte and *Il dito di Dio e il potere di Satana: L'esorcismo* by Father Gabriele Nanni) were written since 2004. These books provided not only detailed theological analysis, but also firsthand accounts of what performing an exorcism is like. And the more I read, the more curious I became. Once Father Gary began participating in exorcisms, I was able to add his interpretations. However, I also knew that if I wanted to tell this story, I would have to enter into the world of the exorcist, and the only way to do that would be to witness an exorcism.

My first behind-the-scenes look at exorcism occurred when I began to interview the various exorcists on their "home turf." Here and there I would catch a glimpse of what existed on the other side—a group of people hounding Father Tommaso outside the sacristy of the Scala Santa; Father Bamonte wiping a puddle of holy water off a chair so that I could sit down for our interview; sitting in Father Carmine's waiting room while a woman screamed and banged around in his office. Perhaps most surprising was that far from being carried out in some hilltop monastery, many of the exorcisms were performed in churches located right in the heart of Rome. In fact, it was common to be talking to an exorcist while groups of tourists paraded around taking photos of religious iconography. One bizarre aspect of researching this book was this juxtaposition of two worlds— talking to a victim of demonic possession or hearing an exorcism and then emerging into the bright sunshine and chaotic streets of Rome.

Each exorcist I interviewed was compelling in his own right. I warmed to Father Bamonte's boyhood exuberance, Father Nanni's movie-star good looks and intellectual demeanor, Father Amorth's avuncular joviality and penchant for dramatic rejoinders, and Father Carmine's salt-of-the-earth unpretentiousness. All were patient and gracious with me no matter how many questions I stumbled through in my less-than-perfect Italian.

I also found their candor to be refreshing. Many of the books I'd read had ordered everything into neat little boxes, yet here were exorcists with years of experience telling me that there were still things that couldn't be known.

Then there were the victims. Like Father Gary, not only did I find their apparent normalcy surprising, but I also found them credible, even likable people. These were not people who struck me as trying to pull a fast one; they were sincere, heartfelt individuals who were struggling with something even they seemed at a loss to understand. Later, when I participated in exorcisms, this impression was only re-inforced.

Many people assume that an exorcist is out to prove that people are possessed; however, with each of the Italian exorcists I talked to, I found the opposite to be true. It is also wrong, I think, to assume that the Church is on one side promoting the belief in spirits while the secular world is on the other, trying to debunk such notions. Stroll down to the local New Age bookshop to see the tremendous popu-larity of angels, "channeling," and "astral travel," not to mention the numbers of "ghost whisperers" and therapists who practice "spirit re-leasement." Take away officially appointed exorcists, and people will still seek out exorcisms, or pay "psychics" to rid their homes from evil spirits. Seen in this light, the concept of an exorcism course offering lectures by psychologists and other experts in the field to help train priests is a good idea, even if only to give people some sort of stan-dards.

The writing of this book became a journey of sorts for me as well. It helped me to reconnect with my faith in a way that I never ex-pected when I began researching exorcism. Over the course of the three years I spent writing and conducting my research, I met many incredible individuals like Father Gary, whose service and dedication to those who suffer showed me how much good we can do when we set aside our egos and reach out to help people.

While I was writing, people often asked whether anything strange had happened to me. Besides the odd shutter bang on a windless day or the ill-timed power outage costing me some of my work, both of which I attribute to coincidence, there was an experience I cannot explain.

I was driving home one afternoon, after an interview with a woman who suddenly entered into the trance state and started screaming at a picture of Mary on the wall. All at once my car was filled with the scent of flowers. In an offhand way I thought, *Oh, that's nice. Where is this coming from?* Then I found myself unconsciously grinning. I remembered that before the exorcism took place, Father Bamonte had told me that the Virgin Mary often came to the aid of the woman, and so during her outburst I'd said a little prayer asking Mary to help. I certainly didn't imagine this tiny gesture had any real impact on her case. Father Bamonte went on to perform the exorcism, and the woman continued to scream for nearly an hour.

At the time, I had only a vague recollection that certain people reported smelling flowers in connection with Mary and other mystical experiences. Was my car being flooded by the scent of flowers somehow connected to what had happened earlier in the morning? I wasn't so sure. The smell certainly wasn't coming from outside the car (when it happened I'd been driving by a sheep farm, infamous for its foul odor). It could have been coming from my air conditioner (though I had never smelled it before). It could have been an olfactory hallucination, for all I knew. But in hindsight I've come to realize that an explanation is beside the point. Even though this experience lasted only a few minutes, it touched me deeply. Was this Mary or some angelic being trying to tell me that she'd heard the pathetic cry of a person struggling to come to grips with his own faith in order to help a fellow human being? Was some part of my subconscious feeding impulses to another to convince myself of my own transcendence? I guess I'll never know. One thing is certain, whatever it was filled me with an immense sense of joy.

ACKNOWLEDGMENTS

I AM GRATEFUL BEYOND MEASURE to the courageous and candid contributions of Father Gary Thomas, and to his indefatigable generosity and kindness. Quite simply this book would not have been possible without him.

I am very grateful to all the people who appeared in this book but especially to Father Francesco Bamonte, Father Gabriele Nanni, and Father Carmine De Fillipis, who not only took time out of their busy schedules to answer my questions, but were also vital in opening up the world of exorcism to me. Special thanks also to Father Gabriele Amorth, Father Aldo Buonaiuto, Father Jeremy Davies, Father François Dermine, O.P., Father Giancarlo Gramolazzo, Father Kevin Joyce, Father Vince Lampert, and Father Tiziano Ripetto.

Numerous other priests shared with me their time and personal stories. Some made it into the book but many did not. Thanks to Father Avelina, Father Pedro Barrajon, Father Steve Bigler, Father Bernie Bush, Monsignor John Esseff, Father Paul Hrezzo, Father Brenden Lally, Father James LeBar, Father Gerardo Menchaca, Father John Michet, Father Bill O'Callaghan, Father Serge Propst, O.P., Father Mike Simone, Father Johanus Sweetzer, Father Mike Tomaseck, and Father Antonius Wall.

Father Basil Cole, O.P., not only helped me to navigate the teachings of Thomas Aquinas on the angels, but also read sections of the manuscript and offered valuable feedback. The same can be said for Father Jeffrey Grob, who provided invaluable insight into the exorcism *Ritual,* and Father A. Farren, O.P., who donated his time and expertise to give the manuscript a critical read.

Thanks also to Monsignor James F. Checchio at the North American College for allowing me access to the NAC library, and to Sister Rebecca for making the difficult task of wading through all that material less daunting.

Dr. Richard Gallagher gets my sincerest thanks for sharing with me his knowledge and expertise. I was very sorry to hear that Dr. Barry L. Beyerstein had passed away in the spring of 2007. He was doing amazing work in the field of biopsychology and I know he will be missed.

A special thank-you to all the victims who were willing to share their stories with me. Baring one's soul to a complete stranger is never an easy thing to do, and I was truly humbled by the courage of these people.

I cannot say enough about my amazing agent, Christy Fletcher, who got on board at the very beginning and whose determination and dedication never faltered. She patiently guided me through my first foray into the world of publishing with an almost Zen-like calm.

Thanks also to my wonderful editor JillEllyn Riley, who made a tough situation seem like a walk in the park. It was a real pleasure to work with such a talented and committed professional.

At Doubleday Religion, many thanks to John Burke for fielding my numerous calls and e-mails, to my copy editor Ruth Younger for all the hard work she put into the manuscript, and especially to Trace Murphy for his words of encouragement and unwavering support of the book.

Thanks also to Paolo Alei, Lori Armstrong, Pierpaolo Balani, Richard Brener, Dr. Tonino Cantelmi, Melissa Chinchillo, Carlo Climati, Sam Copeland, Marta Falconi, Merideth Finn, Beau Flynn, Elizabeth Hazelton, Natalie S. Higgins, Mara Lander, Swanna MacNair, Jim Michaletti, Lory Mondaini, Michael Petroni, Nora Reichard, Peter Robinson, Howard Sanders, Kate Scherler, Claudio Vignozzi,

Tripp Vinson, Lorien Warner, Christopher Winner, and Sara Wolski. Thanks also to the Thomas family for their time and memories.

Every writer needs a good support group. Thanks to Scooter Leonard for helping to instill in me a love of writing, and to my good friend and mentor Randolph Wright, who through skill and tact was able to steer me through the minefields of some of the earliest drafts.

I owe a huge debt of gratitude to Eric Blehm, who opened door after door for me and helped to keep me afloat throughout the whole process with his encouragement, sage advice, and commiseration. A simple thank-you would not be enough.

To my parents, Tom and Nancy Baglio, who have always believed in me and supported me over the years. And to my entire American and Italian families for their unconditional support and enthusiasm, I could not have done it without you guys. My son, Noah, who constantly reminded me what really mattered. And lastly to my brilliant and multitalented wife, Sara, who not only translated and transcribed most of my interviews but who also put up with my long absences and never-ending doubts. I know it wasn't easy, but your support never wavered. For that, and so much more, I offer you my eternal love and gratitude.

NOTES

About the citations: For the sake of maintaining the narrative flow, I have kept citations in the text to a minimum. Unless specifically noted here in the end-notes, direct quotations appearing in the text are taken from my interviews.

PROLOGUE

2: **The thirty-five-year-old woman:** The material for this exorcism came primarily from two sources: the transcript of an audio recording of the exorcism made by Father Bamonte and an interview with the victim, in which she recounted her visions and feelings during the exorcism.

2: **Saint Gemma Galgani:** Saint Gemma is one of the few Catholic saints reported to have been attacked by the Devil during her lifetime. As a result, possessed people often pray to her for strength. Born near the Italian town of Lucca on March 12, 1878, Gemma had many mystical experiences. At a very early age, she dedicated herself to a life of intense prayer and claimed that Jesus, Mary, and her guardian angel appeared to her. Constantly ill, she developed meningitis when she was twenty and attributed her cure to the intervention of deceased Passionist priest Gabriel Possenti, later canonized. At twenty-one she received the stigmata, which appeared on Thursday evenings and healed by Saturday mornings, leaving a whitish mark where the deep wounds had been. Throughout her life she felt constantly tormented by the Devil. In one diary entry, she describes the Devil raining blows down upon her back for several hours. She died at the age of twenty-five.

In this case, the woman had always felt a strong connection to Gemma, having visited her tomb in Lucca, Italy, on her honeymoon.

6: *Catechism of the Catholic Church:* The first version of the book was published in French in 1992, translated into English in 1994. The creation of the *Catechism* was undertaken in 1985 when Pope John Paul II, guided by the "spirit of the Second Vatican Council," convoked an extraordinary assembly of the Synod of Bishops to "study its teachings in greater depth in order that all the Christian faithful might better adhere to it and to promote knowledge and application of it," *Catechism of the Catholic Church*, p. 2. In 1986, Pope John Paul II entrusted the drafting of it to a group of twelve cardinals and bishops led by then Cardinal Joseph Ratzinger, who became Pope Benedict XVI in 2005. The book is considered the source of all authentic Catholic doctrine.

6: **By 2006, that number was said to have risen:** Chas S. Clifton, *Her Hidden Children: The Rise of Wicca and Paganism in America*, p. 11.

6: **Sales of occult and New Age books:** Numerous self-help spirituality books have become best sellers in recent years, such as Eckhart Tolle's *The Power of Now: A Guide to Spiritual Enlightenment*, New World Library, 2004, and *A New Earth: Awakening Your Life's Purpose*, Penguin, 2008, both of which had sales into the millions.

6: **According to the Association of Italian Catholic Psychiatrists and Psychologists:** as reported in "God Told Us to Exorcise My Daughter's Demons. I Don't Regret Her Death," by Elizabeth Day, *The Daily Telegraph*, November 26, 2005.

7: **a Romanian nun . . . was found dead:** "Crucified Nun Dies in 'Exorcism,'" June 18, 2005, BBC. The story was originally reported in the *Agence France-Presse*, 2005. In February 2007, the priest was sentenced to fourteen years in jail for the crime. See "Priest Jailed for Exorcism Death," BBC, February 19, 2007.

In another famous case in Germany in 1976, two priests were charged with negligent homicide when a young girl they were exorcising, Anneliese Michel, starved to death. The episode provided the basis for the movie *The Exorcism of Emily Rose*. For more, see *The Exorcism of Anneliese Michel*, by Felicitas D. Goodman.

CHAPTER ONE: ROME

10: **more than 15,000 of them:** John L. Allen, Jr., *All the Pope's Men*, p. 161.

12–13: **At his Jesus Caritas monthly priest support group:** A group based on the teachings of Charles de Foucauld, who was born in Strasbourg, France, in 1858. Losing his faith as a youth, Foucauld served as an officer in the army in North Africa and went to explore Morocco in 1883. After returning to France, he undertook a pilgrimage to Jerusalem, where he became a Trappist monk for seven years. Ordained in 1901, he desired to live as Jesus had, among "the most abandoned." He spent his time in the deserts of northern Africa and established the groundwork for founding a religious family, centered on the Gospels. He died before its creation, however, when he was killed by marauders in 1916. Today, Jesus Caritas continues Charles de Foucauld's desire to "live in the presence of God and at the same time in the midst of humankind."

Members of the group meet once a month to share scripture, pray before the Eucharist, and share a review of life. http://www.jesuscaritasusa.org/.

15: **Father Gabriele Amorth [. . .] official exorcist of Rome and best-selling author:** The latest of these appearances occurred on June 6, 2008. Both his books, *An Exorcist Tells His Story* (1999) and *An Exorcist: More Stories* (2002), were European best sellers. Father Amorth has been featured in many publications including *The Daily Telegraph* ("Vatican to Create More Exorcists to Tackle 'Evil'" by Nick Pisa, December 30, 2007) and the *New York Times*, January 1, 2002.

15: **including the Harry Potter books:** In 2002, Father Amorth originally told the ANSA Italian News Agency that "behind Harry Potter hides the signature of the king of the darkness, the devil." He also decried the books' attempt to differentiate between "white" and "black" magic when "the distinction does not exist because magic is always a turn to the devil." The diatribe was then picked up and ran in numerous periodicals and Web sites, most notably in an article in the *New York Times*, January 1, 2002: "A Priest Not Intimidated by Satan or by Harry Potter." As recently as January 15, 2008, an Italian scholar spoke out on the Harry Potter books in the official Vatican newspaper, *L'Osservatore Romano*, saying that the books fall into "the old Gnostic temptation of confusing salvation and truth with secret knowledge." In addition to attacking Harry Potter, Father Amorth has also been quoted as saying that both Hitler and Stalin were possessed by the devil, *Daily Mail News*, London, by Nick Pisa, August 28, 2006.

15: **"are treated as though they are crazy, as fanatics":** "The Smoke of Satan in the House of the Lord," by Stefano Maria Paci, first printed in *30 Days*, June 2001, p. 30.

15: **"For three centuries, the Latin Church":** Ibid, pp. 30–31.

15: **"There are countries in which":** Ibid.

16: **According to the Associazione Comunità Papa Giovanni XXIII:** Founded in 1968 by Don Oreste Benzi, the association was established as a way to reach out to young people who "would never have managed to make it on their own." Now present in eighteen countries, the association works for the betterment of the marginalized, including former drug addicts, prostitutes, and victims of cults. http://www.apg23.org/cgi-bin/pagina.cgi.

16: **still practice Tarantism:** For more information on Tarantism, see *Ecstatic Religion: A Study of Shamanism and Spirit Possession* by I. M. Lewis, pp. 36–38, 80–83.

16: **50,000 tax-paying citizens:** Marlise Simons, "Paris Journal; Land of Descartes Under the Spell of Druids?" *New York Times*, April 30, 1996.

16: **some would say exaggerated:** Given the secretive nature of sects, it is hard to know if these numbers reflect an accurate picture. In *Sette Sataniche (Satanic Sects)*, Italian psychiatrist Vincenzo Maria Mastronardi and psychologist Ruben De Luca point out the near impossibility of knowing the true numbers of satanic sects in existence, p. 92. To further complicate matters, some scholars cast a wide net when it comes to categorizing certain beliefs as "satanic," including voodoo and Wicca. According to one expert, Satanism can be seen as a form of extreme cynicism: "It is a way of seeing the world as a jungle, where only the strongest survive. A world in which all limits are absent, bad examples are on offer and in which the perfection of television's role models is countered with the search for extremes, for power at all costs" (Carlo Climati, as quoted by journalist Nicholas Rigillo, "Satanic Murders Just the Tip of an Iceberg, Claims Roman Church," from the Australian Web site "The Age," January 5, 2005).

17: **the Church's approach to appointing and training exorcists:** Father Gramolazzo told me that the International Association of Exorcists had been looking at the possibility of starting a training program for many years as well, but had been unable to organize it.

17: **Legionaries of Christ:** Founded in 1941 in Mexico by Father Marcial Maciel, the Legionaries of Christ is currently one of the fastest-growing Catholic organizations in the world, with a presence in over twenty countries, and a large lay movement known as Regnum Christi. The Legion is mostly considered "right wing" because it is dedicated to advancing the Church's social agenda as expressed by the Holy See. It has always been strongly supported by the Vatican, especially Pope John Paul II. Liberals see the group as antithetical to the modernization that was ushered in by the Second Vatican Council. For more on the Legionaries go to: www.legionariesofchrist.org/.

Chapter Three: Going Back to School

33: **a struggle between "two cities":** A concept developed by Saint Augustine, in his work *The City of God*, in which he contrasted the declining glory of the Roman Empire and its citizens' worldly pursuits to that which will be won by the inhabitants of the City of God, who shun all such earthly pleasures in favor of a spiritual path.

34: **The New Testament is full of stories of Jesus exorcising demons:** Four of Jesus' exorcisms are presented in great detail: (1) the man in the synagogue at Capernaum (Mark 1:21–28; Luke 4:33–36); (2) the Gerasene demoniac (Mark 5:1–20; Matthew 8:28–34; Luke 8:26–39); (3) the Syrophoenician woman (Mark

7:24–30; Matthew 15: 21–28); and (4) the epileptic boy (Mark 9:14–29; Matthew 7:14–21; Luke 9:37–43).

34: **the Gerasene demoniac:** Although the story labels the man as the Gerasene demoniac, Matthew locates the exorcism in the town of Gadara, closer to the Sea of Galilee than Gerasa is. Much has been made of the obvious exaggeration associated with this exorcism. For instance, in his book *Mary Magdalene,* Bruce Chilton suggests "legion" is really a stand-in for Rome and all the "evils" that the Roman Empire represented to the Jews at the time, pp. 38–40.

34: **not the only exorcist:** The Jews also believed in exorcism, as documented by the historian Flavius Josephus, who lived in Palestine (circa 37–100). In one exorcism recounted by him, the Jewish exorcist Eleazar used a root attached to a sacred ring to draw out a demon though a person's nose, Josephus's *Antiquities* 8.46–48.

34: **impossible for a demon to cast out a demon:** Jesus was charged by the Pharisees with invoking the name of Beelzebul, "the chief of demons," also known as "Beelzebub," which was tantamount to an accusation of witchcraft. Some scholars say the name "Baal Zebub," meaning "Lord of the flies," is actually a corruption of "Baal Zebul," "Lord in high places." It is first used in 2 Kings 1:2–16, to denote a foreign god. It has been reported by scholars that during the exorcisms of the time, certain exorcists did invoke Beelzebul's name. See Bruce Chilton's *Mary Magdalene,* p. 29; and *By the Power of Beelzebub: An Aramaic Incantation Formula from Qumran (4Q560)* by Douglas L. Penney and Michael O. Wise, pp. 627–50.

35: **for believers to win converts:** Saint Irenaeus, writing in the second century C.E. (Christian Era), says, "By invoking the name of Jesus Christ . . . Satan is driven out of men." In his *Apology,* Tertullian writes: "Let a person be brought before your tribunals, who is plainly under demonical possession. The wicked spirit, bidden to speak by a follower of Christ, will as readily make the truthful confession that he is a demon, as elsewhere he had falsely asserted that he is a god" (Chapter 23). And in his apologetical work *Against Celsus,* Origen counters the pagan philosopher Celsus's view that Christian exorcisms are accomplished through magical rites, stating that "the strength of the exorcism lies in the name of Jesus, which we pronounce while, at the same time, we announce the facts of his life." Origen even claims that the name of Jesus is so powerful that a non-Christian can use it with success (as witnessed by the Jewish exorcists in the Gospel of Mark 9:38–41).

35: **in the early ceremonies of baptism:** In *The Prince of Darkness,* Jeffrey Burton Russell quotes Tertullian as saying, "If the Son of God has appeared . . . to destroy the works of the Devil, he has destroyed them by delivering the soul through baptism." Russell also notes that until the year 200, baptism was preceded by a series of exorcisms that were separate from the rite itself, reflecting the belief of early Christians that the Devil had a hold over mankind thanks to original sin, p. 72. Among other things, Tertullian incorporated a formal renunciation of Satan into the baptismal rite about 200 C.E. The early Church did differentiate between an exorcism performed on a candidate for baptism (known as a catechumen) and a person who was possessed (known as an energumen), a belief that persists today in the form of a "simple" exorcism performed at baptism and the "solemn" exorcism performed on energumens. For more on the importance of exorcism in the ritual of baptism, see Jeffrey Burton Russell's *Satan: The Early Christian Tradition*, pp. 100–103; and H. Kelly, *The Devil at Baptism: Ritual, Theology, and Drama*.

35: **continue to believe in such things:** Satan had already begun to be "phased out" from popular thought even earlier, when critics like Voltaire and David Hume had attacked the foundations of Christianity during the Enlightenment. Later, with the advent of psychoanalysis, the concept of the Devil took another blow. Sigmund Freud called him "nothing other than the personification of repressed, unconscious drives," while for Carl G. Jung he was a mythical, psychological symbol or archetype, which Jung called the "shadow."

35: **the Devil was a "person":** *Catechism of the Catholic Church*, 2851, "Evil is not an abstraction, but refers to a person, Satan, the Evil One, the angel who opposes God," p. 753.

35: **"We cannot use electric light and radio":** Rudolf Bultmann, *New Testament & Mythology*, p. 110.

35: **Herbert Haag, Bas van Iersel, and Henry Ansgar Kelly:** Haag's important works are *Abschied vom Teufel* (1969) and *Teufelsglaube* (1974). Bas van Iersel wrote the book *Engelen en duivels* (Angels and Devils) in 1968; and H. A. Kelly's seminal work is *The Devil, Demonology and Witchcraft* (1968). In an even earlier work by Arturo Graf, *The Story of the Devil* (1931), the author states: "The devil is dead or about to die; and, dying, he will not reenter the kingdom of heaven, but he will reenter and become dissolved in the imagination of man, the same womb whence he first issued forth," p. 251.

36: **on November 15, 1972, Pope Paul VI:** A general audience entitled "Liberaci dal male" (Deliver Us from Evil), in which the pope spoke about, among other things, the mystery of evil and the defense against the Devil.

36: **why would he misinform his followers:** This question seems all the more pertinent since the belief in exorcism was by no means universal during Jesus' time. The Sadducees, for instance, did not believe in angels or spirits and, as a corollary, demonic possession. The Bible also makes a clear distinction between those times when Jesus heals certain illnesses, such as blindness or leprosy, as opposed to when he casts out an evil spirit. For example, in none of the instances when he simply heals people do they manifest any of the symptoms described in the cases of demonic possession (such as unnatural strength or the demon addressing Jesus directly).

In addition, many critics of exorcism simply assume that all disease was attributed to the presence of "evil spirits." The Greek Hippocrates (460–377 B.C.E.), for one, wrote in his treatise *The Sacred Disease* that mental illnesses have natural causes. About epilepsy, known as "sacred disease" at the time, he wrote: "It is not in my opinion, any more divine or more sacred than other diseases, but has a natural cause, and its supposed divine origin is due to men's inexperience, and to their wonder at its peculiar character" (from *The Sacred Disease* I, W. H. S. Jones and E. T. Withington, *Hippocrates*, 4 vols., Loeb Classical Library, 1923).

36: **a kind of existential relativism:** Existentialism's emphasis on individual interpretation undercut the foundation for ontological truth, which Thomas Aquinas said formed the "essence" of a thing. As John Nicola wrote in *Diabolical Possession and Exorcism*, "Relativism in ethics urged the individual to judge the morality of a given act not on general principles of law but in its concrete moral milieu," p. 77. In this way, priests became less bound by tradition and more apt to follow their own interpretations.

36: **Charles Baudelaire's well-known phrase:** "My dear brothers, never forget, when you hear *the progress of enlightenment* vaunted, that the devil's best trick is to persuade you that he doesn't exist!" *"Le Joueur généreux,"* February 7, 1864; trans. Cat Nilan, 1999.

37: **Father Daniel:** This is a pseudonym.

38: **the Scala Santa, a church:** For many years, it was used by Father Candido Amantini, a Passionist priest who was the chief exorcist in Rome during the 1960s, '70s, and '80s.

CHAPTER FOUR: KNOW YOUR ENEMY

40: **to explain the existence of evil:** Evil is considered to be the lack of good that should otherwise normally be present in an object. Theology typically divides evil into two categories: physical and moral. Examples of a physical evil would be something harmful such as an accident, illness, or disaster. But moral evil occurs when an individual knowingly makes a choice to commit an evil act. In the Church, moral evil is considered more base than a physical evil because it stems from the free-will choice of man. In other words, when we commit a moral evil, we intentionally commit that sin. For more see *Catechism of the Catholic Church,* 309–14, pp. 91–93.

40: **tempt them to worship false idols:** Thomas Aquinas writes in the *Summa Theologiæ,* "Augustine says (De Civ. Dei xi, 50) that the angels were not passed over in that account of the first creation of things, but are designated by the name 'heavens' or 'light.' And they were either passed over, or else designated by the names of corporeal things, because Moses was addressing an uncultured people, as yet incapable of understanding an incorporeal nature; and if it had been divulged that there were creatures existing beyond corporeal nature, it would have proved to them an occasion of idolatry, to which they were inclined, and from which Moses especially meant to safeguard them" (*Summa Theologiæ* I, 61:1).

40: **the Israelites had a strict law:** Gabriele Nanni, *Il dito di Dio e il potere di Satana: L'esorcismo* [The Finger of God and the Power of Satan: Exorcism], p. 15.

40: **his name is really just a title:** Any number of books address this topic. See, for example, Jeffrey Burton Russell's books, *The Prince of Darkness,* p. 33; and *Satan: The Early Christian Tradition,* pp. 26–28; also Edward Langton, *Essentials of Demonology: A Study of Jewish and Christian Doctrine, Its Origins and Development.*

41: **dedicated to incantations and conjurations:** The ancient world was rife with fear of demons. In addition to the Assyrians, the Babylonians also believed in a complex hierarchy of evil spirits. For instance, there was *Pazuzu,* a god associated with the howling north winds who was responsible for leaching the soil and destroying crops. Another was *Lilitu* (an early forerunner of the witch of medieval tradition), a creature that was part human and part bird who "roamed the night draining men of their bodily fluids." See Jeffrey Burton Russell, *The Prince of Darkness,* pp. 15–16.

41: **"The Apostles' Creed professes":** *Catechism of the Catholic Church,* 325, p. 95.

41: **"There must be some incorporeal creatures":** For more on Thomas Aquinas's extensive writings on the subject, see *Summa Theologiæ* I, 50, 1; I, 14, 8; I, 19, 4.

41–42: **"It would be most extraordinary":** Pie-Raymond Régamey, O.P., *What Is an Angel?* Translated from the French by Dom Mark Pontifex, pp. 20–21.

42: **Satan was a good angel:** See the *Catechism of the Catholic Church* 391, p. 110.

42: **"render [themselves] similar to God":** Pope John Paul II, "Creator of the Angels Who Are Free Beings," Catechesis on the Angels, general audience, July

23, 1986, as published in *L'Osservatore Romano* weekly edition in English. One theologian says, "Pure spirit is pure love . . . Love has created them and controls them; and their perfection consists in their likeness to God," Pie-Raymond Régamey, O.P., *What Is an Angel?* Translated from the French by Dom Mark Pontifex, p. 42.

42: **"By creating the pure spirits":** General audience by Pope John Paul II, on July 23, 1986, titled "Creator of the Angels Who Are Free Beings," from the Global Catholic Network (EWTN) Web site.

42: **choosing to place themselves before God:** Though no specific passage in the Bible dealt directly with the "sin" of the fallen angels, various theories abounded among the early Apostolic Fathers: Justin Martyr (died between 163 and 176) thought the sin to be lust, while Irenaeus (died in 202) thought it was envy. Over time, the most widely accepted theory would be the one promulgated by Origen (born in 185), that the fallen angels sinned through pride, which made them think they could place themselves above God. Though as Thomas Aquinas says, this pride was less a belief that they could become God, which would be impossible, but that they wanted to be "as God," beings who could attain ultimate happiness through their own powers (*Summa Theologiæ* I, 63, 3). Because of the exalted nature of the angels, once they sinned, they could never go back on their decision. Thomas Aquinas deals with this point extensively and equates the angelic fall with human death: "Now it is clear that all the mortal sins of men, grave or less grave, are pardonable before death; whereas after death they are without remission and endure for ever" (*Summa Theologiæ* I, 64, 2).

42: **Theologians call this punishment "the pain of loss":** From *Catholic Encyclopedia: The New Advent*: "The *poena damni*, or pain of loss, consists in the loss of the beatific vision and in so complete a separation of all the powers of the soul from God that it cannot find in Him even the least peace and rest."

43: **Lucifer and Satan are two distinct demons:** There is no mention in the Bible of Satan being connected to Lucifer. In *Satan: The Early Christian Tradition*, Jeffrey Burton Russell notes that the association was most likely established by Origen when he linked the Prince of Tyre and the Dragon to Satan, pp. 131–33. According to Father Amorth, Lucifer is a very common name among demons, while Satan is rare. In Father Amorth's opinion, during an exorcism, if the eyes of the victim roll upward, this signifies the presence of Lucifer or his army, while if they roll down it means that the person has been possessed by Satan or members of his army.

43: **"transplant[ed] into man the insubordination":** Pope John Paul II, in a general audience on August 13, 1986, taken from *L'Osservatore Romano*, weekly edition in English.

43: Satan has been given some degree of dominion over man: The Council of Trent (1545–63) affirms this story as a dogmatic element of the Church. "Let him be an anathema who does not admit that the first man, Adam, after having transgressed God's commandment, in the earthly paradise, immediately lost his holiness and the justice in which it had been established, and incurred, by committing such an offence, the wrath and indignation of God and subsequently death, with which God had previously threatened him, and with death, captivity under the dominion of him who, from that instant after that, had dominion over death, that is to say the Devil, and that Adam, by committing this offence, suffered a fall both in his body and his soul." From the Eternal World Television Web site, "The Council of Trent, Session V, June 17, 1546," http://www.ewtn.com/library/councils/trent5.htm.

43: fallen angels had denser bodies: For more see Jeffrey Burton Russell's *Satan: The Early Christian Tradition*, p. 73; and *The Angels*, by Pascal P. Parente, pp. 20–23.

44: "'Angel' is the name": *Catechism of the Catholic Church* 329, p. 96.

44: not according enough importance to intelligence: Thomas Aquinas addresses the intelligence of angels in the *Summa Theologiæ* I, 58, 1–7.

44: endowed with intellect and free will: Thomas Aquinas says, "Only a being endowed with an intellect can act with a judgment which is free" (*Summa Theologiæ* I, 59, 3).

44: their knowledge is derived from the intellect: In *Summa Theologiæ* I, 54, 3, Thomas Aquinas writes, "An angel is called 'intellect' and 'mind,' because all his knowledge is intellectual: whereas the knowledge of a soul is partly intellectual and partly sensitive."

44: "An angel possesses such penetration": A. M. Lepicier, *The Unseen World*, p. 27, from *The Angels*, by Pascal P. Parente, p. 29.

44: the demon is *acting* on that object: Thomas Aquinas addresses this notion extensively in question I, 52, 1 of the *Summa Theologiæ*. "A body is said to be in a place in such a way that it is applied to such place according to the contact of dimensive quantity; but there is no such quantity in the angels, for theirs is a virtual one. Consequently an angel is said to be in a corporeal place by application of the angelic power in any manner whatever to any place."

45: likened this movement to the human mind: Pascal P. Parente, *The Angels*, p. 38.

45: Satan has only "preternatural" power: Preternatural is derived from the Latin *prætor*, meaning outside the normal laws of nature, as opposed to supernatural, which comes from the Latin *supra,* meaning above or beyond the laws of nature. In this way, an angel's abilities are said to be outside the understanding of humans, though still within the confines of the natural world, while God's are above nature.

45: create the appearance of a miracle: Thomas Aquinas writes: "For even a man by doing what is beyond the power and knowledge of another, leads him to marvel at what he has done, so that in a way he seems to that man to have worked a miracle" (*Summa Theologiæ* I, 114, 4).

45: accurately "predicting" what will happen: Thomas Aquinas addresses this in the *Summa Theologiæ* I, 57, 3. "This manner of knowing future events exists in the angels, and by so much the more than it does in us, as they understand the causes of things both more universally and more perfectly."

46: God permits the Devil to act: "It is a great mystery that providence should permit diabolical activity, but 'we know that in everything God works for good with those who love him'" (*Catechism of the Catholic Church* 395, p. 111). Thomas Aquinas called the Devil's work part of the natural order: "In another way, indirectly, as when anyone assailed is exercised by fighting against opposition. It was fitting for this procuring of man's welfare to be brought about through the wicked spirits, lest they should cease to be of service in the natural order" (*Summa Theolgiæ* I, 64, 4).

46: "The devil is not the cause of every sin": Thomas Aquinas, *Summa Theologica* I, 114, 3.

47: The Devil's extraordinary activity: It is important to note that according to the International Association of Exorcists (IAE), these categories do not constitute a sequence of events that lead automatically to possession, which some authors have suggested.

48: this kind of direct attack is aimed at people who are closest to God: Born in Siena, Catherine was a mystic who was said to have received visions of Hell, Purgatory, and Heaven. The Devil supposedly appeared to Catherine in various forms, including once as an angel of light, to tempt and assault her. She wrote extensively on the discernment of spirits.

A powerful reformer of the Carmelite order, Teresa was born in Avila, Spain. Considered to be one of the foremost writers on mental prayer, Teresa later became one of only three women ever to be named as a doctor of the Church. A mystic, Teresa was troubled by demonic visions as well as physical attacks that she attributed to the Devil. Once the Devil attacked her in the form of a small black "creature" that she chased away with a jar of holy water.

The Curé d'Ars, Saint John Vianney, was born near Lyons, France, in 1786.

Patron saint of parish priests, Vianney was reputed to have a preternatural gift of knowing the past and future, and was also said to have a gift for healing. Vianney was also believed to have been attacked by the Devil, who would harass him all night with shouts and loud noises and in one famous incident set his bed on fire. During the last ten years of his life, he spent between sixteen to eighteen hours a day in the confessional.

49: **"Some are thoughts and impulses":** Francesco Bamonte, *Possessioni diaboliche ed esorcismo*, p. 76.

49: **Also known as "involuntary possession":** Anthropologists refer to demonic possession as being "involuntary" so as not to confuse it with the various rituals in which a shaman or witch doctor is said to invite a possession to take place (usually for the purpose of imparting knowledge or healing). The same also goes for the practice of glossolalia (or speaking in tongues), in which individuals are said to be possessed by the Holy Spirit.

49: **more people are becoming possessed:** Father Amorth compares the cultural atmosphere of today to the decadence of the declining years of the Roman Empire.

50: **"People who are possessed can keep undergoing":** This quote is taken from a personal interview with Italian exorcist Father Gabriele Nanni. For more on Father Nanni, see Chapter Six.

51: **"In this case," says an Italian exorcist:** Ibid.

51: **"like a demon walking on the earth":** The person is not literally taken over by the demon, but his actions comply with the demonic. For example, he is full of pride, hate, rage, or engages in illicit activity, crime. In this case, say exorcists, the demon does not need to make his presence known. It is only when the person wishes to turn his life around that the demon manifests to put a stop to that.

CHAPTER FIVE: OPENING THE DOOR

55: **the Cathars took up this theory once again:** The Cathars were a dualist sect that took hold primarily in northern Italy and southern France in the twelfth century. Influenced by Gnosticism, the Cathars essentially believed that the material world was too evil and corrupt to have been created by God. Instead, in order to account for the existence of both good and evil, the Cathars stipulated that the true God created only the spirit, while the Devil created the material world. As a corollary, the Cathars believed that the God of the Old Testament was too cruel to be the true God. In response, the Catholic Church labeled the Cathars as heretics and, during the Fourth Lateran Council (1215), established a canon delineating that the Devil had indeed been created by God, and was not a principal or entity independent from him. For more on the Cathars, see Jeffrey Burton Russell's *The Prince of Darkness*, pp. 135–136, 164.

55: **this view was easily perverted:** Jeffrey Burton Russell and Brooks Alexander, *A History of Witchcraft, Sorcerers, Heretics and Pagans*, p. 61. The authors write: "Evidence that this [misinterpretation of Catharist doctrine] occurred comes from fourteenth century Italy, where heretics believed that the Devil created the material world. Since the Devil was the creator of the world, he was more powerful than God, and should be worshipped in his place."

55: **the infamous Hellfire Club:** For more on the Hellfire Club, see Geoffrey Ashe's *The Hell-Fire Clubs*, 2001.

55: **Father Bamonte, who also authored a book:** *Cosa fare con questi maghi?* (What Do We Do with These Magicians?), Ancora, Milan, 2000.

56: **seven capital sins:** Pride, avarice, lust, wrath, envy, gluttony, and sloth.

56: **" 'Do what you want' ":** Francesco Bamonte, *Possessioni diaboliche ed esorcismo*, p. 46. A variant of the famous phrase "Do what thou wilt," by Aleister Crowley, who called himself "The Great Beast."

57: **"satanic panics" that gripped the United States:** According to author Michael Cuneo, a variety of factors contributed to this phenomenon, including, among other things, an explosion in charismatic-style deliverance ministries coinciding with the growth in psychotherapy that took place during the 1980s. A few scandalous testimonials—some later debunked as fabrications—such as *Michelle Remembers*, which detailed the horrors of ritual abuse, also fanned the flames. For more see *American Exorcism* by Michael Cuneo, pp. 51–55, 195–209.

57: **the McMartin Preschool trial:** This phenomenon was well covered in Paul and Shirley Eberle's The *Abuse of Innocence: The McMartin Preschool Trial* (1993); Debbie Nathan and Michael R. Snedeker's *Satan's Silence: Ritual Abuse and the Making of a Modern American Witch Hunt* (1995); and Jeffrey S. Victor's *Satanic Panic: The Creation of a Contemporary Legend* (1993).

58: **According to exorcists:** The information in this section is compiled from interviews with Fathers Francesco Bamonte, Gabriele Amorth, Gabriele Nanni, Giancarlo Gramolazzo, François Dermine, Fra Benigno, Jeremy Davies, and Carmine De Filippis.

59: **"Possessed persons can obtain":** *Patrologia graeca*, ed. P. J. Migne, LX, p. 293, from Corrado Balducci, *The Devil*, p. 119.

60: **"All forms of divination":** *Catechism of the Catholic Church* 2116, pp. 569–70.

61: **The first people to be affected by a curse:** In the Bible, Jesus rebukes his disciples James and John when they wish to "bring down fire from heaven" in order to punish the Samaritans who refuse them hospitality. For more on this concept see Francis MacNutt, *Deliverance from Evil Spirits*, pp. 97–119.

67: **"Whenever I express a fear":** John Nicola, *Diabolical Possession and Exorcism*, p. 95.

Chapter Six: In My Name

71: **a documentary on exorcism:** Series *Is It Real?* on exorcism, Episode 8, season 1, August 29, 2005.

72: **exorcism is a sacramental:** According to the *Catechism of the Catholic Church*, "Sacramentals are sacred signs which bear a resemblance to the sacraments. They signify effects, particularly of a spiritual nature, which are obtained through the intercession of the Church," 1667, p. 464. For more on sacramentals, see *Catechism of the Catholic Church* 1668–1679, pp. 464–67.

72: **"In a simple form, exorcism":** *Catechism of the Catholic Church* 1673, pp. 465–66.

72: **According to the Christian deliverance minister:** Francis MacNutt, *Healing*, p. 167.

72: **"The priest [. . .] should carry out this work":** Praenotanda, No. 13, *De exorcismis et supplicationibus quibusdam*, translated by Pierre Bellemare of Saint Paul University. Also, number 1172 of the Code of Canon Law states that a potential exorcist should have piety, knowledge, prudence, and integrity of life.

73: **The earliest mention of the office:** Jeffrey Grob, unpublished dissertation, "A Major Revision of the Discipline on Exorcism: A Comparative Study of the Liturgical Laws in the 1614 and 1998 Rites of Exorcism," Saint Paul University, Ottawa, Canada, p. 53.

73: **The Council of Laodicea:** Ibid., p. 54.

73: **the practice of blowing on the person:** In his *Apologetics*, Tertullian added this practice, which some experts say is connected to the act of Jesus breathing on his disciples after the Resurrection. For more see *Apologetics* 23.16; *Tertullian: Apologetical Works and Minucius Felix: Octavius*, p. 74; 1, 415.

74: **an exorcist who uses complicated or lengthy invocations:** Grob, p. 48.

74: *Statuta Ecclesiae Latinae,* **a collection:** Corrado Balducci, *The Devil*, translated by Jordan Aumann, O.P., p. 167.

74: **growing climate of superstition:** As early as the eleventh century, people began to augment the official formulas of the Church with their own gestures, incantations, and medicines. A general sense of superstition grew attached to the rite of exorcism, which fed into the already growing hysteria of the age, marked by an exaggerated fear of the Devil and witchcraft. Perhaps one of the most infamous cases illustrating the hysterical climate surrounding exorcism during the sixteenth century was Marthe Brossier, a twenty-five-year-old woman who alleged that her neighbor had bewitched her, causing her to become possessed. The neighbor was jailed and Brossier was paraded from village to village by her father—as a sort of traveling sideshow—and repeatedly exorcised in public. Jeffrey Grob, p. 78. See also Sarah Ferber, *Demonic Possession and Exorcism in Early Modern France*, pp. 40–59.

74: **diverse formulas were compiled into the *Roman Ritual*:** Though a number of people were involved in this process, two stand out as having contributed much of what would later come to be known as the *Ritual*. The first was a Franciscan named Girolamo Menghi (1529–1609) born in Viadana, Italy, and considered to be one of the most important exorcists of the sixteenth century. Menghi's work, the *Flagellum daemonum* (Scourge of Devils), contains seven exorcism prayers as well as helpful advice for exorcists on discerning spirits. For more on Menghi, see *The Devil's Scourge*, Weiser Books, 2002. The second figure was Peter Thyraeus (1546–1601), a Jesuit from Germany who was instrumental in revising the criteria used for determining whether a person was possessed or not. Prior to Thyraeus, the signs used by exorcists to determine possession varied greatly from region to region. His most important work was *Daemoniaci, hoc est: de obsessis a spiritibus daemoniorum hominibus*, published in 1598. Thyraeus divided the signs of possession into two categories, those that are attributed to the intellect and those to the body.

For this information, I am indebted to the research conducted by Father Jeffrey Grob, and his unpublished dissertation, "A Major Revision of the Discipline on Exorcism."

74: **the *Ritual* has gone through a few adjustments:** In 1952 Pope Pius XII released the new edition of the *Roman Ritual*, slightly updating some of the language in the criteria section pertaining to mental illness and psychology. In addition, the strictures on what constitutes demonic possession were loosened up. Where the original states, "Signs of possession are the following . . . ," the revised language states, "Signs of possession may be the following . . ." Considerable consternation followed the release of the 1998 *Ritual*. Father Amorth was perhaps the most vocal critic of the revision, characterizing it as watered down.

Much less important, the order of the prayers was also reversed. In January 1999, a year after the *Revised Ritual* was released, the Congregation for the Divine Worship and the Discipline of the Sacraments announced that if requested by the diocesan bishop, it would grant a priest the permission to use the former rite of exorcism contained in the 1952 edition of the *Roman Ritual*. Many exorcists prefer to pray the older *Ritual* for a variety of reasons, some simply because they know the older *Ritual* by heart. The 1998 *Ritual* has also gone through various revisions since it was released, the most recent in 2005 (Grob, "A Major Revision of the Discipline on Exorcism").

74: **only when he is "morally certain":** In certain difficult cases where the presence of a demon may be hard to diagnose, some exorcists, including Father Amorth and Father Bamonte, prefer to use the deprecatory prayer as a tool for discernment. In addition, other exorcists might incorporate elements of the deprecatory prayer into spontaneous prayers of deliverance. Not, however, the imperative formula.

75: **confused with a magic ceremony:** *Praenotanda* No. 19, *De exorcismis et supplicationibus quibusdam,* trans. Pierre Bellemare of Saint Paul University.

77: **indicative of full demonic possession:** Gabriele Amorth, *An Exorcist Tells His Story,* pp. 79–80.

77: **there are five traps:** Father Nanni, *Il dito di Dio e il potere di Satana: L'esorcismo,* pp. 257–62.

77: **Father Amorth has been threatened:** Being threatened by demons is quite common, so much so that some exorcists have devised little "tricks." One exorcist prefers to recite Luke 10:17–20 when intimidated: "And the seventy returned again with joy, saying Lord, even the devils are subject unto us through thy name. And he said unto them, I beheld Satan like lightning falling from heaven. Behold, I give unto you power to tread on serpents and scorpions, and over all the powers of the enemy: and nothing shall by any means hurt you."

78: **who is almost always a woman:** Anthropologists, such as I. M. Lewis and Lesley A. Sharp, have also noted the frequency of spirit possession among women in native societies, which they claim can be attributed to its use as a tool of empowerment. For instance, in some male-dominated societies, there is no outlet for a woman to express her outrage except through possession. For example, Somalis believe that evil spirits (jinns) often lie in wait to take possession of unsuspecting passersby. "These malevolent sprites are thought to be consumed by envy and greed and to hunger especially after dainty foods, luxurious clothing, jewelry, perfume and other finery . . . The prime targets for the unwelcome

attentions of these malign spirits are women, and particularly married women"
(*Ecstatic Religion, A Study of Shamanism and Spirit Possession*, p. 67).

80: **after the demon threatened him:** Gabriele Amorth, *An Exorcist Tells His Story*, pp. 194–95.

80: **this last point has perhaps been exaggerated:** For its sheer level of hysteria, no book has perhaps surpassed Malachi Martin's *Hostage to the Devil*, in which the author, a former Jesuit priest, describes in lurid prose the physical and spiritual dangers that await any priest who dares to perform this ministry. Numerous critics have cast doubt on the veracity of Malachi's claims, including even some of his disciples. In his book *People of the Lie*, psychiatrist M. Scott Peck, who credits Martin as one of his sources for his knowledge about exorcism, writes: "From my experience I suspect Martin may have overemphasized the physical dangers [of exorcism]" (M. Scott Peck, *People of the Lie*, p. 189).

CHAPTER SEVEN: SEARCHING FOR AN EXORCIST

84: **outside the Scala Santa:** The building was once a part of the Lateran Palace. In the sixteenth century, Pope Sixtus V renovated the site and had the steps moved to their present location. Upon entering the building, the visitor is immediately faced with three flights of stairs, the one in the center being the Holy Steps. The sanctum sanctorum, which is protected by a large grille, and a small chapel are all located on the second floor.

87: **Medjugorje in Bosnia-Hercegovina:** Similar to Fatima in Portugal, six villagers at Medjugorje claim to have seen Mary on the mountainside daily since 1981. While the Catholic Church still has yet to make any kind of official statement as to the authenticity of the claims, the site has become a major pilgrimage destination on par with other Marian sites. Many people have claimed that their rosary beads have turned to gold, or that they have seen strange lights. On a trip to Medjugorje in 1998, Father Gary, along with his parents, saw the sun spin (a common miracle associated with the site), although nothing similar happened this trip.

89: **"These charismatic gifts":** *Lumen Gentium,* No. 12, from Gabriele Amorth, *An Exorcist Tells His Story*, p. 157.

92: **little about the building has changed:** The porch had to be rebuilt when the church, which was located next to a Nazi supply dump, was accidentally bombed during World War II by the Allies in 1943. More than three thousand citizens were killed during the attack.

Chapter Eight: The First Night

100: **Padre Pio:** Born in Pietrelcina, in the south of Italy, in 1887, Padre Pio became a Capuchin novice at sixteen and was ordained in 1910. In 1920 Padre Pio was purported to have been kneeling in front of a crucifix when he received the stigmata. The blood from the wounds carried with it the particular scent of flowers, and when he died in 1968, the wounds miraculously healed without leaving a mark. Padre Pio was also said to have the ability to read the inner hearts of the people who confessed to him, and numerous miracles—such as bilocation—were attributed to him. The gloves that Padre Pio wore to cover the stigmata were also said to effect miraculous cures. On more than one occasion during his life, he was said to have fought with the Devil who appeared to him in various forms—including a "monstrous dog" with smoke billowing from its mouth—in order to torment him.

Chapter Nine: Discernment

108: **"fixing" them in this state:** Cognitive therapists use this rationale to illustrate how a person claiming to have Multiple Personality Disorder (MPD) might have that condition reinforced by a therapist who requires that an individual "inhabit" these personalities through hypnosis and past-life regression. This in turn not only legitimizes those personalities in the person's mind, they say, but also can create an "alter" where none existed. As Nicholas Spanos points out, a majority of MPD cases (80 percent in one study) do not enter therapy complaining about having more than one personality. It's because of this that Spanos says, "the procedures used to diagnose MPD often create rather than discover the multiplicity" (*Multiple Identities & False Memories: A Sociocognitive Perspective*, p. 235). Another problem, according to academic psychiatrist Dr. Richard Gallagher, is that a person suffering from a mental disease might not get the proper medical treatment if he is led to believe his problem is "spiritual."

109: **"the exorcist should not proceed":** No. 16 of the Praenotanda, *De exorcismis et supplicationibus quibusdam (DESQ)*, translated into English by Pierre Bellemare of Saint Paul University.

109: **"must above all exercise necessary":** No. 14 of the Praenotanda, *DESQ*, translated into English by Pierre Bellemare of Saint Paul University.

110: **It is like a "holy light":** Matteo La Grua, *La preghiera di liberazione*, p. 70. *"Il discernimento è una 'luce' particolare che ci fa vedere in Dio come stanno le cose."*

110: **fruits of the Holy Spirit:** Wisdom, knowledge, faith, healing, working of miracles, prophecy, discerning of spirits, speaking in tongues, understanding tongues.

110: **demons often disguise their attacks:** Saint Teresa of Avila writes: "The devil comes with his artful wiles, and, under color of doing good, sets about undermining [the soul] in trivial ways, and involving it in practices which, so he gives it to understand, are not wrong; little by little he darkens its understanding, and weakens its will, and causes its self-love to increase, until in one way and another he begins to withdraw it from the love of God and to persuade it to indulge its own wishes" (*Interior Castle*, 4. 4, 5).

Along with the impulses sent by spirits, theologians say, a person must take into consideration the state of the soul itself, especially because of the imperfections that have resulted from original sin. Concupiscence drives us toward committing "sins of the flesh," while the higher functions of the soul such as the intellect receive graces from God that lead us back to goodness (Romans 7:22–25).

110: **"These signs can offer some indication":** No. 16 of the Praenotanda, *DESQ*, translated into English by Pierre Bellemare of Saint Paul University.

111: **People seek exorcists:** This information is based on personal interviews with exorcists.

113: **while in a real possession:** Adolf Rodewyk, *Daemonische Besessenheit heute*, pp. 17–18, as quoted in Gabriele Nanni, *Il dito di Dio e il potere di Satana: l'Esorcismo*, p. 272.

114: **"one of the determining factors":** Gabriele Amorth, *An Exorcist Tells His Story*, p. 70.

115: **"Most demons will manifest with a simple prayer":** If the demon does not manifest during the initial diagnosis but the exorcist suspects that he is present, then he will most likely advise the person to return to church, pray daily, receive the Eucharist as often as possible, and above all, go to confession. If, after two months, the person continues to have problems but the demon has not manifested, then the cause is most likely "natural," say exorcists; therefore the person doesn't need an exorcism.

115: **"There are cases in which [obsession]":** Francesco Bamonte, *Possessioni diaboliche ed esorcismo*, pp. 77–78.

116: **Historically, *epilepsy*:** Barry L. Beyerstein, "Dissociative States: Possession and Exorcism," *The Encyclopedia of the Paranormal*, Gordon Stein, ed. (Buffalo, NY: Prometheus Books, 1995), pp. 544–52, reprinted on the Web site for the Committee for Skeptical Inquiry, http://www.csicop.org/.

117: **In simple terms, disassociation:** David H. Gleaves, "The Sociocognitive Model of Dissociative Identity Disorder: A Reexamination of the Evidence,"

Psychological Bulletin 120, no. 1 (1996): 42. See also, "An Examination of the Diagnostic Validity of Dissociative Identity Disorder," by David H. Gleaves, Mary C. May, and Etzel Cardeña, *Clinical Psychology Review* 21, no. 4 (2001): 577–608.

117: **underestimate just how much of our behavior:** Barry L. Beyerstein, "Dissociative States: Possession and Exorcism," p. 3.

118: **Dr. Beyerstein is also on the board:** Dr. Beyerstein was often quoted on the correlation between dissociation and demonic possession, and interviewed on the History Channel among others. These comments by Beyerstein are taken principally from two sources, an article he wrote for *The Encyclopedia of the Paranormal* (1995), and two interviews conducted over the phone in the fall of 2006. In the spring of 2007, Dr. Beyerstein died unexpectedly of a heart attack.

118: **traditional disease view:** For a summation of this position, see Gleaves, May, and Cardeña, "An Examination of the Diagnostic Validity of Dissociative Identity Disorder"; and *Adult Psychopathology and Diagnosis*, 5th edition, Chapter 13, "Dissociative Disorders" by Etzel Cardeña and David H. Gleaves, 2007.

118: **the sociocognitive model:** For a description of the sociocognitive perspective, read *Multiple Identities & False Memories: A Sociocognitive Perspective*, by Nicholas Spanos, 1996.

119: **According to proponents of this view:** The sociocognitive theory of how dissociation works offers the best answer about a number of phenomena associated with possession, including why the victim may not remember what transpired during an exorcism, and feel as if he or she had been taken over by an "alien" presence. In explaining how this might work, Spanos compares the process to "a stage actor who becomes immersed in his character [and who] tries to see the world the way his character would see it. The actor attempts to feel what his character would feel and to take on the mind-sets that his character would likely develop in different situations" (*Multiple Identities & False Memories: A Sociocognitive Perspective*, p. 217).

119: **In Puerto Rico, for instance,** *espiritistas:* Spanos, *Multiple Identities & False Memories*, p. 150–51.

119: **These experiences teach them the behaviors:** Spanos, *Multiple Identities & False Memories*, pp. 150–151.

119: **"The notion provided a culturally":** Spanos, *Multiple Identities & False Memories*, p. 171.

119: **Anthropologists, for instance, have documented:** For more, see I. M. Lewis, *Ecstatic Religion: A Study of Shamanism and Spirit Possession*, 3rd ed., p. 77.

120: **"produces strongly cued demon self-enactments":** Spanos, *Multiple Identities & False Memories*, p. 162.

120: **In one such study:** Giuliana A. L. Mazzoni, Elizabeth F. Loftus, Irving Kirsch, "Changing Beliefs about Implausible Autobiographical Events: A Little Plausibility Goes a Long Way," *Journal of Experimental Psychology: Applied* 7, no. 1 (2001): 51–59.

Chapter Ten: Crossing Over

125: **her name would later be revealed:** The woman's identity has been changed to ensure her anonymity.

Chapter Eleven: The Fall

136: **"Whenever we are with people":** Joseph Cardinal Bernardin, *Gift of Peace*, p. 47.

143: **EMDR (eye movement desensitization and reprocessing):** A treatment combining known psychotherapies with external stimuli, in which the patient is asked to identify a negative memory and then to focus on that image, while at the same time rapidly moving the eyes back and forth, following the fingers of the therapist. For more on EMDR read Francine Shapiro and Margot Silk Forrest's *EMDR: The Breakthrough "Eye Movement" Therapy for Overcoming Anxiety, Stress, and Trauma* (New York: Basic Books, 1997).

Chapter Twelve: Suffering of the Soul

153: **pure spirits do not occupy space:** Thomas Aquinas, *Summa Theologiæ* I, 52, 1.

153: **"In this way, [the demon] tries to":** Francesco Bamonte, *Possessioni diaboliche ed esorcismo*, p. 40.

153: **"Every exorcism is like hitting the demon":** Gabriele Amorth, *An Exorcist Tells His Story*, p. 97.

154: **"Of course the object itself has no power":** Father José Antonio Fortea, *Interview with an Exorcist*, pp. 66–67.

154: **"The strongest and most lasting impression":** Gabriele Amorth, *An Exorcist: More Stories*, p. 11.

154: **Anna, now thirty-five:** Her name has been changed at her request to protect her anonymity.

Chapter Thirteen: A Pastoral Approach

163: **enters through the person's senses:** Other exorcists have observed the unusual connection demons have with the senses of their victim. "It is as if the demon, while possessing the body, feels whatever the body senses at a given moment. Whatever upsets the body also upsets the demon," José Antonio Fortea, *Interview with an Exorcist*, p. 69. In this way, however, the demon will also unwittingly reveal his presence, by reacting to the prayers of the exorcism.

164: **Hebrew tradition is believed to give:** Joshua Trachtenberg, *Jewish Magic and Superstition: A Study in Folk Religion*, p. 91. For more on names see Gabriele Nanni, *Il dito di Dio e il potere di Satana: L'esorcismo*, p. 186; and S. Vernon Mc-Casland's *By the Finger of God: Demon Possession and Exorcism in Early Christianity in the Light of Modern Views of Mental Illness*, pp. 96–109.

164: **"the number and name of the spirits":** No. 14 in the guidelines of the 1952 *Roman Ritual*.

168: **"I always say that the exorcism is ten percent":** Gabriele Amorth, *An Exorcist Tells His Story*, p. 112.

Chapter Fourteen: Windows to the Soul

174: **threw herself out the window:** Gabriele Amorth, *An Exorcist Tells His Story*, pp. 83–84.

175: **"He need only enter into":** Antonin-Gilbert Sertillanges, Catéchism des Incroyants I, 186, from *Who Is the Devil?* by Nicolas Corte, *The Twentieth Century Encyclopedia of Catholicism*, p. 88.

176: **"partly so that he may do that":** Pie-Raymond Régamey, O.P., *What Is an Angel?* Translated from the French by Dom Mark Pontifex, p. 75.

177: **"A priest who is afraid":** Gabriele Amorth, *An Exorcist Tells His Story*, p. 194.

177: **"If this Lord is powerful":** Saint Teresa of Avila, *The Book of Her Life*, Chapter 25, p. 19, as quoted in Gabriele Amorth, *An Exorcist Tells His Story*, pp. 64–65.

177: **"Throughout her life":** *Catechism of the Catholic Church* 149, p. 46.

177: **"God made [Satan] magnificent":** Fr. José Antonio Fortea, *Interview with an Exorcist*, p. 42.

178: **"if she weren't stopping me!":** Many people accuse the Catholic Church of practicing idolatry in its veneration of Mary. The dogma of the Church is quite clear. Mary should be honored for her service to God, but never worshiped. To establish a relationship with Mary, theologians say, is to be better united with Jesus Christ, who chose Mary as a partner to his earthly ministry. Pope Paul VI confirmed this when he said in an address on April 24, 1970, "If we want to call ourselves Christians we must be Marian, that is, we must recognize the essential, vital and providential relationship that unites Our Lady to Jesus, and that opens up a pathway to us that leads to him."

In one exorcism Father Bamonte recorded the demonic voice saying: "Under the cross, she gathered with her hands the flooding blood [of Christ] and with those hands she prayed to God, she praised and thanked the Father, she forgave and loved the ones who nailed her son [to the cross] and said that she wanted to feel that pain to alleviate the pain of her son but she knew she couldn't and I suffered, I've never suffered that much." Another time, "We wanted to rejoice [at Christ being crucified] but instead she killed us with her crying; her tears are like fire that kills us."

180: **the woman, Giovanna:** This is a pseudonym.

185: **called Pseudo-Dionysius:** The name Pseudo-Dionysius denotes an unknown theologian who wrote in the late fifth or early sixth century C.E. As a neo-Platonist, Dionysius synthesized elements of Greek philosophy, most notably the teachings of Plotinus and Proclus into a Christian worldview. The breadth of his knowledge suggests that he was a learned man (possibly a student of Proclus) who probably lived in Syria. Dionysius completed four major works, *Divine Names*, *Celestial Hierarchies*, *Ecclesiastical Hierarchies*, and *Mystical Theology*. Though rejected by some within the Church, the writings were later used during the Lateran Council (649) to defend certain tenets of the faith, and in the Middle Ages influenced important Scholastic writers like Peter Lombard and Thomas Aquinas.

186: **"receives the rays of the supreme Deity":** Dionysius the Areopagite, *Celestial Hierarchies*, p. 3

186: **"That there are in heaven Thrones":** Pie-Raymond Régamey, O.P., *What Is an Angel?* Translated from the French by Dom Mark Pontifex, p. 48.

188: **an actual Satanic possession:** While Satan is the leader of all the fallen angels, it is very rare for him to physically be present in a demonic possession. Most times, explain exorcists, he pulls the strings from afar, sending lesser demons to do his bidding. But occasionally, Satan himself is present. Father Daniel believes he was in this instance because of the length and ferocity of this case.

Chapter Fifteen: Liberation

192: **Silvia, a hollow-eyed woman:** Any identifying traits have been changed to protect the victim's anonymity.

194: **"Liberation is a gift from God":** Father Matteo La Grua, *La preghiera di liberazione*, p. 105. *"Liberazione è un dono di Dio, e Dio può liberare quando vuole e come vuole, anche senza l'intervento dell'uomo e di intermediari umani."*

194: **Not everybody has to be a Catholic:** All major religions believe in some form of exorcism. Islam specifies that people can become possessed by jinns, spirits that can be either good or bad. In order to cast out an evil jinn, the exorcist performs an official ceremony in which he reads passages from the Quran to the possessed person. In the Hindu tradition, numerous holy books contain ceremonies for casting out spirits, which is accomplished by reciting names of the Narasimha and reading from the *Bhagavata Purana* (scriptures) aloud. In Judaism, a *dybbuk* is a wandering soul with the ability to attach itself to a living person. Erich Bischoff documents a Jewish possession and exorcism in the Middle Ages: "The spirit was the soul of a drunken Jew, who died without prayer and impenitent. Having wandered for a long time it was permitted to him to enter into a woman as she was in the act of blaspheming, and since that moment the woman (an epileptic-hysteric) suffered terribly. Lurja speaks to the tormenting spirit and treats him as Christian exorcists treat the devil; he reprimands him, makes him tell his story, etc. By means of the 'Name' he at length obliges him to come forth by the little toe of the possessed, which the spirit thus handled with his habitual vehemence," from *Die Kabbalah, Einführung in die jüdische Mystik und Geheimwissenschaft*, Leipzig, 1903, p. 87, as quoted in T. K. Oesterreich, *Possession: Demonical and Other Among Primitive Races in Antiquity, the Middle Ages, and Modern Times*, p. 185.

For more on Islamic and Jewish demonology, see T. Witton Davies's *Magic, Divination, and Demonology among the Hebrews and Their Neighbors*, pp. 95–130.

194: **"Exorcism can drive a demon":** Father José Antonio Fortea, *Interview with an Exorcist*, p. 70.

195: **"Sincere forgiveness, which includes prayer":** Gabriele Amorth, *An Exorcist Tells His Story*, p. 113.

197: **In 2003, Beatrice, a forty-six-year-old:** All details have been changed to protect the identity of the individual.

200: *which I will continue to do:* Father Bamonte believes that Beatrice's involvement in the occult opened her up to a curse placed on her while she was on vacation. During the exorcisms, her face would contort, with her lips turning black and sometimes curling inward, seeming to disappear.

200: **numerous anthropologists have documented:** On p. 367 of Etzel Cardeña, Stephen Jay Lynn, and Stanley Krippner, *Varieties of Anomalous Experience: Examining the Scientific Evidence* (Washington, D.C.: American Psychological Association, 2000), Stanley Krippner and Jeanne Achterberg cite a study done by Achterberg in 1985, titled "Imagery and Healing."

200: **life-threatening diseases:** In a documented case, a Filipino American woman whose lupus (a chronic autoimmune disease that can be fatal) had not responded to traditional medical treatment went into remission after visiting a Filipino healer, who claimed to have removed a curse put on her by a jealous lover. R. A. Kirkpatrick, "Witchcraft and Lupus Erythematosus," *Journal of the American Medical Association* 245 (1981), as cited in *Varieties of Anomalous Experience: Examining the Scientific Evidence,* Stanley Krippner and Jeanne Achterberg, p. 359.

Likewise, scores of studies have been done on people reporting cures being effected at the shrine of Lourdes, France: R. Cranston, *The Miracle of Lourdes* (New York: Popular Library), as cited by Stanley Krippner and Jeanne Achterberg in "Anomalous Healing Experiences," in *Varieties of Anomalous Experience,* p. 363.

201: **for many indigenous people "healing" means:** Taken from Stanley Krippner and Jeanne Achterberg's "Anomalous Healing Experiences," in *Varieties of Anomalous Experience,* p. 359.

201: **voodoo possession can be considered a kind of psychotherapy or "folk therapy":** Steve Mizrach writes: "It might also allow a person to integrate parts of his personality otherwise jeopardized by narrow social roles—a man's possession by *Erzulie* might allow him 'to get in touch' with his 'feminine side,' so to speak. A quiet, mousy woman who was told that she had become *Ogoun* might find her 'inner fierceness' after the experience." "Neurophysiological and Psychological Approaches to Spirit Possession in Haiti," http://www.fiu.edu/~mizrachs/spiritpos.html.

201: **the "psychologically highly charged atmosphere":** I. M. Lewis, *Ecstatic Religion: A Study of Shamanism and Spirit Possession,* 3rd ed., p. 47.

202: **reattributing is a particularly effective technique:** Schwartz and Begley, *The Mind and the Brain,* p. 84, as quoted in *The Spiritual Brain,* Mario Beauregard and Denyse O'Leary, p. 130.

204: **the results of his experiments are far from conclusive:** E. Rodin, "A neurobiological model for near-death experiences," 1989, as quoted by Bruce Greyson, "Near-Death Experiences," in *Varieties of Anomalous Experience,* pp. 335–36.

204: **Even British author . . . Richard Dawkins, who used the helmet:** As seen on the BBC Two *Horizon* program, "God on the Brain," 2003.

204: **"Correlating a brain state with an experience":** Bruce Greyson, "Near-Death Experiences," in *Varieties of Anomalous Experience*, p. 337.

204: **knowing how a television set works:** R. Strassman, "Endogenous Ketamine-like Compounds and the NDE: If So, So What?" *Journal of Near-Death Studies* (1997), p. 38; as quoted in Bruce Greyson, "Near-Death Experiences," in *Varieties of Anomalous Experience*, p. 338.

205: **John Haught describes a concept:** John Haught, *Is Nature Enough? Meaning and Truth in the Age of Science* (New York: Cambridge University Press, 2006).

206: **"the experience of certain mystical contact":** Beauregard and O'Leary, *The Spiritual Brain*, p. 346.

206: **the experiences neurally engaged different regions:** Beauregard and O'Leary, *The Spiritual Brain*, pp. 274–76.

206: **"Is the ego perceiving something":** From a forthcoming book by Dr. Craig Isaacs, *Revelations and Possession: Distinguishing the Spiritual Experience from the Psychological*, pp. 67–68.

207: **depending on the therapist's school of thought:** Dr. Isaacs references the theories of John Weir Perry, as documented in *Trials of the Visionary Mind*, (New York: SUNY Press, 1999), in which Perry evaluates five contending approaches to psychosis. Dr. Isaacs summarizes them as "a fear and mistrust of the disorder; viewing brain disorders as primarily causing psychosis; viewing psychosis as a disorganized and unnecessary emotional response to stimuli; a complete negation of existence of an inner life; and finally as a desire for quick fixes which leads to faulty theory." In Perry's opinion, the first approach usually wins out, and as such, he claims that most theories are designed to "suppress" the behavior rather than to heal it. Isaacs, *Revelations and Possession*, pp. 79–80.

207: **This understanding can then be carried:** Isaacs, *Revelations and Possession*, p. 114.

207: **"Thus, spiritual illness may also be seen":** Isaacs, *Revelations and Possession*, p. 114.

CHAPTER SIXTEEN: ORGANIZING THE MINISTRY

213: **fourteen officially appointed exorcists:** This number is based on estimates taken as of April 2006.

213: **the old titular houses, original house churches:** Up until the fourth century, when Christianity was officially recognized, secret Christians worshiped privately. Wealthy Roman citizens often turned their private residences into places of worship. Later these houses became known as "titular churches," and each took the name of its owner. Paul mentions the *Titulus Priscae* in his letter to the Romans (Romans 16:3–5).

216: **the two agreed to stay in touch:** Father Daniel continued his graduate studies in Rome. In 2006 he performed exorcisms for two years at a church in Rome before finally being relocated out of the country in 2008. They met once more in Rome in the fall of 2007 as Father Daniel was preparing to leave for his new post.

CHAPTER SEVENTEEN: THE EXORCIST

223: **The woman, Stephanie . . . the man, Chris:** Any identifying traits have been changed to protect the couple's anonymity.

225: **he was allowed to do it in English:** Any translation for the revised rite of exorcism must be officially approved by the Congregation for Divine Worship and the Discipline of the Sacraments. So far the only versions that have been approved are Latin and Italian. It would also fall to the U.S. Conference of Catholic Bishops to request that such a translation be undertaken, which hasn't yet happened.

226: **one of the unused offices:** I have purposely changed the location of the exorcism.

227: **rosary beads turned the color of gold:** This is one of the miracles that has been associated with Medjugorje, in Bosnia-Hercegovina.

227: **run by a group of Charismatic laypeople:** The "charismatic renewal" is the name commonly given to Pentecostal-style groups, both Catholic and Protestant, that promote the belief that special "charismatic" gifts, such as speaking in tongues, prophecy, discernment of spirits, and healing, are imparted directly to those believers who are baptized in the Holy Spirit. Chief among these gifts is the power to cast out evil spirits, a power held by all baptized individuals according to early Christians. Adherents practice a watered-down form of exorcism known as "deliverance." By the 1980s the movement had come to dominate the deliverance scene in America.

For more on the charismatic approach to deliverance see: Francis MacNutt, *Deliverance from Evil Spirits* (Grand Rapids, MI: Chosen Books, 2005); and Michael Scanlan, T.O.R., and Randall Cirner's *Deliverance from Evil Spirits* (Ann Arbor, MI: Servant Books, 1980).

In the 1980s the Catholic hierarchy took steps to rein in the practice of deliverance. Most notably, in 1983, Cardinal Leon-Joseph Suenens of Belgium, a charismatic himself, wrote a report entitled *Renewal and the Powers of Darkness* in which he decried, among other things, the tendency of some charismatics to ascribe a majority of everyday problems to a demon—demon of impulsivity, demon of depression, demon of anxiety, and so on. In 1985, the Congregation for the Doctrine of the Faith, at that time headed by Cardinal Ratzinger, issued "Instruction on Prayers for Healing," reminding bishops and laypeople alike that solemn exorcism should be left to those priests nominated by the bishop.

231: **originally from Honduras:** I have removed identifying details in these cases to protect the identity of the individuals.

Author's Note

238: **therapists who practice "spirit releasement":** For more on spirit releasement, see William J. Baldwin, D.D.S., Ph.D., *Spirit Releasement Therapy: A Technique Manual*, 1992.

238: **to give people some sort of standards:** Numerous misguided individuals have turned the concept of casting out demons into murder. Among the most recent, in 1997, a five-year-old girl from the Bronx was killed when she was forced to drink a mixture of ammonia, pepper, olive oil, and vinegar by her mother and grandmother, who then bound and gagged her with duct tape in an attempt, they said, to "poison" the demon out of her. Michael Cooper, "Mother and Grandmother Charged with Fatally Poisoning Girl," *New York Times*, May 19, 1997.

Then in November 2007, in a ceremony involving nearly forty people, a woman in New Zealand was drowned during an Anglican exorcism ceremony when a member of her "healing group" held her under water in an attempt to drive out an evil spirit. Simon Winter, "Exorcism Death Shocks Archdeacon," *The New Zealand Herald*, November 12, 2007.

SELECTED BIBLIOGRAPHY

BOOKS

Allen, John L. *All the Pope's Men: The Inside Story of How the Vatican Really Thinks*. New York: Doubleday, 2004.

Allen, Thomas. *Possessed: The True Story of an Exorcism*. New York: Doubleday, 1993.

Amorth, Gabriele. *An Exorcist: More Stories*, N. MacKenzie (trans.). San Francisco: Ignatius Press, 2002.

——. *An Exorcist Tells His Story*, N. MacKenzie (trans.). San Francisco: Ignatius Press, 1999.

Aquinas, Thomas. *Summa Theologiæ*, J. Cunningham (trans.). Blackfriars series, vol. 57. London: Eyre & Spottiswoode, 1975.

——. *Summa Theologiæ*, T. Gilby (trans.). Blackfriars series, vol. 59. London: Eyre & Spottiswoode, 1975.

Ashe, Geoffrey. *The Hell-Fire Clubs*. Gloucestershire: Sutton Publishing, 2005.

Athanasius: The Life of Antony and the Letter to Marcellinus, R. Gregg (trans.). New York: Paulist Press, 1980.

Balducci, Corrado. *The Devil: Alive and Active in Our World*, J. Auman (trans.). Staten Island, NY: Alba House, 1990.

Baldwin, William. *Spirit Releasement Therapy: A Technique Manual*, 2nd edition. Terra Alta, WV: Headline Books, 1992.

Bamonte, Francesco. *Possessioni diaboliche ed esorcismo*. Milan: Figlie di San Paolo, 2006.

——. *Cosa fare con questi maghi? Come liberarsi dalla superstizione e difendersi dai truffatori*. Milan: Ancora, 2000.

Bangley, Bernard. *Butler's Lives of the Saints*. Orleans, MA: Paraclete Press, 2005.

Baumeister, Roy, Ph.D. *Evil: Inside Human Violence and Cruelty*. New York: Henry Holt and Company, 1997.

Benigno, Fra. *Dalla filosofia all'esorcismo*. Roma: Associazione Rinnovamento nello Spirito Santo, 2006.

Bernardin, Joseph Cardinal. *The Gift of Peace*. New York: Doubleday, 1997.

Bultmann, Rudolf. *New Testament & Mythology, and Other Basic Writings*. Minneapolis: Augsburg Fortress Publishers, 1984.

Buonaiuto, Aldo. *Le mani occulte: viaggio nel mondo del satanismo*. Rome: Città Nuova Editrice, 2005.

Cardeña, Etzel, Stephen Jay Lynn, and Stanley Krippner. *Varieties of Anomalous Experience: Examining the Scientific Evidence*, Washington D.C.: American Psychological Association, 2000.

Catechism of the Catholic Church, with Modifications from the Editio Typica, English trans. New York: Doubleday, 1994.

Chadwick, Henry. *The Early Church*, rev. edition. New York: Penguin Books, 1993.

Chilton, Bruce. *Mary Magdalene*. New York: Doubleday, 2005.

Clifton, Charles S. *Her Hidden Children, The Rise of Wicca and Paganism in America*. Landham, MD: AltaMira Press, 2006.

Codex Iuris Canonici, Auctoritate Ioannis Pauli PP. II promulgatus fontium annotatione et indice analytico-alphabetico auctus, Libreria editrice Vaticana, 1989. English trans. Code of Canon Law, Latin-English edition, New English trans., prepared under the auspices of the Canon Law Society of America, Washington D.C.: Canon Law Society of America, 1999.

Cole, Basil, O.P. *The Hidden Enemies of the Priesthood: The Contributions of St. Thomas Aquinas*. Staten Island, NY: The Society of St. Paul, Alba House, 2007.

Corte, Nicholas. *Who Is the Devil?* D. Pryce (trans.), *The Twentieth-Century Encyclopedia of Catholicism*, Henri Daniel Rops (ed). New York: Hawthorn Books, 1958.

Cozzens, Donald B. *The Changing Face of the Priesthood: A Reflection on the Priest's Crisis of Soul*. Collegeville, MN: Liturgical Press, 2000.

Cristiani, Léon. *Evidence of Satan in the Modern World.* Rockford, IL: Tan Books and Publishers, 1977.

Cuneo, Michael. *American Exorcism: Expelling Demons in the Land of Plenty.* New York: Doubleday, 2001.

Dante. *The Inferno,* trans. Robert Pinsky. New York: Farrar, Straus and Giroux, 1994.

Davies, Steven L. *Jesus the Healer: Possession, Trance, and the Origins of Christianity.* New York: Continuum, 1995.

Davies, Thomas Witton. *Magic, Divination, and Demonology Among the Hebrews and Their Neighbors.* London, J. Clarke & Co., 1898; reprint, Whitefish, MT: Kessinger Publishing, 1997.

Davis, Winston. *Dojo: Magic and Exorcism in Modern Japan.* Stanford, CA: Stanford University Press, 1980.

Delbanco, Andrew. *The Death of Satan: How Americans Have Lost the Sense of Evil.* New York: Farrar, Straus and Giroux, 1995.

Diagnostic and Statistical Manual of Mental Disorders, 4th edition. Michael B. First (ed.). Washington, D.C.: American Psychiatric Association, 2000.

Dickason, Fred C. *Angels, Elect & Evil.* Chicago: Moody Press, 1975.

Dolan, Monsignor Timothy M. *Priests for the Third Millennium.* Huntington, IN: Our Sunday Visitor Publishing Division, 2000.

Drane, John. *What Is the New Age Still Saying to the Church?* London: Marshall Pickering, 1999.

Eberle, Paul, and Shirley Eberle. *The Abuse of Innocence: The McMartin Preschool Trial.* Amherst, NY: Prometheus Books, 2003.

Esorcismo e preghiera di liberazione, edited by the Instituto Sacerdos of the Ateneo Pontificio Regina Apostolorum, in collaboration with the Gruppo di Ricerca e Informazione Socio-religiosa (GRIS), Rome: Edizioni Art, 2005.

Ferber, Sarah. *Demonic Possession and Exorcism in Early Modern France.* New York: Routledge, 2004.

Ferguson, Everett. *Demonology of the Early Christian World,* symposium series, vol. 12. New York: Edwin Mellen Press, 1984.

Fortea, Fr. José Antonio. *Interview with an Exorcist: An Insider's Look at the Devil, Demonic Possession, and the Path to Deliverance.* West Chester, PA: Ascension Press, 2006.

Gibson, David. *The Coming Catholic Church: How the Faithful Are Shaping a New American Catholicism*. New York: HarperCollins, 2003.

Goodman, Felicitas D. *The Exorcism of Anneliese Michel*. Eugene, OR: Wipf and Stock Publishers, 1981.

Graf, Arturo. *The Story of the Devil*, trans. from the Italian by Edward Noble Stone. New York: MacMillan Company, 1931; reprint, Whitefish, MT: Kessinger Publishing, 2005.

Haddock, Deborah Bray M.Ed., M.A., L.P. *The Dissociative Identity Disorder Sourcebook*. New York: McGraw-Hill Books, 2001.

Hersen, Michael, Samuel M. Turner, and Deborah C. Beidel. *Adult Psychopathology and Diagnosis*, 5th edition. Hoboken, NJ: John Wiley & Sons, 2007.

Huxley, Aldous. *The Devils of Loudun*. New York: Harper & Brothers, 1952.

Josephus. *Antiquities*. Thackeray, H. St. John and Ralph Marcus (trans.), vol. 5. Cambridge, MA: Harvard University Press, 1988.

Kaplan, Harold I., and Benjamin J. Sadock. *Synopsis of Psychiatry, Behavioral Sciences/Clinical Psychiatry*, 10th edition. Philadelphia: Lippincott Williams & Wilkins, 2007.

Kelly, Henry Angsar. *The Devil, Demonology, and Witchcraft: The Development of Christian Beliefs in Evil Spirits*. Garden City, NY: Doubleday & Company, 1968.

———. *The Devil at Baptism: Ritual, Theology, and Drama*. Ithaca, NY: Cornell University Press, 1985.

Klass, Morton. *Mind over Mind: The Anthropology and Psychology of Spirit Possession*. Lanham, MD: Rowman & Littlefield Publishers, 2003.

La Grua, Matteo. *La preghiera di liberazione*. Palermo, Italy: Herbita editrice, 1985.

Lane, Anthony N.S. *The Unseen World: Christian Reflections on Angels, Demons and the Heavenly Realm*. Grand Rapids, MI: Paternoster Press and Backer Book House, 1996.

Langton, Edward. *Essentials of Demonology: A Study of Jewish and Christian Doctrine, Its Origin, and Development*. London: Epworth Press, 1949.

———. *Satan, A Portrait: A Study of the Character of Satan Through All the Ages*. Folcroft, PA: Folcroft Library Editions, 1974.

LeBar, Rev. James J. *Cults, Sects, and the New Age*. Huntington, IN: Our Sunday Visitor Publishing Division, 1989.

Lecky, W. E. H. *History of the Rise and Influence of the Spirit of Rationalism in Europe, Part 1.* New York: D. Appleton and Company, 1882; reprint, Whitefish, MT: Kessinger Publishing, 2003.

Lewis, C. S. *The Screwtape Letters.* New York: Macmillan, 1944.

Lewis, I. M. *Ecstatic Religion: A Study of Shamanism and Spirit Possession*, 3rd edition. New York: Routledge, 2003.

Lynn, Steven Jay, and Irving Kirsch. *Essentials of Clinical Hypnosis: An Evidence Based Approach.* Washington, D.C.: American Psychological Association, 2005.

MacNutt, Francis. *Healing*, rev. and expanded edition. Notre Dame, IN: Ave Maria Press, 1999.

———. *Deliverance from Evil Spirits: A Practical Manual.* Grand Rapids, MI: Chosen Books, 1995.

Martin, Malachi. *Hostage to the Devil: The Possession and Exorcism of Five Living Americans.* San Francisco: Harper, 1992.

Mastronardi, Vincenzo M., Ruben de Luca, and Moreno Fiori. *Sette Sataniche.* Roma: Newton Compton editori, 2006.

McCasland, S. Vernon. *By the Finger of God: Demon Possession and Exorcism in Early Christianity in the Light of Modern Views of Mental Illness.* New York: Macmillan, 1951.

Menghi, Girolamo. *The Devil's Scourge: Exorcism During the Italian Renaissance*, Gaetano Paxia (trans., intro., and ed.). York Beach, ME: Weiser Books, 2002.

Métraux, Alfred. *Voodoo in Haiti*, trans. Hugo Charteris. New York: Schocken Books, 1959.

Michela. *Fuggita da Satana.* Casale Monferrato, Italy: Edizioni Piemme, 2007.

Morabito, Simone. *Psichiatra all'inferno.* Tavagnacco, UD, Italy: Edizioni Segno, 1995.

Nanni, Gabriele. *Il dito di Dio e il potere di Satana: L'esorcismo.* Città del Vaticano: Libreria Editrice Vaticana, 2004.

Nathan, Debbie, and Michael R. Snedeker. *Satan's Silence: Ritual Abuse and the Making of a Modern American Witch Hunt.* New York: Basic Books 1995.

Nicola, John. *Diabolical Possession and Exorcism.* Rockford, IL: Tan Books and Publishers, 1974.

Origen. *Contra Celsum*, H. Chadwick (trans.). Cambridge, England: Cambridge University Press, 1980.

Osterreich, T. K. *Possession: Demonical and Other Among Primitive Races in Antiquity, the Middle Ages, and Modern Times,* D. Ibberson (trans.). New Hyde Park, NY: University Books, 1966.

Oxford Dictionary of the Christian Church. Ed. F. L. Cross and E. A. Livingstone. New York: Oxford University Press, 2005.

Parente, Fr. Pascal P. *The Angels.* Rockford, IL: Tan Books and Publishers, 1961.

Peck, M. Scott. *People of the Lie: The Hope for Healing Human Evil.* New York: Simon & Schuster, 1983.

Pseudo Dionysius: The Complete Works. Trans. Karlfried Froehlich, and Jean Leclercq. Mahwah, NJ: Paulist Press, 1987.

Régamey, Pie-Raymond O.P. "What Is an Angel?" *The Twentieth-Century Encyclopedia of Catholicism.* New York: Hawthorn Books, 1960.

Rodewyk, Adolf. *Possessed by Satan: The Church's Teaching on the Devil, Possession, and Exorcism.* Trans. M. Ebon. Garden City, NY: Doubleday, 1975.

Roman Ritual: Complete Edition. Trans. P. Weller. Milwaukee, WI: Bruce Publishing Company, 1964.

Russell, Jeffrey Burton. *Witchcraft in the Middle Ages.* Ithaca, NY: Cornell University Press, 1972.

——. *The Devil: Perceptions of Evil from Antiquity to Primitive Christianity.* Ithaca, NY: Cornell University Press, 1977.

——. *Satan: The Early Christian Tradition.* Ithaca, NY: Cornell University Press, 1981.

——. *Lucifer: The Devil in the Middle Ages.* Ithaca, NY: Cornell University Press, 1984.

——. *Mephistopheles: The Devil in the Modern World.* Ithaca, NY: Cornell University Press, 1986.

——. *The Prince of Darkness: Radical Evil and the Power of Good in History.* Ithaca, NY: Cornell University Press, 1988.

Russell, Jeffrey Burton, and Alexander Brooks. *A History of Witchcraft, Sorcerers, Heretics and Pagans,* 2nd edition. London: Thames & Hudson, 2007.

Saint Augustine. *City of God.* Ed. Vernon J. Bourke, trans. Gerald C. Walsh, Demetrius B. Zema, Grace Monahan, and Daniel J. Honan. Garden City, NY: Image Books/Doubleday, 1958.

Salvucci, Raul. *Cosa fare con questi diavoli? Indicazioni pastorali di un esorcista.* Milan, Italy: Ancora Editrice, 1992.

Satan. Ed. Bruno de Jesus-Marie. New York: Sheed & Ward, 1952.

Scanlan, Michael T. O. R., and Randall Cirner. *Deliverance from Evil Spirits: A Weapon for Spiritual Warfare.* Cincinnati: St. Anthony Messenger Press, 1980.

Shapiro, Francine, and Margot Silk Forrest. *EMDR: The Breakthrough "Eye Movement" Therapy for Overcoming Anxiety, Stress, and Trauma.* New York: Basic Books, 1997.

Sharp, Lesley A. *The Possessed and the Dispossessed: Spirits, Identity, and Power in a Madagascar Migrant Town.* Berkeley, CA: University of California Press, 1993.

Spanos, Nicholas. *Multiple Identities & False Memories: A Sociocognitive Perspective.* Washington, D.C. American Psychological Association, 1996.

St. Justin Martyr: The First and Second Apologies. Trans. L. Barnard, Ancient Christian Writers, no. 56. Mahwah, NJ: Paulist Press, 1997.

Suenes, Léon-Joseph. *Renewal and the Powers of Darkness.* Trans. O. Prendergast. Ann Arbor, MI: Servant Books, 1983.

Synan, Vinson. *The Century of the Holy Spirit: 100 Years of Pentecostal and Charismatic Renewal.* Nashville: Thomas Nelson Publishers, 2001.

Tertullian: Apologetical Works and Minucius Felix: Octavius. Trans. R. Arbesmann, E. Daly, and E. Quain. The Fathers of the Church, vol. 10. New York: Fathers of the Church, 1950.

Turch, Michael E. M. *Considering a Career in Mortuary Science.* West Hartford, CT: Graduate Group, 1995.

Victor, Jeffrey S. *Satanic Panic: the Creation of a Contemporary Legend.* Chicago, IL: Open Court Publishing, 1993.

Vogl, Carl. *Begone Satan! A Soul-Stirring Account of Diabolical Possession.* Trans. C. Kapsner. Rockford, IL: Tan Books and Publishers, 1973.

Walker, Daniel P. *Unclean Spirits: Possession and Exorcism in France and England in the Late Sixteenth and Early Seventeenth Centuries.* London: Scolar Press, 1981.

ARTICLES AND OTHER SOURCES

Allison, Ralph B. "The Possession Syndrome on Trial." *American Journal of Forensic Psychiatry* 6, no. 1 (1985), pp. 46–56.

——. "If in Doubt, Cast It Out? The Evolution of a Belief System Regarding Possession and Exorcism." Submitted to the *Journal of Psychology and Christianity*, April 1999.

Beck, J., and G. Lewis. "Counseling and the Demonic: A Reaction to Page." *Journal of Psychology and Theology* 17 (1989), pp. 132–34.

Beyerstein, Barry L. "Dissociative States: Possession and Exorcism." *The Encyclopedia of the Paranormal*. Ed. Gordon Stein. Buffalo, NY: Prometheus Books, 1995, pp. 544–52.

Collins, James M. A. "The Thomistic Philosophy of the Angels." *The Catholic University of America Philosophical Studies* 89 (1947).

Congregation for Divine Worship and the Discipline of the Sacraments. "Decree *Inter sacramentalia*." *Notitiae* 35 (1999), p. 137.

——. *De exorcismis et supplicationibus quibusdam*, editio typica. Vatican City: Typis Vaticanis, 1999.

——. *De exorcismis et supplicationibus quibusdam*, editio typica emendata. Vatican City: Typis Vaticanis, 2004.

——. Notification. *De ritu exorcismi*. *Notitiae* 35 (January 27, 1999), p. 156.

Congregation for the Doctrine of the Faith. Instruction on Prayers for Healing. *Instructio de orationibus*. *Notitiae* 37 (September 14, 2000), pp. 20–34; English translation in ibid., pp. 51–65.

Congregation for the Doctrine of the Faith. Letter. *Inde ab aliquot annis* [On the Current Norms Governing Exorcisms]. *Acta Apostolicae Sedis* 77 (September 29, 1985), pp. 1169–70: English translation in *Canon Law Digest* 11, pp. 276–77.

Ferrari, Giuseppe. "Phenomenon of Satanism in Contemporary Society." *L'Osservatore Romano*, January 29, 1997.

Gleaves, David H. "The Sociocognitive Model of Dissociative Identity Disorder: A Reexamination of the Evidence." *Psychological Bulletin* 120, no. 1 (1996), pp. 42–59.

Gleaves, David H., Mary C. May, and Etzel Cardeña. "An Examination of the Diagnostic Validity of Dissociative Identity Disorder." *Clinical Psychology Review* 21, no. 4 (2001), pp. 577–608.

Grob, Jeffrey S. "A Major Revision of the Discipline on Exorcism: A Comparative Study of the Liturgical Laws in the 1614 and 1998 Rites of Exorcism." Ontario, Canada: Saint Paul University, 2006.

Halligan, Rev. Nicholas, O.P. "What the Devil!" *This Rock* (November 1995).

Hauke, Manfred. "The Theological Battle over the Rite of Exorcism: 'Cinderella' of the New *Rituale Romanum*." *Antiphon* 10, no. 1 (2006), pp. 32–69.

Henneberger, Melinda. "A Priest Not Intimidated by Satan or by Harry Potter." *New York Times*, January 1, 2002.

Hyland, Michael E., Ben Whalley, and Adam W. A. Geraghty. "Dispositional Predictors of Placebo Responding: A Motivational Interpretation of Flower Essence and Gratitude Therapy." *Journal of Psychosomatic Research* 62, (2007), pp. 331–40.

"Interview with Carlo Climati: When Young People Fool with Satanism." *Zenit*, September 11, 2001.

James, Susan Donaldson. "People Need Both Drugs and Faith to Get Rid of Pain." ABC News, August 1, 2007, ABC News Internet Ventures.

John Paul II. General audience. "La caduta degli angeli ribelli." *Insegnamenti di Giovanni Paolo II 9* (August 13, 1986), pp. 361–66; English trans. in *L'Osservatore Romano* 19, no. 33 (1986), pp. 1–2.

John Paul II. General audience. "La vitttoria di cristo sullo spirito del male." *Insegnamenti di Giovanni Paolo II 9* (August 20, 1986); pp. 395–98; English trans. in *L'Osservatore Romano* 19, no. 34 (1986), pp. 1–2.

Langley, M. "Spirit-Possession, Exorcism and Social Context: An Anthropological Perspective with Theological Implications." *Churchman* 94 (1980), pp. 226–45.

Lilienfeld, Scott O., et al. "Dissociative Identity Disorder and the Sociocognitive Model: Recalling the Lessons of the Past." *Psychological Bulletin* 125, no. 5 (1999), pp. 507–23.

Macchitella, Sara. "Italy Rocked by Satanic, Drug-Induced Sexual Abuse in Kindergarten." *Malta Star*, April 28, 2007.

Mayaram, Shail. "Recent Anthropological Works on Spirit Possession." *Religious Studies Review* 27 (2001), pp. 213–22.

Mazzoni, Giuliana A. L., Elizabeth F. Loftus, and Irving Kirsch. "Changing Beliefs About Implausible Autobiographical Events: A Little Plausibility Goes a Long Way." *Journal of Experimental Psychology* 7, no. 1 (March 2001), pp. 51–59.

Medina Estévez, J. "Il rito degli esorcismi." *Notitiae* 35 (January 26, 1999), pp. 151–55; English trans. in *L'Osservatore Romano* 32, no. 5 (1999), p. 12.

National Conference of Catholic Bishops. "New Rite of Exorcism." *Committee on the Liturgy Newsletter* 35 (1999), pp. 58–60.

New Advent Catholic Encyclopedia (online version), Kevin Knight, 2008, http://www.newadvent.org/.

Nicola, John J. "Is Solemn Public Exorcism a Viable Rite in the Modern Western World? A Theological Response." *Exerpta ex dissertatione ad* Doctoratum in Facultate Theologiae Pontificiae Universitatis Gregorianae, Washington, D.C., 1976.

Paci, Stefano. "The Smoke of Satan in the House of the Lord: An Interview with Rome's Exorcist, Father Gabriele Amorth." *30 Days* 19, no. 6 (2000), pp. 52–59.

Paul VI. Address. *"Liberaci dal male."* *Insegnamenti di Paolo VI* 10 (November 15, 1972), pp. 1168–73; English trans. in *The Pope Speaks* 17 (1973), pp. 315–19.

Penney, Douglas L. and Michael O. Wise. "By the Power of Beelzebub: An Aramaic Incantation Formula from Qumran *(4Q560)." Journal of Biblical Literature* 113, no. 4 (Winter 1994), pp. 627–50.

Pisa, Nick. "Hitler and Stalin Were Possessed by the Devil, Says Vatican Exorcist," *Daily Mail News*, August 28, 2006.

——. "Pope's Exorcist Squads Will Wage War on the Devil." *Daily Mail News*, December 29, 2007.

——. "Italian Priests Join the War on Satanic Crime," *Sunday Telegraph*, January 8, 2007.

Sacred Congregation for the Doctrine of the Faith. "Christian Faith and Demonology." *L'Osservatore Romano*, July 10, 1975, pp. 6–9.

Taylor, A. "Possession or Dispossession?" *The Expository Times* 86 (1974–75), pp. 359–63.

Van Slyke, D. "The Ancestry and Theology of the Rite of Major Exorcism, 1999/2004." *Antiphon* 10, no. 1 (2006), pp. 70–116.

"Why Another Course on Exorcism and Satanism?" *Zenit*, September 9, 2005.

INDEX